D1560395

CLARA DRISCOLL

BOOKS BY MARTHA ANNE TURNER

White Dawn Salutes Tomorrow

The City and Other Poems

Tools of the Earthmover
(Edited by Martha Anne Turner)

Sam Houston and His Twelve Women

The Life and Times of Jane Long

The Yellow Rose of Texas: The Story of a Song

William Barret Travis: His Sword and His Pen

Women of Texas
(In collaboration with others)

Texas Epic

The Yellow Rose of Texas: Her Saga and Her Song

Old Nacogdoches in the Jazz Age

Richard Bennett Hubbard: An American Life

Clara Driscoll: An American Tradition

Clara Driscoll

AN AMERICAN TRADITION

BY

Martha Anne Turner

MADRONA PRESS · AUSTIN

ISBN 0-89052-025-9
Library of Congress Catalog Card No. 79-89214
Copyright 1979 by Martha Anne Turner. All rights reserved.

FIRST EDITION

Manufactured in the United States of America

MADRONA PRESS, INC.
Box 3750
Austin, Texas 78764

Frontispiece: Portrait of Clara Driscoll which hangs
in the Driscoll Foundation headquarters in Corpus Christi, Texas.

All photographs in this book are courtesy of the Driscoll
Foundation unless otherwise noted.

THIS BOOK IS A MEMORIAL

TO THE GREAT AMERICAN WOMAN

Clara Driscoll

ALL ROYALTIES FROM ITS SALE HAVE BEEN

ASSIGNED BY THE AUTHOR TO

DRISCOLL FOUNDATION CHILDREN'S HOSPITAL

CORPUS CHRISTI, TEXAS

Contents

ILLUSTRATIONS

Picture sections following pages 44, 76, and 108

Preface

IT WAS SIXTY-SEVEN YEARS AFTER WILLIAM Barret Travis and the 182 other patriots defended the Alamo through the thirteen-day siege to insure Texas's independence in 1836, that a slender girl bought the property to save the neglected site from commercial exploitation. The girl was Clara Driscoll, a redheaded, hazel-eyed beauty of scarcely twenty-two—the daughter of the wealthy Texas cattleman Robert Driscoll, Sr. Already a belle in Texas, she went on to become a legend, then the toast of New York upon the success of her comic opera *Mexicana* on Broadway, and eventually a power in the Democratic party.

While Clara Driscoll's relationship to the Texas shrine in San Antonio had a lifelong influence, her patriotic ardor projected beyond it. In an era when woman's place was subservient and still believed to be in the home, she held the national spotlight for almost two decades as Texas's Democratic committeewoman and made a notable contribution to American life.

Clara Driscoll's name will remain irrevocably linked with that of Franklin Delano Roosevelt. She helped to elect the man said to have been one of the most loved and most hated in United States history to the presidency four times, even though she did not agree with all of his New Deal policies. In fact, Roosevelt's election to the office for his fourth term proved to be the final victory for both. The grind of the campaign, coupled with the stress and strain of the war, exacted its toll; and death came for both in 1945 within a space of three months. Roosevelt died on April 12 in Warm Springs, Georgia, where he had gone for polio therapy after his return from the Yalta Conference. Clara Driscoll died on July 17 in Corpus Christi, Texas. Both succumbed to a cerebral hemorrhage and both were of practically the same age. He was 63; she was 64.

In Clara Driscoll's declining years she—like the president—was physically impaired. Her lameness, from which she never completely recovered, was sustained from an automobile accident in 1931. Roosevelt's disability, more serious and long-lived, resulted from a severe paralytic attack at the vacation retreat on Campobello Island, New Brunswick, in August, 1921. Both had a scientific interest in the disease of polio. In 1927 he established the Warm Springs Foundation as a nonprofit institution for the treatment of polio victims, and she supported it generously as one of her favorite charities.

Just as Roosevelt served the country through two wars, so did Clara Driscoll. As assistant secretary of the navy during World War I, he served efficiently, if controversially, under his superior, Josephus Daniels. She assisted her husband, Hal Sevier, in his diplomatic assignment to combat German propaganda in South America for the duration. Her mastery of Spanish and knowledge of Latin-American psychology contributed to the tremendous success of the work. At the end of the war she lent moral support as Sevier assisted U. S. diplomat and President Wilson's confidential adviser, E. M. House, at the European peace conference. During the Second World War Mrs. Driscoll, as she was legally known after her divorce in 1937, was active in fund raising at bond rallies and in other patriotic activities.

But the major reason to connect the names of Driscoll and Roosevelt is that their deaths underscored the end of the era that was perhaps the most flamboyant and innovative in United States political and cultural history. In fewer than three decades—from the close of World War I to the end of World War II—America survived the depression and emerged from behind a facade of isolationism to win international recognition. After the Pearl Harbor attack December 7, 1941, the country took a stand for intervention in the war and assumed its place of leadership among the great nations of the world. What was more, regardless of Roosevelt's detractors or supporters, he implanted permanently in the minds of the American people the idea that federal government should accept the responsibility for the national welfare.

Altogether it was an exciting era—an age of tragedy and an age of triumph—punctuated by incredible extremes and sweeping changes. As the nation moved away from the effects of the First World War into the twenties, jazz reached its peak through the magic trumpet and gravel voice of Louis Armstrong, and Americans pondered the exhortation of Austrian psychoanalyst Sigmund Freud to free themselves from their sexual inhibitions and repression of natural behavior. Then by 1935, before bandleader Benny Goodman could convert jazz into an improvisation called swing, composer George Gershwin elevated it to operatic proportions with the American classic *Porgy and Bess*.

Sum-mer time—an' the liv-in' is eas-y,
Fish are jump-in'—an' the cot-ton is high.

Oh yo' dad-dy's rich, an' yo' ma is good-look-in',
So hush, lit-tle ba-by, don'—yo' cry.

It was the period in which Roosevelt later used radio to introduce Americans to symphony broadcasts conducted by Arturo Toscanini and to performances of the Metropolitan Opera. His Federal Music Project employed fifteen thousand persons who brought concerts into the homes of one hundred million people Nor was it surprising that in 1940 radio audiences subscribed over $300,000 to help "save the Met."

After the depression, Roosevelt used the Federal Theater Project to put 12,500 unemployed actors back to work. Though Congress killed the project in 1939 to discourage vocal leftists and pinks, many of the Broadway playwrights had already begun to appraise social problems negatively. Foremost among them, Robert E. Sherwood ridiculed intellectual impotence in *The Petrified Forest* and blasted war in *Idiot's Delight* in 1936, and doctrinaire Lillian Hellman dissected graft in *The Little Foxes* in 1939. Meanwhile Thornton Wilder collected a Pulitzer prize with his highly innovative *Our Town* in 1938 and Eugene O'Neill—disciple of Freud and winner of the Nobel award in 1936—took command of the American theater.

Nor were the novelists silent. A young genius by the name of Ernest Hemingway denounced war in *A Farewell to Arms* in 1929 and repeated his excellent performance in *For Whom the Bell Tolls* in 1940. Also in 1929 Thomas Wolfe, the gangling, introspective mountain boy from North Carolina, erupted with a scathing anatomy of his hometown of Ashville in *Look Homeward Angel,* then rediscovered himself as central to the universe in the magnificent *Of Time and the River* in 1936. In that same year little Margaret Mitchell found nostalgic escape from her sickbed in re-creating the Civil War (from the Southern viewpoint, you all!) in *Gone With the Wind.* Three years later, in 1939, lusty John Steinbeck castigated the machine age with his sentimental and escessive portrayal of the Oklahoma migrants—the "Oakies"—in *The Grapes of Wrath.*

It was the epoch in which the government stimulated a resurgence of interest in sculpture and in painting. Before his decease in 1941, the unpredictable Gutzon Borglum was enabled, through a federal subsidy, to add a new dimension to nationalism—and indeed to iconology—with his colossal portraits of Theodore Roosevelt, Washington, Jefferson, and Lincoln chiseled across the Black Hills of Mount Rushmore. The upsurge of interest in painting was due partly to art instruction sponsored by the Federal Art Project and partly to the opening of new museums. An impetus came in 1937, when Andrew W. Mellon, secretary of the treasury from 1921 to 1932, gave to the nation his

European art collection valued at $35 million, and in 1941 the National Art Gallery in Washington, D.C., was opened to house it.

It was, moreover, the era in which Clara Driscoll, who preferred to think of herself as a cattlewoman, assumed control of the Driscoll empire—comprised of cattle, oil wells, land, banks, hotels, stocks, and bonds—and became one of the most successful businesswomen of her time. When she undertook active operation of the two-year-old Corpus Christi Bank and Trust Company in 1929, its assets were modest. By 1939—the tenth year under her management—the bank's resources exceeded $3 million.

Also in 1939, while she was revitalizing South Texas economy through the development of her oil and gas interests, she matched—two for one—donations toward the establishment of a United States Naval Air Force base at Corpus Christi. Today the Naval Air Station at the south end of Corpus Christi Bay is reputed to be the largest in the nation. In 1943 Mrs. Driscoll sponsored the launching of the U.S.S. *Corpus Christi* at Wilmington, California. After earning a reputation as one of the nation's outstanding philanthropists, she gave Corpus Christi the luxurious twenty-story Robert Driscoll Hotel in 1941 at a cost of $3.5 million.

Toward the end of the period, even though she staunchly supported Roosevelt as the party's candidate, she tried to win the 1940 Democratic presidential nomination for Vice-President Garner. Roosevelt had held the office two terms and the party's opposition to a third was traditional. Furthermore, she considered the vice-president a man of broader intellect than Roosevelt and a superior leader better equipped to serve the country's interests during the critical war period. Her abortive attempt to dethrone Roosevelt cost her $250,000.

In addition to Roosevelt and Garner, others in the national limelight with whom Mrs. Driscoll maintained close relations included Reconstruction Finance Corporation chairman Jesse H. Jones, Postmaster General James A. Farley, Secretary of State Cordell Hull, Speaker of the House Sam Rayburn, and World War I president, Woodrow Wilson. All of these friends respected Clara Driscoll's views on national and world affairs and did not hesitate to seek her counsel. Her friendship with Wilson dated from her brother's university days at Princeton in the early nineties when Wilson was a favorite professor. Wilson was among the first to discover Mrs. Driscoll's talent for diplomacy and political finesse.

As an active clubwoman and philanthropist, Mrs. Driscoll enjoyed the friendship of many women. She was known to most of them affectionately as "Miss Clara." However, her most intimate woman friend was the artist Florence (Flo) Eagar Roberts of San Antonio. Before her marriage Mrs.

Roberts was a frequent traveling companion and the illustrator of Mrs. Driscoll's second book, *In the Shadow of the Alamo*.

Ardent patriot, successful author in her early twenties, financier, and gifted stateswoman, Mrs. Driscoll had a deep compassion for humanity. A burning desire to help persons less fortunate than she was a part of her code. Making money was important to her for what she could accomplish with it in the service of her fellowman. She literally gave away millions in her lifetime; but she did it cautiously, wisely, and for the most part, privately.

Clara Driscoll is still giving. She was the last of her line, and the era she halped to make memorable bears the brunt of receding time. But the children's hospital, which she endowed with a foundation named for her parents and brother, continues to attest to her love for mankind. Now in its twenty-fifth year of operation, the institution has provided free medical care for over forty thousand underprivileged children who have been admitted to the hospital and more than one million who have been treated on an outpatient basis, at a cost of more than $30 million.

Acknowledgments

WHEN I BEGAN THE RESEARCH FOR THIS biography, an archivist of one of the most prestigious libraries of the Southwest tried to discourage me. "You do select the most interesting subjects to investigate," he observed. "The latest, Clara Driscoll, is a classic case in point."

Then he informed me that his library carried references to articles in its general index and a folder of newspaper clippings in the General Biographical File, in addition to slight documentation in the papers of Coppini, Adina de Zavala, Hally Bryan Perry, and a few others. "These, however," he pointed out, "are not sufficient to support a full-scale study . . . which is probably why no one has undertaken the task before."

He assured me that he was not taking a dim view of my choice of a subject. "The reverse is true," he said. "I would be deeply grateful if you could find enough supporting evidence to write a good biography of the lady. One is badly needed."

I was fortunate. My problem was not a sparsity of material. On the contrary, it was a preponderance of it. First through the aid of my librarian friends I began to comb this country for information. Clara Driscoll left her impact on the West Coast. Politicians in Washington, D.C. listened to her. She turned heads in the upper echelons of New York society. She contributed to two wars and was active in foreign service. As the evidence began to pour in, I petitioned for permission to use the Driscoll Archives administered by the members of the Driscoll Foundation and housed on the sixteenth floor of the Bank and Trust Tower in Corpus Christi.

The immense mass of material comprising the Driscoll Archives is staggering, much of it uncatalogued and virgin. A capable writer herself aware of the value of primary sources, Clara Driscoll never threw anything away. She literally preserved everything from a simple cornbread recipe to her cancelled checks for the purchase of the Alamo, pinned, not clipped, to the deed of trust.

xviii / *Acknowledgments*

It is no exaggeration to say that I could not have produced this book without the munificent cooperation of the trustees of the Robert Driscoll and Julia Driscoll and Robert Driscoll, Jr. Foundation: Dr. McIver Furman, Mr. W. Preston Pittman, and Mr. T. S. Scibienski, and the ladies who grace their offices—executive secretary and accountant, Nettie Ruth Hoskins; Betty De Brosse and Jimmie Nicholson. My thanks go also to Brenda Hefly, editor of *The Driscollite* and director of public relations.

It would be remiss of me not to make my manners to those kind friends who took time to endorse me to the Foundation: Elliott T. Bowers, president, and Robert G. Brooks, former vice-president of academic affairs and dean of faculties, of Sam Houston State University; Jewel Gibson, novelist-playwright of Corsicana; Edwin W. Gaston, dean of the graduate school and Ralph W. Steen, president emeritus, of Stephen F. Austin State University; Joseph Milton Nance, professor of history, Texas A&M University; Gwin Morris, academic dean of East Texas Baptist College; and W. L. Thompson, president of Shoal Creek Publishers, Inc. I requested references from a few of these wonderful people and learned later that others had volunteered to recommend me.

I remain in the debt of libraries. My greatest indebtedness for research assistance is to members of the Sam Houston State University Library staff: John P. Nunelee, director; Charles L. Dwyer, in charge of rare documents and books housed in the Colonel John W. Thomason Room; Dong H. Ko, director of interlibrary loan; Diana Bennett and Paul Culp, reference librarians.

Other librarians who went far beyond the call of professional duty to help me include James Stewart, former head of information services, Corpus Christi Public Libraries; the staff of La Retama Public Library of Corpus Christi; and Miss Mary Fleischer, librarian of the Texas Collection of the Barker Texas History Center of the University of Texas at Austin.

I appreciate the interest of various chapters of the Daughters of the Republic of Texas in this project and particularly that of the Clara Driscoll Chapter of Corpus Christi. I desire also to express my warmest gratitude for the interest of Mary Jane Addison of Huntsville, retiring president general of the Daughters of the Republic of Texas, and her worthy successor, Opal Hollis of Coldspring.

Finally, I desire to acknowledge the courtesies of my publishers, Clois W. Bennett and Bob Mallas of Madrona Press, and my efficient and loyal secretary of many years, Jeanette Koger of Huntsville.

CLARA DRISCOLL

1

Antecedents

 CLARA DRISCOLL WAS BORN APRIL 2, 1881,
in the little South Texas coastal town of St. Mary's, which no longer exists.
Her father, Robert Driscoll, Sr., and her mother, Julia (Fox) Driscoll, were
married December 7, 1870. Clara was the couple's second child. Their first,
a son, Robert Driscoll, Jr., was born on December 21, 1871. Robert Driscoll,
Sr., a pioneer cattleman and landbuyer, was the son of Daniel O'Driscoll. Julia.(Fox) Driscoll, an attractive blonde woman with scholarly tendencies, who
was educated in the Ursuline Convent in San Antonio, was the daughter of
James Fox, who was also a rancher. Her brother, Charles P. Fox, the sheriff
of Refugio County, was for a number of years the foreman in charge of the
Driscoll ranches in Goliad and Bee counties.

On her father's side Clara Driscoll was descended from Irish forebears, and
on her mother's, English. Both paternal and maternal grandfathers were early
settlers who helped to colonize the Power and Hewetson land grants in Refugio and Goliad counties. Colonel James Power and Dr. James Hewetson
formed a partnership and applied for an empresario contract to colonize
twenty-two littoral leagues along the Texas coast with immigrants from Mexico and Ireland in 1829. The grants, however, were not actually issued until
1834.[1] Meanwhile, the Mexican government of Coahuila and Texas granted
the empresarios a concession on April 21, 1830, to colonize the ten littoral
leagues of Texas between the Guadalupe and Nueces rivers.[2]

Powers, who took over the active operation of the colony, went to Ireland
in 1833 to recruit immigrants. He returned with 350, but a large number of
these succumbed to cholera when the contingent reached New Orleans.[3] A-
mong the cholera victims was Clara Driscoll's paternal grandmother's first
husband.

Upon reaching Texas, part of the survivors remained at Copano Bay while
others received their legal allotment of land from Commissioner José Jesús

Viduarri in 1834. Clara Driscoll's paternal grandparents were among those hardy Irish pioneers who began the colonization of that part of Texas. Two hundred land titles were issued before the Congress of the Republic of Texas in 1836 declared all of the public lands to be the property of the state.[4] Inasmuch as Clara Driscoll's forebears were among those fortunate 200, they had the advantage of getting a headstart in planting roots in the new world—a rich tradition of leadership that bears fruit today.

Both grandsires Fox and O'Driscoll immigrated to America in time to participate in the Battle of San Jacinto, April 21, 1836. The more prominent of the two was apparently the latter. At the end of the Texas Revolution, Daniel O'Driscoll settled in Refugio County. "Among the earliest ranchers in this area [Refugio County] was Daniel O'Driscoll, a Power colonist, sergeant at San Jacinto, public official, and ancestor of Clara and Robert Driscoll and Birdie [Roberta] Rooke."[5] He is listed on the San Jacinto muster roll as Daniel O. Driscoll, third sergeant of Company A of the Regulars.[6] The family dropped the Celtic O, followed by the apostrophe, in favor of the Anglicized initial O.

Before his discharge from the Texas Army in 1838, Driscoll was promoted to lieutenant. Immediately after his discharge, he first settled in Victoria. Here he married Catherine Duggan, a widow whose husband had succumbed to the cholera epidemic en route. Mrs. Duggan had a daughter, Lizzie. Both sons, Jeremiah O. (Jerry) and Robert (Bob) were born to the couple in Victoria. It was in 1843 that the elder Driscoll moved his family to Refugio, where he operated an inn for a time in addition to his ranching activities. One of the first county officials to serve after statehood, he was elected as justice of Refugio County in 1846 and served until his accidental death in 1849. His wife Catherine died three years later, and the young sons, Jerry and Bob, were reared by their older half-sister, Mrs. Daniel C. Doughty.[7]

When Clara Driscoll was born in 1881, Texas independence, for which her grandsires fought at San Jacinto, was less than fifty years old; and some aging veterans scattered around still remembered the Alamo. In 1881 O. M. Roberts, the pay-as-you-go politician, was serving his second term as governor of Texas, the capitol was accidentally burned and would be rebuilt in 1888, and the organization identified as the Daughters of the Republic of Texas was as yet unorganized.

In the year of Clara Driscoll's birth the Civil War, in which Jerry and Bob Driscoll fought for the Confederacy, had been over sixteen years and the South had emerged from the harsh penalties of reconstruction. In 1881 James A. Garfield, the compromise choice of the Republican party had been removed from the presidency by an assassin's bullet four months after his inauguration, and Chester A. Arthur, another political misfit, became president.

But 1881 was a good year and certainly the closeknit Driscolls were not complaining. After almost a decade they had produced a girl—a little lady with sparkling hazel eyes, like her father's, and reddish-black hair—who increased their happy family to four. Robert Driscoll, Jr., their son, was a manly young fellow going on ten.

Clara Driscoll's birthplace perched on a bluff on the northwestern shore of Copano Bay in the heart of the Karankawa and Copane Indian country. Since Copano Bay was considered a part of Aransas Bay, the town was sometimes referred to as "St. Mary's of Aransas." Two miles southwest of St. Mary's was the village of Bayside. Because of its Indian background, the location was for many years the haunt of archeologists.

The erstwhile seaport and titular county seat of Refugio County had its heyday between 1850 and 1886, as the town, along with Rockport and Fulton in the coastal area, enjoyed a boom for more than fifteen years.[8] During this period St. Mary's became the major lumber mart of South Texas and also shipped hides, tallow, cattle, and cotton by water and through freight lines overland to Refugio, Goliad, Beeville, San Antonio, Uvalde, and other points.[9] Although the town of Refugio had served as the seat of government in Refugio County since 1836, the Constitutional Convention adopted an ordinance changing the county seat to St. Mary's on January 18, 1869.[10] The records were not moved, however; and on March 15, 1871, influenced by an increase in coastal population, the legislature changed the county seat to Rockport. But the older citizens inhabiting the inland area objected so strenuously that the legislature compromised on April 18, 1871, by creating Aransas County with Rockport as the seat of government and restored the county seat of Refugio to the remainder of Refugio County.[11]

In 1857 the townsite, which was originally plotted by Joseph Smith, consisted of ninety-one blocks, each 400 feet square, arranged in seven tiers of thirteen blocks each. The first thirteen blocks were separated from the bay by a wide beach below the bluff called "The Strand."[12] The Driscoll brothers had built comfortable two-story homes on Block 12, and in addition to Clara, the daughters of Jeremiah O. Driscoll—Roberta, Laura, and Kathleen—were born here.

Also below the bluff were the wharf and the warehouses. The 1200-foot wharf extended to the deep serpentine-shaped channel that bulged in front of El Copano and twisted through the comblike reefs beyond Live Oak Point and Lamar, into Aransas Bay and thence over a perilous bar to the Gulf. Although the channel was navigable for seagoing vessels, the Aransas bar was difficult to cross and its maritime history is laced with stories of shipwrecks.[13]

Still the port flourished as some old seasalts became skilled at navigating the bar and St. Mary's, as indicated, had its golden age. At one time the town boasted a two-story concrete building known as the "Opera House," several hotels, including one of three stories, the customary mercantile houses, lumber yards, blacksmith shops, livery stables, even a photography studio, and a celebrated barrel house, or quart shop, whose proprietor, George S. Sherman, had a ribald wit and sense of humor "that made him as popular locally as Will Rogers was nationally."[14] *The Vaquero*, Refugio's first newspaper, was founded at St. Mary's and was published until 1870. St. Mary's had the convenience of telegraph service from about 1870 to 1890. The last operator was Frank B. Rooke, who married Jeremiah O. Driscoll's daughter Roberta.[15] By the time of the Civil War St. Mary's had a population of three hundred and had grown considerably by the 1880s.

St. Mary's streets were constantly glutted by teamsters, carters, and cattle drovers in town to make contact with incoming vessels and to ship their own wares by water and inland freighters. Among the prominent cattlemen were the familiar faces of the Driscolls and their friends Jim McFaddin, "Coon" Duncan, and John Young, protagonist of J. Frank Dobie's *A Vaquero of the Brush Country*. Between 1837 and 1885 lumber schooners and cattle boats docked frequently at the wharves of St. Mary's.[16] Some of the seagoing ships that made St. Mary's their regular port of call had such names as the *Waterloo*, the *Fairy*, *Belleport*, and the *Hannah*. But the all-time favorite was the schooner *Frances*, a post-bellum ship owned and captained by Theodore (Charley) Johnson and about which the poem "A Night in Tilden" was written.[17]

St. Mary's also had its lighter side as its citizens took time out to entertain themselves. There was the annual horse-racing tournament, usually climaxed by a dance in the evening at one of the hotels, which drew people from all sections of the coastal area. The fine hard sand below the bluff served as the racetrack and spectators did not hesitate to evaluate the horseflesh and lay their bets. Another popular diversion was the moonlight dance on the deck of a great lumber schooner docked at the wharf. Customarily the arrival of any big three-masted schooner was the occasion for a dance that same evening. Sometimes the sailors themselves provided the music, usually stringed instruments. At others, local talent did the fiddling. At least one old-timer could make the music on his fiddle and cut the "buck and wing" at the same time, without missing a note, until his considerable talent was sacrificed on the alter of religion.[18]

Still a third form of recreation was the moonlight oyster bake. Copano

Bay was well supplied with oyster reefs; and while certain gregarious inhabitants made a specialty of gathering the seafood in vast quantities, others made of the bake per se a gastronomic masterpiece. They baked the oysters in their shells over hot coals in the ground according to a recipe handed down from past generations. This popular activity attracted people from miles inland.[19]

There were particular places of amusement usually reserved for the gentlemen. The most famous barrel house has been mentioned. Not only did the male population of St. Mary's and their guests refresh themselves with hard liquor, they also indulged in gambling for both fun and profit. Until the storm of 1886 destroyed it, one of the largest gaming houses on the Texas coast was located at St. Mary's.[20] Many well-known stockmen and professional gamblers patronized it.

But the decline of St. Mary's was inevitable. Despite the tenacity with which some of the older settlers tried to hold on to it, a combination of events spelled out its extinction. The first of these was the eventual failure to cope with the Aransas bar. The Morgan steamship line had been forced to discontinue business because of it. Another decisive factor was St. Mary's inability to obtain the rail connection she had been promised by the San Antonio and Aransas Pass Railroad, while Rockport, Beeville, and Corpus Christi were successful. Finally—and worst of all—there was a series of disastrous storms—in 1869, 1875, 1886, and 1887—which wiped out port facilities.

The storm of 1875 began on September 15 and mushroomed to the proportions of a cyclone on the sixteenth. The most devastating to lash the Texas coast up to that time, the storm completely destroyed the town of Saluria and almost demolished the port of Indianola.[22]

St. Mary's made partial recovery from the damage inflicted by the storms of 1869 and 1875. This fact may have had some bearing on the Driscoll family's residence there in 1881 at the time of Clara's birth. However, the exodus from St. Mary's after 1887 was rapid, and the Robert Driscoll family was among those to evacuate the town by that time if not earlier. As late as 1890, on the other hand, Jeremiah O. Driscoll and his son-in-law, Frank B. Rooke, had elected to remain.[23]

By the turn of the century only a few struggling remnants of the port of St. Mary's remained to testify to its former glory, among them, the old Sherman barrel house, the Neel Hotel, and the Jerry Driscoll residence. In 1907, with the closing of the post office and general store, the demise of St. Mary's had become official.[24]

When the Civil War ended in 1865 and Bob and his older brother Jerry returned home, after serving four years in the Virginia theater, their sole possessions, except for two small tracts of land heired from the family, were the tattered regimental uniforms they were wearing and the spent ponies they were riding back to Texas. What they knew of ranching, they had learned before the war from their older brother-in-law, Captain Daniel C. Doughty.

Since the Driscoll brothers had started as common cowhands, they had collaborated as a team. As diverse as the two were in personality—Jerry, calm and easygoing but positive when occasion warranted; and Bob, restless, adventurous, and sometimes quick tempered—they both had inherited Daniel O. Driscoll's unconquerable spirit. Like him, they were men of vision with faith in the future. Immediately they appraised conditions, continued to pool their modest resources, and began to build up an estate. When the war ground to a close, the Great Plains still belonged to the Indians, whether it was the Comanche or Apache in the Southwest or the Sioux or Cheyenne in the North. But there remained the vast Texas frontier, and Texas was itself a part of the Plains, which comprised about 44 percent of the area of the United States.[25] Theoughout the first half of the nineteenth century, the Plains were equated in the American mind with the myth of the Great American Desert—a boundless wasteland populated by wild beasts and savages, a land of cactus and prairie dogs, of shifting sands and unpredictable dust storms.

Moreover, an integral part of the so-called Great American Desert was the original land from which Nueces County was carved—that enormous trapezoidal area running westward from San Antonio to Laredo, down the Rio Grande to Brownsville, up along the Gulf Coast to Indianola (once a significant entrepôt before tropical hurricanes leveled it) and then northward back to San Antonio. From 1850 to the war's end, in this huge region between the Nueces River and the Rio Grande, the open range cattle industry was spawned. Eventually it spread over all of the Great Plains and revolutionized ranching. Over millions of acres of free land thousands of herds of the fleet-footed longhorns and wild mustangs roamed. There were no windmills, no fences, no roads—only miles and miles of open pasture land with sufficient mesquite and scrub to protect the cattle in inclement weather plus the lush grass and water for sustenance. More, in this rattlesnake- and coyote-infested brush country, called the Brasada, the animals had reproduced without risk of decimation during the four years of war while the men and boys were away shouldering guns. How the cattle, coyotes, and rattlesnakes managed to live so amicably together and proliferate is one of nature's riddles.

True enough, the first longhorns had been introduced to the continent in 1493 by Columbus and later in 1540 by Cortes, along with the Spanish mustang, from which the noted Texas cow pony had evolved. But these cattle had probably gravitated to South Texas from all over the state and perhaps other states in the North and West. The animals had a tendency to drift before bad weather and, finding the South Plains of Texas pleasant, had remained. Here, then, free for the taking were thousands of head of cattle. But it required men of courage and stamina and hours of hard labor to rope and brand the wild animals. By the same token, the yearly increase went to the men whose brand the mother cows bore. All that was necessary was for cattlemen to transfer their brands to the mother cow and wait for the calves to drop. Bob and Jerry Driscoll were such men. Once a year they branded the calves whose mothers carried the Wrench brand, soon to become one of the most famous in the Southwest. Occasionally the Indians raided, two- and three-year drouths set in, and depredations on the herds by cattle rustlers were not uncommon. But these were all calculated risks which the Driscolls took in stride and overcame.

Once their herds were built up, the brothers sought an adequate market. Another aggressive man with an optimistic outoook, Joseph G. McCoy, helped to provide that. He had heard of the ingenuity of Jesse Chisholm, the half-breed trailblazer and wagonmaster, got in touch with him, and thus came into existence the Chisholm Trail that opened up Northern markets to Texas cattlemen.[26]

All of this had a monumental impact on the economy of the Southwest, as men with such names as Driscoll, King, and Kleberg made ranching history. Thus not only did the enterprising Driscolls witness this exploding of the Great American Desert myth, they had been a viable part of it.

Although the Driscoll brothers worked as a team, at the outset of their collaboration Jerry usually handled the land buying while Bob directed the ranching operations. However, Bob Driscoll had demonstrated early qualities of both leadership and business ability. In the spring of 1872, when cattlemen of Refugio County were called upon to fill a United States government contract for 1,200 big steers, the "crowd," as the cattlemen called themselves, named Bob Driscoll as leader. "Robert Driscoll, although among the younger men of the outfit, was unanimously chosen as boss, and no better choice could have been made."[27] Because of the business ability of the Driscoll brothers, cattlemen, who provided packing companies with beef, had them to negotiate the trade. One such transaction reveals that the brothers realized early the value of land. Offered a fee of $5,000 or 5,000 acres of land, the Driscolls opted for the latter.[28]

Eventually Robert Driscoll took over the Nueces County ranches, making his home base Corpus Christi, while Jerry managed the Refugio, Bee, and Goliad ranches. By 1890, or shortly before, the brothers had begun to partition their immense holdings. They were engaged in the process when Jerry and his wife, Anna Elizabeth Allen Driscoll, died of tuberculosis and their son-in-law, Frank Booth Rooke, helped with the final division of the estate. In the partition, the children of Jeremiah O. Driscoll received the ranches in Refugio and Goliad counties and most of the holdings in Bee. The major portion of Robert Driscoll's share was the 83,000-acre Palo Alto ranch.[29] With its black, waxy soil, which produced excellent grass, it was one of the most valuable properties in all of the Southwest. Not only was Robert Driscoll able to stand in the center of Palo Alto and, as far as he could look in four directions, see grazing herds that bore his brand, he would subsequently add the 53,000-acre Sweden ranch and the La Gloria ranch in Duval County; the 20,000-acre Los Machos ranch near Alice in Jim Wells County, and the 8,000-acre Clara ranch near Skidmore, Texas.[30] Robert Driscoll seemed to have the Midas touch. Everything he put his hands to turned to money. An innovative cattleman of the first order, he soon thinned out the lean and shaggy longhorns and replaced them with whitefaces and herds of the Brahman strain. In fact, he was one of the first to cross native cattle with the Brahman breed. Another thing, Driscoll never overstocked his ranches. Consequently, his ranches always had grass when many others were bare. Thus Bob Driscoll was well on his way toward a $10 million empire later to be compounded of "equal parts of land and oil and the trail-driven cattle."[31]

But Driscoll—a proud, straight-limbed man of medium height with fair complexion, piercing brown eyes and brown hair, who picked up the title of colonel because of his military bearing—never forgot his modest beginnings. A self-educated and self-made man, he relished the memory of driving the big herds up the trail to the northern markets; recalled with gusto the days when he could round up his own cattle on his various ranches with no governmental interference. Ranching was as much a pleasure to him as a business and he virtually lived in the saddle. He also loved to hunt for wild game so plentiful in the brush country. Moreover, he was expert at handling a rifle, shooting from either shoulder with equal skill. He kept packs of deer hounds and greyhounds for running coyotes. One of the main amusements at Palo Alto was coyote chasing. For the sport, Colonel Driscoll, with his young daughter, and son Robert, Jr., would saddle up and join several cowhands behind a pack of twenty-five greyhounds on a chase.

Driscoll often regaled his friends with stories of his early ranching experiences. There was of course much "mavericking" and brand changing, along with wire cutting after fencing was introduced. He especially enjoyed telling the yarn of how he traded a pocketknife for his first cow. He conceded that it sounded like a hard deal to consummate, but that he was the one "trading" (pulling) the knife. Even though mild mannered, Driscoll could be tough when occasion demanded.

Not the least of Driscoll's recommendations was his genuine love for animals. He was a connoisseur of horses as well as cattle and equally fond of both. As a matter of fact, even when modern ranching switched to mechanization, he stuck to horses, convinced that motor vehicles were against the finest traditions of the industry. Because of his concern for animals, he had his cowboys dispense with their quirts and spurs and manage the beasts with kindness. He believed in gentling the herd on the trail and avoiding overexciting the cattle. On long, hard drives he was known to insist upon the cattle being fed before the men.

Driscoll's range hands had a deep respect for their employer's principles and his seriousness on the trail. Even in his younger days some of them referred to him as "the old man" without disrespect. As serious as Driscoll was at roundup and on the trail, he never pulled rank. He usually dressed in similar range garb to that of his outfit, wearing blue pants and a yellow shirt; and he never expected a hand to perform a task that he couldn't handle himself. More often than not, he reserved for himself the difficult and dangerous jobs. In short, he was a regular cowboy. At roundup he would crack his eggs in a shovel, cook them over the campfire, then eat them from the same "utensil," as the other cowhands did.

But on his trips to Corpus Christi and other towns, the colonel was strictly the businessman sans chaps, boots, and bandana. By his excellent grooming and conservative dress he would not have been taken for a cattleman, but a banker, which indeed he soon became.

No sooner had Robert Driscoll, Sr., established Palo Alto as his base of operations than he began to map plans for the development of South Texas. As early as 1904, he, together with Robert J. Kleberg, Sr., John G. Kenedy, and a few others, was instrumental in bringing the first railroad to the south Gulf Coast. The men pledged land and other inducements to arouse capitalistic interest. As a result, the tracks of the St. Louis, Brownsville, and Mexico Railroad linked the people to the north in Corpus Christi with their neighbors southward.

Realizing that people and trade were the lifeblood of the railroad, Driscoll was the first man in the area to offer land for townsites and agricultural development.[32] For this purpose he sold 78,000 acres from his Palo Alto ranch, and the towns of Robstown (named for his son, Robert, Jr.) and Driscoll (named for himself) came into existence.[33] Where once were thousands of head of cattle a score of cotton gins sprang up and farmhouses dotted square miles of rich prairie. This section opened up a rich storehouse of natural fertility and the country began its first step toward eventual industrialization.

Another commercial development which Driscoll initiated was the movement to convert the port of Corpus Christi into a safe and adequate harbor for oceangoing ships.[34] Among Driscoll's most successful enterprises in downtown Corpus Christi was the Corpus Christi National Bank, the largest banking institution in that section of the state.[35]

Through their ranching activities the Klebergs and the Driscolls became close friends. In the early days of ranching the country was pretty well divided at the Nueces and Kleberg county line by the only fence in the area. Everything to the north belonged to Driscoll, and everything to the south belonged to Kleberg. So at roundup time cowhands from both outfits would work together to help each other out. The two families remained good friends through three generations.

Mrs. Driscoll, said to have been an unusually attractive woman of slight stature, was a devoted housewife and mother. When her husband was getting started in the ranching industry, she and the two children accompanied him as he traveled around to contract to sell beef and purchase land. Later at Palo Alto, after the family fortune was secure, she became a gracious hostess to visiting dignitaries and her husband's business associates. Of a scholarly disposition, she took particular interest in the children's education. She enrolled each in excellent private schools in San Antonio for their early training. Robert Driscoll, Jr., took his law degree from Princeton in 1893 when he was twenty-two. It was said that he took especial pride in having the signature of Professor Woodrow Wilson on his diploma. Mrs. Driscoll later enrolled Clara in the select Miss Peebles and Thompson's School in New York before taking her abroad to complete her education in a convent, the Chateau Dieudonne, an hour's drive from Paris. At the latter school young Clara studied German and French along with other subjects.

But the Texas area central to the Southwestern cattle tradition (before barbed wire came into common use in the mid-eighties) was also steeped in earlier history as it involved Spain, as well as Mexico, France, and the United States. The 775-square-mile stretch of land comprising Nueces County, originally inhabited by Lipan-Apache and Karankawa Indians, was the first part of Texas to be explored when Alonzo Alvarez de Piñeda dropped anchor in Corpus Christi Bay in 1519, mapped the Gulf of Mexico, and took possession in the name of the Spanish crown.[36] Cabeza de Vaca, who discovered the tuna region near Corpus Christi and named the Nueces the "River of Nuts," reinforced Spain's claim by further exploration before ending his seven-year odyssey in Mexico City in 1536.[37]   Likewise, Rene Robert Cavelier, Sieur de la Salle, who named the river "Riviere D'Or," tagged the rich area for France before his untimely end in 1687.[38]

José de Escandón, the Spanish colonizer responsible for the first successful settlement along the Rio Grande between the present towns of Laredo and Brownsville, made the initial attempt to set up a colony—villa de Vedoya—on the Nueces. He sent Captain Pedro Gonzales Paredes in 1749 with fifty families to locate on the lower left bank of the river near the present site of Corpus Christi.[39]   Although the attempt failed and many of the settlers relocated across the Rio Grande, ranchers with grants from the Spanish crown occupied the area intermittently until the Texas Revolution.

Mexican soldiers attempted to garrison "Lipan Land," or Lipantitlán, as the Indian village on the Nueces was called, to enforce the Law of April 6, 1830, prohibiting further Anglo-American immigration into Texas. In 1831 Francisco Ruiz commanded the fort. In 1835 Texas volunteers under Ira J. Westover captured it. The site was occupied briefly by Francis W. Johnson and the New Orleans Greys on the ill-fated Matamoros Expedition.

Because of its proximity to Mexico and its predominantly Mexican population, Nueces County was vitally affected by the war for Texas independence. After the Republic of Texas came into existence in 1836, skirmishes between the Texans and the Mexicans became more frequent as a result of the boundary controversy. Mexico claimed the Nueces River as the Texas boundary while Texas and the United States claimed the Rio Grande. The contested area between the rivers developed into a sort of no man's land and the boundary dispute eventually embroiled the United States and Mexico in a war.

Despite the border dissension, Henry L. Kinney purchased ten leagues of land on the west bank of the mouth of the Nueces River from Enrique Villareal and established a trading post. Although the date is disputed, Kinney sailed into the crescent-shaped bay in either 1838 or 1839. W. S. Henry, a contemporary, insists that the date Kinney came was 1838. However, an affidavit bearing Kinney's signature and published in the Houston *Telegram and Texas Register* on August 25, 1841, confirms the date of 1839.[40]   Kinney and his partner, William Aubrey of Alabama, established a trading post that became known as Kinney's Ranch and provided the nucleus for the present city of Corpus Christi.

Kinney chose the site of his trading post with exceeding care. First, its physical features were assets: the beach of white shell and sand to the north, the very imposing 40-foot-high bluff to the south, the 21-mile-wide bay, self-landlocked with narrow islands protecting it from tidal waves and intruders. Then the strategic location made the site an excellent outlet for shipping goods by horseback or wagon train to and from the interior of Mexico as well as Texas. Finally, it was easy to evade payment of the customs duties of both Texas and Mexico.

Thus Kinney was able to carry on a profitable trade in smuggled goods with both countries. Aware of the disputed territory, or in spite of it, the colonizer was the first to establish regular trade routes in defiance of the customs collectors of Mexico and Texas. The Mexicans brought in droves of horses and mules, saddles and bridles, blankets and silver, and returned with bolts of unbleached domestic and tobacco.

Most of the schooners shipped out of New Orleans, thus enabling Kinney to observe both ends of the trade and any problems or obstacles that might arise.

The Mexican law of 1824 had prohibited the settlement of foreigners within ten leagues of the coast without consent of the Mexican government. Kinney knew that the time of reckoning was imminent. But to forestall any interference with his enterprise he made a successful trip to Matamoros. His diplomacy paid off and by 1840 the trading post was considered permanent. With Kinney's permission other businesses sprang up as a small colony of venturesome settlers developed. For protection against warring bands and Indian raiders, Kinney maintained a small body of armed men. Captain Villareal of Matamoros, who claimed a grant of 400 square miles on the shores of Corpus Christi Bay, from the Oso to the Nueces, attempted to dispossess Kinney. Desperate but determined, Kinney met Villareal's envoy, who demanded surrender and delivery of all goods at the post as the price of peace. Concealing his men to disguise their inferior number, the American made a display of strength by exploding mined bombs with a loud uproar. He warned Villareal's envoy to inform his leader "that his bones would bleach on the prairie if he attacked."[41] The ruse worked and arrangements were made for the transfer of Villareal's grant to Kinney. Final papers for the transaction were drafted on January 4, 1840. It was not until 1847, however, that Kinney made the last payment on the property to Villareal's widow.

Meanwhile Kinney's competitors tried to undermine him and discredit him to both the Texas and Mexican governments. To compound his troubles, an outgrowth of Indian and outlaw Mexican raids led to the formation, north of the Rio Grande, of companies of "volunteers," consisting of lawless Anglo-Americans that began to raid the settlement indiscriminately and to prey upon his trading trains. His business suffered. But Kinney, who by this time had become a goodwill agent for President Lamar, was more concerned for the safety of the settlers. He continued to work as peacemaker and ultimately the tide turned and Corpus Christi Bay reflected the colonizer's prosperity.

For a time, as the boundary dispute waged, Corpus Christi became a town without a country. Then when the war between the United States and Mexico began it became the base from which the action was launched to settle the boundary dispute. When General Zachary Taylor set up a supply depot—Fort Marcy—and established the first federal burial place—Bay View Cemetery—for eight casualties sustained en route, at the location in July, 1845, Corpus Christi assumed strategic significance. Taylor's subsequent nine-month encampment at the mouth of the Nueces in the disputed territory added further to the town's historic importance in American history.

During General Taylor's occupation of Corpus Christi Bay he mustered several companies of John C. Hays's Texas Rangers into the United States Army. Aside from the incredible courage demonstrated in guerrilla fighting and derring-do, for which they were noted, the Nueces County mounted men performed invaluable reconnaissance duty for the American forces because of their familiarity with the terrain and the character of its inhabitants.[42] A number of these same intrepid rangers joined General Winfield Scott later in the drive on Mexico City, captured the fortress of Chapultepec, and celebrated the American victory in the halls of Montezuma on September 14, 1847.[43]

The military depot at Corpus Christi continued to be of service and was not abandoned until 1857. In fact, at one time Nueces County maintained five federal forts.

The first bloodshed of the Mexican War was spilled at Palo Alto, twelve miles north of the Rio Grande, on May 8, 1846. Here brave American troops aggregating twenty-three hundred, under Taylor's command defeated a Mexican force twice their size. Many of the soldiers had been recruited in the immediate vicinity of Corpus Christi. The encounter, essentially an artillery action, demonstrated the superiority of Taylor's cannon and strengthened American morale.

With the recognition by the Treaty of Guadalupe Hidalgo (February 2, 1848) of the Rio Grande as the Texas border, the area of Corpus Christi began a period of rapid expansion. Once the Texans had established their claim to the Rio Grande, they confiscated the Spanish stock which the Mexicans retreating southward were unable to transport across the river. Legislation enacted by the Texas Congress declared that all unbranded cattle were to be public property.[44]

Nueces County also contributed to the Civil War. Before the main hostilities between the North and South began, the Battle of the Nueces was fought at sunrise on August 10, 1862. Sixty-five Union sympathizers en route to Mexico had bivouacked for the night on the west bank of the river without choosing a defensive position or posting a strong guard. Ninety-four mounted Confederate soldiers, composed mostly of Germans, under the command of Lieutenant C. D. McRae, attacked the camp. Casualties consisted of nineteen Unionists killed and nine wounded (later executed), two Confederates killed and eighteen wounded, including McRae. Of the thirty-seven Unionists who escaped, six were killed by Confederates on October 18, 1862.[45]

The Eighth Texas Infantry Battalion was assigned to guard the Texas coast between Lamar and Corpus Christi, where various units were concentrated. In the winter of 1862 a regiment known as the Eighth Texas Infantry Regiment was organized with Alfred M. Hobby as commander. The regiment guarded the coast for three years, fought skirmishes on the islands and in the bays and inlets, defended Corpus Christi twice, participated in the Battle of Galveston Island, and saw action in the Louisiana campaign.[46] The contingent was so successful that it was awarded a special citation by the state legislature.

Banquete, in the western portion of Nueces County, became a strategic point as a crossroads for trade with Mexico after the restoration of normal relations. Texans shipped cotton to Mexico in exchange for medical and other necessities for the use of the Confederacy.

It was in this environment of the range and scene of centuries of history that Clara Driscoll's formative years were shaped. History to her was not confined to a textbook. She cherished the fact that her family had lived it. Quite literally Clara Driscoll attained young girlhood with the bawl of a yearling in her ears and the acrid smell of hot burning cowhide in her nostrils. By her own admission she was equally skilled behind a revolver or a rifle, was born and bred to the saddle, proficient with a lariat. In fact, she was capable of doing almost anything her father's ranch hands could do except bulldog a steer.[47] But even as a girl in her teens Clara Driscoll possessed no qualities of the hoyden to which such a background is sometimes conducive. On the contrary, she gave the impression of having spent her life in the fashionable capitals of the world. Not only had she studied abroad, she had visited Europe several times and had been around the world before she was eighteen.

As a young girl Clara Driscoll possessed a wisdom that belied her tender years. Still she found the quiet peace that she associated with grazing cattle to be a perennial font of inspiration. It was also during her early years at Palo

Alto that she came to appreciate Mexican culture, especially the aspects of folk music and the dance, and learned to speak the language like a native. For that matter, by the time she was sixteen, she had a command of four languages—English, Spanish, French, and German. While Clara Driscoll inherited her intellectual tendencies and the classic beauty of her oval face and flawless complexion from the distaff side of the family and her firm Irish chin, hazel eyes, and independence from her father, she never forgot that it was this legacy of the range and atmosphere of historic legend that engendered within her traits of self-reliance and a profound love of her native state.

Moreover, the product of every cultural advantage that money could provide (excellent schooling, musical training, world-wide travel) and the object of lavish attention from an adoring older brother and devoted parents, Clara Driscoll was not even spoiled. Not by the farthest stretch of the imagination did she typify the stereotype of the pampered little rich girl. In addition to her feeling for history and her patriotic ardor, she developed an affinity for literature and the arts and a deep compassion for humanity. All of these attributes, either singly or in combination, left the young Texan well equipped for the later role she was destined to play.

2

The Birth of a Legend

WHEN CLARA DRISCOLL LEFT AMERICA IN 1892 to complete her education and to travel abroad, in the company of her mother, she was a young girl. As noted, Julia (Fox) Driscoll—a woman of culture and intellectual attainment—took pride in personally supervising her daughter's education. After Clara had finished training in Texas and New York, Mrs. Driscoll enrolled her in a school near Paris to conclude her studies. At the time of her departure the nineteenth century—an era of technical advancement with its increasingly industrialized society—was nearing its close.

When Clara Driscoll returned to America almost a decade later, at the turn of the century, she was a young woman of eighteen. It was on the last lap of their return trip that Mrs. Driscoll suddenly died on May 23, 1899, in London. It was a rapidly changing society to which Clara Driscoll returned. Americans were no longer concerned with the past. They were obsessed with the present. Americans subscribed to the gospel of progress and they equated progress with change.

The years abroad had matured the young Texan. She had visited every country in Europe, had spent time in Kashmir and the Himalayas, and had lived with her mother one summer on the Godavari River in Bombay. In Bombay she had come in contact with an Indian woman whose philosophy made a lasting impression on her life.[1] Certainly Old World respect for antiquity and reverence for national shrines were not misplaced on her. To the contrary, she returned to America with a keener perception of the ancient.

But her exposure to European culture had not diminished Clara Driscoll's love for her native state. When she reached Texas and discovered that the state also had succumbed to the superficial twentieth-century ideas of progress, she was appalled. In San Antonio, the birthplace of Texas independence, were flagrant examples. Widespread indifference to the crumbling ruins of the missions and other relics of the past shocked the young girl. But the worst evidence of neglect was the Alamo. The sacred mission chapel stood in ruins shunted aside, in fact almost obscured by business monstrosities of private ownership. Clara Driscoll initiated the new year—indeed the new century—with a letter to the San Antonio *Express*, January 14, 1901. In part the eighteen-year-old girl's incisive phrases read:

> To live for any length of time in the Old World spoils one for things and places which savor of newness. . . . Their monuments, that speak to them of the valor of their forefathers, are held as things sacred. . . . Every respect and deference is shown to any edifice that boasts of historic interest, by the way they preserve and care for it. . . . We uncover our heads and speak in hushed voices in their pantheons, where are buried their famous heroes. We tread with timid feet the battlefield of Waterloo, and yet, there is standing today, right in our very home, an old ruin, a silent monument of the dark and stormy days of Texas. . . . It is our Alamo . . . and how do we treat it?
>
> How can we expect others to attach the importance to it that it so well deserves, when we Texans, who live within its shadow, are so careless of its existence? There does not stand in the world today a building or monument which can recall such a deed of heroism and bravery, such sacrifice and courage, as that of the brave men who fought and fell inside those historic walls. Today the Alamo should stand out, free and clear. All the unsightly obstructions should be torn away. I am sure that if the matter were taken up by some patriotic Texans a sufficient amount could be raised that would enable something of the kind to be done. Yes, every Texan would give his little mite to see the Alamo placed amid surroundings where it would stand out for what it is . . . the Grandest Monument in the History of the World.[2]

It was deplorable to Clara Driscoll that what should have been the world's most revered shrine had been sacrificed to commercialism under the guise of progress.

> Progress, the essence of prosperity, is the embodiment of Americanism. But from the tourist's point of view progress loses twenty-fold in competition with sacred ruins and picturesque antiquity. . . . And the fame of heroes, won through the Alamo and other missions, neglected . . . and weather-beaten by time, is what will endure in the memory of all who have seen or read of the old city of San Antonio.[3]

At the time Clara Driscoll arrived, the Hugo-Schmeltzer's unsightly property was in the process of exchanging hands. On September 11, 1890, Reagan Houston had tried to purchase it for a consideration of $160,000. He paid $60,000 cash and the remainder in three vendor's lien notes amounting to $100,000. Apparently he had overextended himself, for on April 18, 1892, he relinquished the property to Hugo-Schmeltzer for the return of his vendor's lien notes.[4] Here the title would remain until September 26, 1903, at which time it would be conveyed to Charles Hugo by the other members of the firm for $75,000.[5]

Immediately Clara Driscoll embarked on a project to preserve the Alamo—a battle that would require more than two years just as a beginning. Meanwhile, a group of patriotic women, opposed to the threatened destruction of the old chapel, had organized under the name of the Daughters of the Republic of Texas on November 6, 1891. Eligibility for membership required women to be descendants of Austin's "Old Three Hundred" colonists or the defenders and founders of the Republic of Texas. The essential purposes of the organization were to perpetuate the Texas heritage, to preserve historic landmarks and documents, and to encourage the study of Texas history.[6]

Clara Driscoll, who was represented at San Jacinto by both grandfathers, lost no time in joining the de Zavala Chapter of the Daughters of the Republic of Texas in San Antonio. Then she proposed that the organization buy the Hugo-Schmeltzer Company property and launched a campaign to raise money for the purpose.

The old mission-fortress, known originally as the Mission of San Antonio de Valero and later abridged to the Alamo—the Spanish word for cottonwood which grew along the river and the *acequia* ("water ditch")—had a long and checkered history. Throughout the years, while much has been written on the thirteen-day holding action that paved the way for Texas independence and the heroic roles the defenders played in it, people tend to forget the precise details and particularly the significance of the mission-fortress to later Texas and American history. Accordingly, a brief résumé of the Alamo chronicle from 1847 to 1903 bears scrutiny.

After Texas was annexed to the United States, the federal army converted the Alamo into an arsenal. In April, 1847, notwithstanding, the federal government acknowledged to holding the property as a tenant of the Catholic church under the Right Reverend John M. Odin of the Catholic Diocese of Texas.[7]

Also San Antonio claimed the Alamo mission property basing its title on a direct grant from the king of Spain in 1733.[8] The city insisted that its rights to the property were strengthened by certain acts of the Congress of the Republic of Texas passed in 1837, 1838, and 1842.

However, the Congress of the Republic of Texas passed an act on January 18, 1841, giving the Catholic church specific claim to the Alamo chapel and the entire property of the mission compound.[9] The continued delivery of the Alamo registry of births and deaths to the San Fernando Cathedral indicated further church control of the shrine.

The first suit filed in the district court of Bexar County by the city of San

Antonio for recovery of the property ended in a mistrial. On October 25, 1850, when the case came up a second time and was appealed to the Supreme Court, the judge rendered a verdict in favor of the church.[10]

The United States continued to lease the property from the Catholic church to use as a quartermaster's depot. From this base the United States government supplied its forts in the Southwest until 1861.[11] It is of interest to note here that a placard placed on the walls by the Daughters of the Republic of Texas in 1922 gives the United States credit for making the first improvements on the Alamo during its tenancy. In 1848 and 1849 approximately fifty-eight hundred dollars was spent on improvements.[12] Although this expenditure on doors, windows, roofing, and walls increased the property's effectiveness for military purposes, visitors to San Antonio at the time noted that the Alamo chapel and adjoining buildings were still in ruins.[13]

With the advent of the Civil War and even before the secession of Texas on February 1, 1861, the arsenal and commissary were surrendered to the Confederacy. Colonel Ben McCulloch with fifteen hundred troops, acting under the orders of the Texas Secession Commissioners, took possession on January 16, 1861.[14]

With the close of the Civil War, the United States resumed control of the Alamo using it again as a quartermaster depot. Soon afterward, Bishop C. M. Dubuie, in order to find a place of worship for the German Catholics of San Antonio, requested that the United States government vacate the property. The request was denied, however, and the United States continued to use the Alamo until 1876, when the army depot was built at Fort Sam Houston.[15]

San Antonio grew rapidly after the Civil War as the presence of United States troops stationed in the city freed the vicinity from the Indian menace. Since business expansion demanded room and the chapel and the convent and its garden were not employed, the Catholic church decided to sell them. Thus on June 1, 1871, San Antonio condemned the old granary—the building in the southeast corner of the original walled-in area—and then purchased it for $2,500.

San Antonio repaired the property and used it for a city hall and a jail for some years. Inasmuch as the deed specified that the tract was to be for public use only, the building was later demolished and the land became a part of Alamo Plaza.

In June, 1877, Honore Grenet, a public-spirited businessman of French extraction, paid the Catholic church $20,000 for the old mission convent and courtyard consisting of an acre of ground. At the same time Grenet secured a ninety-nine-year lease on the Alamo chapel, which had remained vacant since the United States government had relinquished it the previous year, and on June 25, 1878, purchased a small tract north and east of the convent yard from Samuel Maverick for $2,750.[16] Grenet repaired the chapel and used it as a warehouse. Until his death in 1882, the Frenchman operated a successful retail and wholesale business on the site. He had stated when he acquired the property that he intended to give the convent to the public as a memorial to the heroes whose blood was shed there. Regardless of his "good intentions," when Grenet died, Major Joseph E. Dwyer, his administrator, conducted the same business on the grounds until it was sold in 1886.[17]

A movement to regain the mission chapel was enacted by the Alamo Monumental Society on January 31, 1883. The Society succeeded in interesting the state legislature in the purchase of the chapel. Accordingly, against some opposition, that body appropriated $20,000 for the purpose and the Roman Catholic church deeded the mission chapel to the state on May 12, 1883.[18] At the same time the state made no effort to purchase additional portions of the property. And though some people felt that much of the original ignominy of sacrificing the mission-fortress to commercialism had been eradicated, there still remained the desecration of what was left of the principal area of the mission-fortress courtyard, where the main bloodletting occurred, and where Travis fell and Bowie succumbed from his sickbed.

Further desecration was perpetrated on the hallowed site when the Hugo-Schmeltzer Company acquired this portion of the property on January 23, 1886, for $28,000 and established a retail/wholesale liquor business on it.[19]

After the state purchased the mission chapel on April 23, 1883, it awarded the custody to the city of San Antonio on the condition that the municipal government maintain it and provide a custodian.[20] This arrangement proved to be ineffectual as no substantial improvements were made. Almost nothing was done except to remove the rubbish that had accumulated during Grenet's occupancy. Though a few public-spirited citizens, from time to time, tried to interest the local authorities in preserving the relic and other historic landmarks in San Antonio, they were unsuccessful. Among the patriotic ladies who urged the conversion of the Alamo chapel into a museum for early Texas relics and a depository for Texas historical records and manuscripts were Mrs. Anson Jones (wife of the former president of the Republic of Texas), Mrs. Andrew Briscoe, and Mrs. A. B. Looscan.[21]

Many San Antonians were convinced that the progress of the city demanded that the shrine be converted into a trade mart.[22] Much of this thinking resulted from the widespread ignorance involving the actual scene of the siege and final struggle on March 6, 1836. No doubt the state's purchase of only the Alamo chapel in 1883 had also contributed to the fallacy that the chapel was *the* Alamo in which the 183 patriots fell. The very heart of the old Franciscan mission compound, where the major battle that ended the thirteen-day siege at six-thirty on the morning of March 6, 1836, occurred, was a rectangular plaza of three acres with its west wall of haphazard huts facing the village of San Antonio four hundred feet away. One hundred and fifty-four yards in length by fifty-four in width, the court was framed by stone walls of from eighteen to forty-two inches in thickness and from six to nine feet in height. A ten-foot-wide porte-cochere, the main entrance to the plaza, divided the long, one-story building on the south side into two parts of housing, later to be called the low barracks.

It was here in this plaza that twenty-seven-year-old William Barret Travis cut with his sword the line into the earth by which he and the other defenders went with God—the line symbolizing supreme sacrifice as the price for free-dom—the line which the poet Tapley Holland jumped over and across which magnificent James Bowie had his cot lifted—the line from which Louis Moses Rose, the single Alamo defector, cowered in terror—the line "that can no more be expunged from popular imagination than the damned spots on Lady Macbeth's hands."[23]

It was here along these walls, in the absence of portholes through which to shoot, that the cannon were mounted on platforms of earth and timber to serve as parapets. The heaviest cannon, the eighteen-pounder, was placed at the southwest angle of the plaza facing San Antonio to the west. Crockett's position was at the palisade of dirt and sticks designed to fortify the south-east side at the entrance to the chapel court. Travis himself manned the stra-tegic position at the north battery near the northern postern. Bowie on his cot, armed with a brace of revolvers and his famed knife, earned his immor-tality in his quarters at the south end of the plaza near the entrance. The hal-lowed cubicle, crimson-splashed with Bowie's blood, has now been absorbed by Alamo Plaza in San Antonio.

It was these same walls that the Mexicans tried to climb with the aid of their scaling ladders only to fall back, time after time, in the barrage of wither-ing fire from the parapets. In fact, Santa Anna's dragoons did not scale those walls until they discovered a crudely constructed redoubt at the east end (to reinforce a breech), which they were able to mount with difficulty by using the chinks and beam ends. Once inside, they opened the postern.[24] Within these walls Adjutant John Baugh, replacement for the fallen Travis, carried the battle to the barracks.

The two structures on the east side of the rectangle—the two-story mission convent and the chapel adjoining it, though fortified, were not major theaters of the siege. The chapel was largely reserved as a sanctuary for the women and children who had taken refuge in the Alamo. The structure, containing a sacristy and vestry room, was mistakenly considered the strongest of the fortifications because of its four-foot-thick walls of solid masonry, twenty-two and a half feet high. On a platform at the back Almeron Dickinson and James Butler Bonham, than whom there were none braver, and their small contingent of gunners gave the riflemen and cannoneers at the plaza walls cover as long as they were able. But Colonel José Morales's reply to their spectacular bravery, when the hole-up action began and carried the battle to the barracks, was to swing the eighteen-pounder around and rake the church, silencing the gunners and reducing the platform, stone walls, and doors to rubble.[25]

Clara Driscoll, who was familiar with these details, tried in her campaign waged through the press to reeducate and enlighten the uninformed public. Her first attempts fell on deaf ears. After meticulously laying the groundwork, she resorted to some of the most impassioned appeals in historic record:

> Could any society have a more worthy, more beneficial object, than that of keeping alive in a country its patriotic enthusiasm, which, after all, is the keynote to a national greatness? By the honoring of a glorious past we strengthen our present, and by the care of our eloquent but voiceless monuments we are preparing a noble inspiration for our future.[26]

At one and the same time, Clara Driscoll could envision the future as predicated by the present. For instance: "But of more significance is the preservation, as memorials for the inspiration of future generations of Texans, of the crumbling monuments and changing battlefields where died in the cause of freedom the fathers of the state. . . ." Witness also: "This is a practical age we live in, yet human nature craves the heroic and the ideal. There are times in the affairs of everyday life when one must stop and ponder over the great and momentous deeds of bygone times. They make one's purpose in life more tangible, more real."[27]

Nor did Clara Driscoll hesitate to address her remarks directly to the Alamo City itself. It is possible that the old shrine has not inspired more eloquent expression than the following passage:

> How many of you in San Antonio today have really contemplated the old Alamo building . . . and learned the wonderful lesson . . . of self-sacrifice? Watch it . . . in the silence of eventide, when the glow of a departing day throws its radiant color like a brilliant crimson mantle about the old ruin. How clearly the old battle scars stand out, vivid and lurid in the stones, red as the blood of the men who fought and died there. Look at it in the busy hurry of everyday life. Calm and majestic it stands amid the haggling of trade and trafficking of commerce.

Then go and stand before it on a night when the moon throws a white halo over the plaza; when the lights of the city are darkened, the winds of heaven hushed. . . . How its sinister old face frowns under the silver beams, as if it were still fighting . . . the siege that ended with the martyrdom of the brave spirits whom it shielded. . . .

How eloquently it speaks to us in its grimness and severity! . . . Search the histories of the world and you will not find a deed to equal that of the men who died within the Alamo that Texas might be free. . . .[28]

Despite the apparent apathy, Clara Driscoll, her indomitable father's daughter, was not discouraged. A letter she penned in longhand on her father's commercial stationery to Mr. Hugo inquiring about terms reveals that as a young woman she pursued a forthright and consistent course toward any endeavor she hoped to accomplish.

> Robert Driscoll
> Palo Alto Ranch
> Banquete, Texas
> Feb. 5th, 1903

Mr. Hugo:

Dear Sir—

While in San Antonio a few days ago I saw Mr. Schmeltzer in regard to the property adjoining the Alamo. He said it was for sale. The Daughters of the Republic are anxious to procure it in order to make a park about the old ruins.

They are about to present a bill to the Legislature asking for an appropriation to assist them in their plans. Would you kindly let me know the price of the property? Also if you would give the Daughters of the Republic the option on it, and if in payment of a certain sum by them, you would hold the property until they could pay full amount?

I am sure you, as well as every Texan, would like to see the property used for this purpose in which the Daughters of the Republic wish to utilize it, and I feel convinced that you will work to the interest of the Daughters in this matter.

It is important that I should hear from you at your earliest convenience.

> Sincerely yours,
>
> Clara Driscoll
> Chairman of Committee on Alamo
> and Mission Improvements

Later Clara Driscoll, accompanied by Miss Adina de Zavala, president of the San Antonio chapter of the Daughters of the Republic of Texas, called upon the owners of the liquor store to discuss specific details of price and terms. The Hugo-Schmeltzer Company consented to sell the property for a consideration of $75,000. Terms were $25,000 down and the balance to be paid in annual installments of $10,000 each, the deferred payments to bear interest at the rate of 6 percent per annum. The firm also agreed to give a year's option on the property for $5,000, with the stipulation that at the expiration of the year the remainder of $20,000 would be due. On March 16, Miss Driscoll returned for further conference with Hugo and Schmeltzer, accompanied by Judge James B. Wells of Brownsville and attorney Floyd Mc-Gown of San Antonio. The upshot of this meeting was that the liquor dealers agreed to give a thirty-day option on the property for $500, which had to be paid immediately, with the understanding that the remainder of $4,500 must be met in thirty days, on April 19, 1903. Accordingly a payment of $20,000 bearing interest at 6 percent would be due on February 10, 1904; and the first of the five notes in the amount of $10,000, at 6 percent interest, would be due February 10, 1905, and one thereafter on February 10 for four years or until the total debt was liquidated.[30]

Convinced that she was right, Clara Driscoll gave her personal check on March 17, 1903, in the amount of $500 as the down payment on the $5,000 option for the property. Whether she had acted precipitately or not, she had obligated the Daughters of the Republic of Texas to contract for the property before the funds were raised. Almost immediately the de Zavala Chapter of the Daughters of the Republic of Texas assembled at the Menger Hotel in San Antonio to formulate plans for a vigorous and concerted drive to raise the purchase price of the Alamo.[31] Clara Driscoll was retained as chairman and treasurer to obtain the balance of the option money due April 19. Serving with Miss Driscoll on the committee were Mrs. H. P. Drought, Mrs. R. A. Coleman, Mrs. F. Paschal, Mrs. H. E. Kampmann, Mrs. J. A. Fraser, Mrs. Fred Herff, Miss Adina de Zavala, Miss Florence Eager, all of San Antonio; and Mrs. J. B. Wells of Brownsville.[32]

The first action of the finance committee was to send out "A Plea for the Alamo."* These were addressed to Texans throughout the state and to others who might possibly be interested. Each recipient was requested to donate fifty cents and to submit names of three friends who might be willing to contribute a similar amount. Signed by Miss Driscoll, the plea stated that the Daughters of the Republic had undertaken to purchase the property in order to improve the surroundings in keeping with the dignity of the old ruin of the church-fortress as a monument to the patriots who fell on the site. The plea

---

Please see text of the "Plea" in Appendixes.

listed the threefold purpose of the organization, then made the simple request.

Since the Legislature was in session, it was decided that Miss Driscoll and Mrs. Coleman should appear before the body and request a state appropriation for the option. Clara Driscoll made the appeal and an amendment was tacked onto the general appropriations bill to provide money for the measure.

Since the money was yet to be disbursed, the ladies went forward in their attempts to raise funds by popular subscription. On April 17, two days before the balance of the option of $5,000 was due, the Alamo pleas had brought in the paltry sum of $1,021.75, an amount less than one-fourth of what was needed by April 19. To complicate matters, news came that an Eastern syndicate had initiated negotiations to buy the Hugo and Schmeltzer property on which to build a hotel—hoping to exploit the historical value—and was prepared to pay the $5,000-option immediately.[33] Equally disheartening was the fact that, in the interest of commercial advancement, progressive citizens of San Antonio preferred the hotel to the restoration. But Clara Driscoll was not one to give up easily.

She issued her personal check for the remainder of the option in the amount of $3,478.25.[34] This obligated the Daughters of the Republic to raise $20,000 by February 10, 1904, at 6 percent interest! But it saved the Alamo from commercial oblivion for the time being.

Although the bill to provide the option money had passed both houses by a sizeable majority, Governor S. W. T. Lanham blue-penciled it because, as he explained, there was no Alamo fund in the state general revenue account to which the $5,000 could be charged.[35] Consequently, the Legislature adjourned without succeeding in its appropriation for the shrine.

Meanwhile the Daughters continued to try to raise funds from benefits, bazaars, chain letters, public subscriptions, and letters of solicitation to their friends. Responses came from as far away as California, New York, and Colorado, and even some donations from "beyond the Rio Grande," but only in modest amounts. Clara Driscoll kept up her appeals through the press and the ladies redoubled their efforts to raise money through patriotic organizations, clubs, the county and state conventions, and schools.[36] A second plea, addressed to school boards, school trustees, superintendents, and teachers and signed by Clara Driscoll, was directed especially to school children.* These were expected to be reached through the categories addressed. To any child contributing or collecting a dollar Miss Driscoll pledged to send the story of "The Fall of the Alamo" and a photograph of the mission.

There were still many persons who felt that the state should appropriate

---

Please note text in Appendixes.

the money for the purchase as the men at the Alamo made the Republic of Texas possible, then ultimately the twenty-eighth state in the nation. There were others, however, who felt that it was unwise to invest taxpayers' money in property to which the title was doubtful. Still a third group believed that, since San Antonio would benefit from the tourist trade the shrine would inspire, the city should pay for the Alamo property.[37]

But Clara Driscoll no longer expected help from the state that declined to honor a $5,000 commitment voted by both houses; and there was no time to lose. If the Daughters of the Republic of Texas defaulted in February, the Alamo would be forever lost to posterity and an Eastern syndicate would exploit the sacrifices of Travis, Bowie, and Crockett. As was her custom in times of trial and difficulty, Clara consulted her father. A successful businessman, Robert Driscoll, Sr., conceded that the price of $75,000 the liquor firm quoted was reasonable, along with the terms. Then looking his daughter straight in the eyes, he said, "But do you know of anyone who will throw away that much money on the slim chance that the state may sometime repay it?"

"Yes," Clara Driscoll answered, "I know such a person."

"Who is it?" Her father was incredulous.

"Myself. I have the money, and I don't care whether the state repays me or not."

"Yes, Clara," her father said reflectively. "You have your own bank account, and far be it from me to tell you how to use your money." He paused. "But are you sure that is what you want to do?"

"I am absolutely sure," Clara told her father.

"Then, my dear, I'll see that you have enough in your account to cover the $75,000."[38]

That settled it. *The Alamo was safe!*

As the date of payment—February 10, 1904—drew nearer, Clara Driscoll knew that nothing short of a miracle could produce the necessary amount of $20,000 to meet the obligation by that time. As chairman of the finance committee, she knew to a penny what all the ladies' frenetic efforts had been able to raise—less than $7,000! Soon after conferring with her father, she paid another call to Charles Hugo and Gustave Schmeltzer. She gave the men her personal check to make up the deficit for the $20,000 plus interest.[39] Not only that, she terminated the deal by signing the five remaining notes of $10,000 each, thus obligating herself to pay the balance of $50,000 in five years at 6 percent per annum. In addition, she assumed responsibility for the taxes and insurance. But young Clara Driscoll made it clear to the gentlemen that she was purchasing the property for the Daughters of the Republic of

Texas and she insisted upon the insertion of a notation to that effect in the deed.[40] In part the document read:

> Charles Hugo, Bexar County, Texas, for and in consideration of the sum of $75,000, paid and to be paid, by Clara Driscoll, as follows: $25,000 cash, and $50,000 as evidenced by five promissory notes of even date, each for the sum of $10,000, and payable on or before one, two, three, four and five years after date, each bearing interest from date until maturity at the rate of 6 percent per annum, and 10 percent after maturity as well as 10 percent attorney's fees.
>
> Failure to pay any installment of interest when due or any of the notes when due shall, at the election of the holder of said notes, or any of them, mature all the said notes.
>
> *It is distinctly understood that this property is purchased by Clara Driscoll for the use and benefit of the Daughters of the Republic of Texas, and is to be used by them for the purpose of making a park about the Alamo, and for no other purpose whatever.*
>
> A vendor's lien is retained against the property to secure the $50,000.[40]

The news of a slender Texas woman buying the Alamo—lock, stock, and barrel—swept over the state like a Texas cyclone. It caught the attention of some people who before had simply ignored the whole thing. It appealed to the fancy of the multitude. *Who was Clara Driscoll?* The question did not go begging, for almost overnight, beautiful, brilliant, vivacious Clara Driscoll— the daughter of a pioneer Texas cattleman and millionaire—had become a legend.

Perhaps Clara Driscoll had been naive at the outset in thinking that Texans would consider it a privilege to help recover and restore the shrine. Yet there is an old maxim in Texas that admonishes a person to put your money where your mouth is. Texans understand that. Whereas many had not bothered to part with a mere pittance of two bits, four bits, six bits, a dollar—another old Texas expression—this twenty-two-year-old girl had put almost seventy-five thousand dollars on the line without so much as batting one of her scintillating hazel eyes.

Another thing—no booted and ten-gallon-hatted Texan likes for a little woman to show him up, even though he may admire her for her intestinal fortitude. No doubt the reaction of most of the Texas men could be summed up neatly in still another old Texas idiom—*well, I'll be damned!* So the public of the state the Alamo heroes made possible began to have second thoughts.

By the following February 19, even lethargic San Antonio began to take notice. On that date the San Antonio Bar Association sponsored a grand ball for the benefit of the Alamo mission fund. After this highly successful event, arrangements were made for other benefits, including a patriotic ball and a carnival during the week of the Battle of Flowers, the annual pageant celebrating the anniversary of the Battle of San Jacinto on April 21.[42]

For that matter, the commemoration of the famous battle was also implemented to benefit the Alamo fund. As a climax to the events of the afternoon of April 21, 1904, Judge Clarence Martin of Lampasas addressed an enormous assembly from an improvised platform at Alamo Plaza in front of the chapel. The climax of his inspiring address was a resolution "demanding that a plank be inserted in the next democratic state platform favoring an appropriation by the Legislature to purchase the property."[43] Rarely have the elements of time, place, and theme been combined so ingeniously to incite such favorable reaction. The immense crowd, to a man, approved the resolution with a tremendous roar of approval.

Furthermore, when the Daughers of the Republic of Texas, encouraged by Judge Martin, persisted in trying to win recognition of the state's heroes by appeals to the counties through Democratic conventions, mass meetings were held to adopt resolutions in their favor.[44] Judge Martin himself received pledges of support from many of the counties, virtually assuring the movement success. Then on June 4, 1904, voters at the primaries endorsed state aid to purchase the Alamo, and in August the state convention at Austin adopted the proposed plank. Even Governor Lanham had subscribed to the idea in his San Jacinto address.[45]

More reassuring, the Legislature, which was in session in January, 1905, cordially requested a committee of the Daughters of the Republic to meet with them to provide information. Once more the organization prevailed upon Clara Driscoll to represent the members. She graciously consented and was warmly received by the body. In her report she showed that the Daughters, through their own efforts, had raised almost $10,000 for the project.[47] Then on January 24, 1905, the long-awaited hour of triumph arrived when the House passed the bill to subsidize the preservation of the Alamo by a vote of 191 to 9.[47]

Senator H. S. Hawkins proposed adding an amendment to reimburse Miss Driscoll for interest and moneys paid from her personal funds, but she refused to sanction the amendment. She and Miss de Zavala also declined to approve another amendment designed to place the Alamo and grounds in the hands of a commission appointed by the governor instead of leaving it in the custody of the Daughters of the Republic of Texas. Miss Driscoll said at the time that before she would agree with that disposition of the property, she would buy it outright herself and give it over to the Daughters of the Republic of Texas without reservation.[48]   Indeed this was precisely what she had already done! *On January 25, 1905, the bill passed the Senate unanimously, and the governor signed it into law the following day.*[49]

The bill authorizing the purchase of the Alamo required a clear title. Consequently, deeds to the tract from the earliest Spanish grants in Texas down to the date of the purchase were submitted to Attorney General R. V. Davidson for his approval. The bill provided further that the governor, upon the receipt of a clear title, proceed to deliver the Alamo property to the Daughters of the Republic of Texas to be maintained in good repair by them without additional cost to the state, and to be remodeled according to plans by these custodians subject to the governor's approval.[50]

Since the state's appropriation of $65,000 was not immediately available, Clara Driscoll advanced funds for the remaining notes with accrued interest in the amount of $41,313. The date of this disbursement was August 30, 1905.[51]

The deeds for the property were delivered to the attorney general on August 30, 1905.[52] Two non-interest-bearing warrants, the first for $25,000, payable on demand, and the second for $40,000, payable in January, 1906, were issued to Clara Driscoll.

On October 5, 1905, Governor Lanham formally conveyed the Alamo property to the Daughters of the Republic of Texas. In his presentation remarks he expressed pride and confidence in their ability and work. He pointed out that the trust was one of confidence inasmuch as the state was conveying to their care "its most sacred and historic possession."[53]

Thus the state of Texas finally redeemed itself of the shame of disavowing the Alamo. Moreover, the girl, who had saved the shrine from further commercial exploitation, became known variously as the Custodian, the Saviour, and the Queen of the Alamo. Not only was she acclaimed a heroine in Texas, she was elevated to the national spotlight as everything she said or did became news. Clara Driscoll took all of the homage in stride, sometimes registering incredulity, at others, amazement, but never impatience or intolerance.

3

Author and Playwright

NOT ONLY DID THE EXPERIENCE OF CLARA
Driscoll in preserving the Alamo convert her into a national legend almost
overnight, it affected her life vitally in other ways. One of the first tangible
results was that it launched her into a writing career. She had always known
that she had a gift for expression, both oral and written. But until she had
begun to use her powers of persuasion to save the historic shrine, she had
written little more than a few travel articles back to the state papers. After
all, she was young when she returned from Europe in 1899—scarcely eighteen. The initial struggle to preserve the Alamo had taken over two years. It
would reaquire many more to complete the work so auspiciously begun.

Now that she had the assurance the Alamo was safe, as she continued to
manifest an interest in its complete restoration, she turned her attention to
further self fulfillment through her pen. At twenty-two, in 1903, she had before her many horizons yet to explore. Not only had the experience in preserving the Alamo strengthened her faith in her writing ability, it had led to
another incentive. When Clara Driscoll appeared before the Texas Legislature in 1903, one of the men who listened to her rousing appeal for financial
support for the Alamo was Henry Hulme Sevier, whose name was abridged
to Hal Sevier.

Under the stimulus in preserving the shrine and the inspiration of the man
she was later to marry, Clara Driscoll wrote in two years *The Girl of La Gloria*
(1905) and *In The Shadow Of The Alamo* (1906) and the comic opera, *Mexicana*, which was produced on Broadway in 1906.

The Girl of La Gloria, published by G. P. Putnam's Sons, New York, is
another product of the range legacy that Clara Driscoll inherited. The knowledge of all aspects of ranch life and the cattle industry reflected in the work
is phenomenal. In the novel the author re-creates the culture of the Texas
plains—"a frontier with a history as replete with romance and rich in incident

as the soil of ancient Scotland or the hills that rim the Rhine." She also portrays "in this flat, treeless land the untamed spirit of lawlessness inherited from vagrant ancestors," who were quick to love and quicker to hate.

The heroine, Ilaria Buckley, a descendant of the Spanish *conquistadores* and the lone survivor of a family, half-Mexican and half-American, is caught up in the duplicity of the *Americanos*, who have appropriated her property until she is left with only a meager sustenance at the shabby remnant of a ranch known as La Gloria.

Ilaria falls in love with an outsider, Randor Walton from New York, who unwittingly is aligned with those who have dispossessed her family from generation to generation. Strong, thrilling scenes move swiftly to a dramatic close, in which Ilaria is sacrificed to the system but has the consolation of knowing before her death that she is loved.

The Girl of La Gloria is a Texas story highlighted by all of the glamour and mystery of the plains and its aborigines. While Clara Driscoll's affinity for romance is preeminent, her unerring ability to identify with an exploited minority group—the Mexican-American—is irrevocable. Certainly her mastery of the Spanish language was a contributing factor. Of the strong Mexican influence in the area, she says:

> . . . even today in Southwest Texas . . . though the soil is owned and dominated by the Americans, the Aztec customs are still being followed, and it is as Mexican in speech and habit as if the War for Independence had never separated the two countries. (72)*

The novel is charmingly, if quaintly, illustrated by Hugh W. Ditzler, but the artist's drawings fail to capture the impact of the scenes as etched by Clara Driscoll's pen which only the reader can visualize for himself. For example, the first meeting of the lovers at La Gloria, the cattle drive, the shooting spree at El Ranchero in Alice, the apparition in the darkness, the Texas wind at noonday from the southwest, and the scene of first parting:

> Ilaria was standing where he had left her—her youth and beauty strangely, sadly out of place amid the decaying surroundings, which represented a rapidly vanishing phase of prairie life; yet in a way, so distinctly was this girl a part of them that the man felt he could not conceive her in any other setting. It was thus that he remembered her always. (103)

But *The Girl of La Gloria* is more than an evocative story of Texas ranch

---

Numerals enclosed in parentheses following quoted matter in this chapter refer to pages of the texts under discussion.

life. It is the saga of the Driscoll family and more particularly a salute to the author's father, to whom it is dedicated. It is also the intimate account of young, impressionable Clara Driscoll in love.

The character of the cowman Edward Benton is based on the image of the author's father. To introduce Benton she gives a profile almost identical to that of Robert Driscoll, Sr.:

> Edward Benton was handsome—exceptionally well preserved . . . and he carried himself like a soldier. He could still ride the wildest horses . . . and his capacity for work was tremendous, as he could tire out any cow crowd working under him. Gentle and kind in disposition, yet he could handle a gun with a quickness that surprised his friends and disconcerted his enemies. When angry, he could outswear any man in the State. He never asked a favor of any one, attending strictly to his own business, and letting other people alone. He was kind to women and children, humane to animals, but hotheaded in his dealings with men. Withal, there was no man in the Southwest country so heartily liked for his good qualities, respected for his power and wealth, feared and justly hated for his faults. (111)

Clara Driscoll's pride in her father's well-earned success is apparent in this passage in which she attributes it to Benton:

> It is a business that must be learned from the beginning, and Benton, like most of the successful cattleraisers, had grown up in the hurly burly of it. He knew every phase of it. From infancy he had had the ambition of every ranch boy—to become a cowman. In early youth he had shown the trader's instinct—marbles for jackknives, jackknives for pistols, a horse for a cow and a calf, and so on up the scale. (114)

As the novel unfolds, Clara Driscoll sees the character typifying her father as a symbol of all reputable cattlemen to whom the Southwest is indebted:

> These men knew every inch of the ground they own. Night after night of their youth has been spent sleeping in the open, or riding hour after hour across lonely plains on the lookout for thieves. Filled with energy, endurance, honesty that is proverbial, a fearlessness that knows no equal, they have left records . . . that shall endure forever; battling not only against evil and wrongdoing; but the law itself, the corruption and injustice of which had forced the cattlemen to become a law unto themselves. It is to these men that the peace and prosperity today of the Southwest is due. (115)

Likewise Daniel Benton, one of the first cattlemen to fence his land, is based on the author's paternal grandfather, whose first name he borrows. The analogy she draws is documentary:

> Like many Southwest Texans, he was of Irish parentage. His father had emi-

grated to Texas in 1836, with the Powers colony . . . who settled on the Nueces River, and founded a town which they called, in the soft Mexican tongue, San Patricio—after Ireland's patron saint. (21)

The luxurious Calveras ranch is obviously the Driscoll spread at Palo Alto, and the heroine Ilaria Buckley is the physical and mental counterpart of Clara Driscoll. Even the girl's first name of Ilaria is but a thinly disguised modification of the author's Christian name, with the *C* altered to *I* and the insertion of a lower case *i* before the concluding *a*. Thus the name assumes the soft Mexican musical effect of four syllables instead of the brusque two in the Anglicized Clara.

The young Mexican girl with her characteristic dark features is almost a facsimile of the author at the time she married. The description from the viewpoint of Walton, when he first meets her at La Gloria, may well have been the way Clara Driscoll, with but slight fictionizing, looked to Hal Sevier the day she came to the state capitol to plead for the Alamo.

> The girl's natural, languorous grace and almost indolent movements fascinated him. Not a detail of her beauty escaped him. The small, full mouth, sensitive nostrils, delicately arched brows and long, sweeping lashes falling on the curved cheeks— and how innocently veiled were the glorious eyes, filled with sadness and longing!
> He marked the fair skin against the black of her eyes, the hot wind playing with the stray wisps of hair—heavy midnight hair, waved back naturally from the low brow. (99)

It was said that Clara Driscoll herself was not pretty when she was a child, that in fact, she was austerely plain, as little girls frequently are before they later blossom into reigning beauties. When Ilaria returns to La Gloria the old Mexican woman Paula, mindful of her superb beauty, reminds her of her plainness as a young girl. "You have changed *muchisimo niñita* in the last year! You were just so high. . . . You were not pretty then as you are now." (87) Ilaria, who had been placed in the convent at nine, had abandoned it at seventeen.

The psychical parallels between the author and heroine are equally strong. Like her model, Ilaria is invested with the same pride of family coursing through her veins. When the old Mexican companion tells her that she will be lonely at the decadent ranch, she answers: "Possibly, but—it is my home, where all my people have lived—ah! I shall like it." (90)

Moreover, in the manner of her archtype, Ilaria is a spirited girl who possesses her own standards and would fight upon just provocation. When she is left at the convent at the age of nine and a nun tries forcibly to remove the beads reminiscent of the child's dead mother—thinking the ornament unsuitable for one so young—Ilaria sinks her sharp teeth into the sister's hand. (39) Later, when Paula informs the girl that sometimes in his drunkenness her American father had beaten her Mexican mother, she exclaims

'Beaten her!' . . . showing all her glittering white teeth like a young tigress. 'Why didn't she kill him? That's what I would have done.' (87)

After Tom Crowley, the ranch foreman, learns of the seriousness of the romance between the two, he tries to dissuade Ilaria from seeing Walton again. Learning that he has come upon his own initiative, Ilaria stands up to him, informs him in no uncertain terms that it is a matter for Mr. Walton and herself to decide. Crowley has no alternative but to withdraw in defeat. (250)

Clara Driscoll's aversion to the Catholic convent as an institution is likewise projected to Ilaria, who finally escapes from the monastery to return to Paula. In a scene at the convent when the reverend mother broaches the subject of the girl joining the sisterhood, Ilaria says most emphatically that the life of the cloister does not appeal to her. Only a little later when the reverend mother asks her if she is happy at the convent, Ilaria avoids replying directly. After a few seconds, "the words came out almost defiantly: 'I do not feel that I have ever been happy in all my life. Certainly never since I have been—'" She leaves the sentence unfinished.

As the author's spiritual counterpart, Ilaria prefers nature in its indigenous state. She tells her sweetheart:

I can never bear to pluck a flower from its branch or stem. It seems as much a crime as the killing of a harmless animal. Surely you rob it of life—life wild and free. In the convent I could not bear to see the flowers cut, even to decorate God's altar. (177)

Like Clara Driscoll, Ilaria loves the prairie. To her lover she says " . . . there is joy in living here . . . the prairie is my garden. What color and perfume is in it! What music about it." (179)

Finally Ilaria, like her creator, is a giver. Convinced that her sweetheart's life is in jeopardy, she risks her own to give warning. Once again, when she learns of Seaton Buckley's insidious schemes to get possession of the Calaveras ranch through her, she bequeaths to her lover any lands that had belonged to her grandfather, Manuel Rodriguez. (270)

Undoubtedly Hal Sevier was the prototype of Randor Walton and the tender love scenes represent more fact than fiction. It was said that Sevier was almost preternaturally handsome. The old Mexican Paula's first reaction to Walton is "*Diocito*, that a man should be so beautiful!" When both Paula and Ilaria get their first glimpse of him

Never had they seen such a handsome boyish face and bright shining hair. It is like gold in the sunlight, Ilaria was thinking to herself . . . his eyes as blue as those in the statue of St. Joseph, that she had so often seen in the chapel of the convent. (98)

After Walton's first declaration of his love, the author states that "It was the first man's kiss the girl had ever known" and

It was growing dark when Walton rode off leaving the girl standing motionless in the twilight, the touch of his lips still on hers, a wild new happiness surging in her heart. (182)

Then later:

Tonight, she could only think of as something unreal—a dream intangible and elusive , from which at any moment she might awaken. . . .
Presently, she took something from the inside of her dress and held it to her lips. It was a little gold locket that Walton had slipped into her hand as he was leaving. (183)

(Photographs of the period show Clara Driscoll wearing a heart-shaped locket.)

With the advent of the next day, "Life had a new meaning for her. Oh! the wonder of it all." (174) Only a girl a few days ago. Now Ilaria has become a woman fulfilled. Suddenly in her newfound happiness she feels compassion for the nuns in the convent:

No wonder they regarded the outside world as they did, having wrung their hearts dry of the very wine of life. (184)

Both race and class could have posed a barrier between the lovers and Walton has the opportunity to choose a young lady of equal social status. But the young author explains his emotional commitment:

It was the old, elemental call of heart to heart, drowning all the wisdom of the world, all the teachings of the centuries. Day followed day in the sweet, dangerous proximity of the girl, until now, even if he had cared, for special consideration, to break the spell that her beauty had cast about him, it would have been too late. (150)

G. P. Putnam's Sons were optimistic about the success of the novel. In a letter dated February 4, 1905, and addressed to the author at the Menger Hotel in San Antonio, they state in part:

It is our hope to bring the book out on the 15th of February. This will mean that the production of the book has taken a very unusually short time. I think that you will be very much pleased with the appearance of the volume. We are also hopeful in regard to sales. We have received a good advance order from London and American dealers seem to be interested. . . .

In a subsequent communication, under date of August 16, 1905, and dispatched to Miss Driscoll at her New York address, the publishers enclose "the most important of the English reviews of 'La Gloria.'" They are especially gratified at the "very intelligent and fair point of view" of the London Academy and include extracts from a number of reviews, all of which must have been exciting for the young author.

With the assured success of *The Girl of La Gloria*, G. P. Putnam's Sons were eager to release another volume under Clara Driscoll's byline. By April 6, 1905, plans were already underway to bring out the volume as soon as the author could submit the manuscript. A letter under that date merits attention:

> . . . Our traveller is in Texas at this moment, and he is sending us orders from day to day from the towns which he visits. I am sorry that I was not able to see you before you went [back to Texas] to talk a little about your next book. It will certainly be desirable to follow up this first success with another volume, —as good as the first, or if possible, better. I hope you will let me know how the work progresses, and if I can be of any service to you in connection with it. As soon as you have the title and some idea of the general character of the work, I think that it would be a good plan to announce it in the various literary columns. I can easily attend to this, if you will give me the necessary information.
> With best wishes for yourself and your books old and new, I am
>
> Sincerely yours,
>
> Constance Huntington

Entitled *In The Shadow Of The Alamo*, the volume was released early in 1906. The volume is a singularly handsome specimen of craftsmanship, with the title, the Alamo motif, and a border of cottonwood leaves stamped in gold leaf on a green cover. The work is profusely illustrated in black and white sketches by Florence Eagar, who was affectionately called "Flo"—one of the author's most intimate friends.

In her second book the young author is once more the consummate romanticist, but she adds dimension to her stature as patriot and philosopher. The contents consist of an opening historical account—to which the Alamo, "wrapped in its own solitude," is central—and seven short stories. As the title indicates, the unifying device is the locale of San Antonio. Part I of "The

Custodian of The Alamo" includes events of Texas history anterior to the thirteen-day siege and a special tribute to the gallantry of Travis, Crockett, Bowie, and Bonham:

> Let us scan the lists of the mighty dead and where can we find names that stand ahead of these? As long as there are people to venerate immortal glory these names will live with the great hero-martyrs of history. . . . (13)

Minute detail comprises the portrayal of Santa Anna as a dictator, the line-drawing ceremony, and Travis's classic letter exhorting a friend to "Take care of my little boy."

To conclude the sketch, Miss Driscoll departs from the arbitrary beginning of the historical exposition to return to the time when the Daughters of the Republic of Texas launched their crusade for the Alamo's salvation. Much of the material here is a repetition of the impassioned appeals first exposed in the state press, some of which have been quoted in Chapter Two. Notably in this portion the author extols the Daughters of the Republic of Texas for the preservation of the shrine. Not once, even through indirect reference, does she credit herself with the purchase of the old mission-fortress in behalf of the organization and the fight for its right to maintain custody.

> To the indefatigable and untiring energy of the Daughters of the Republic, Texas owes the greatest debt of being able to show in what manner she honors and venerates her valiant and heroic dead. . . . (25)

In the other segment of "The Custodian of The Alamo: Part II, The Present" the author is the patriot first and the romanticist second. A visitor to the shrine becomes so impressed with the young custodian's dedication in imparting the Alamo history and in praising the young heroes who died there that he returns to declare his love and propose marriage.

Of the remaining stories all but two—"Tommy Huntress," which involves a reunion of lovers at Fort Sam Houston, and "Phillipa, The Chili Queen"— a local color selection—relate to the mission ruins. All of these reflect the writer's prepossession with the romantic and her uncanny talent for identifying with her feminine characters. Thus in "Sister Genevieve" she becomes the cloistered nun who renounces her vows to desert the convent for the man she loves. She rationalizes, "He was her very life and soul and for his kisses and the warmth of his arms she would renounce . . . heaven. . . ." (61) Further on, as the lover convinces his sweetheart, whom he has been unable to marry because of a living wife, that she is making the right decision, the author describes the scene subjectively: "Holding her to him, he pressed his lips passionately to hers. In their kiss the world was forgotten—they had given themselves to each other for eternity." (67)

Yet once again, the nun justifies her action: "But I am a woman with all a woman's power of loving and longing to be loved in return." (71)

"Juana of The Mission De La Concepción" presents the tragic side of romanticism. When a visitor to the old mission accidentally discovers a demented girl crouching in the tower, he learns from the shriveled old Mexican caretaker that the suicide of the girl's musician-husband there over a fair-haired woman, who came to the dances where he performed, was the reason for her deterioration. The body of the Indian girl's husband was discovered in the tower where he had stabbed himself, a flower from the woman's dress clutched in his hand. The old Mexican custodian, who has some individual views about love herself, assures the visitor that "She was a good girl Juana—but she loved, and when a woman loves it is always like that" and "Juana is an Indian. With us one's loves and one's passions come like the fire of the sun on a still summer day." (93)

In "The Red Rose of San José" the author again reveals her knowledge of the psychology of an ethnic minority when she identifies with the "Little Wild Dove of the Wood"—Paoli. Here in the role of the Indian maiden she experiences her first tender emotions of love instead of the intense passion of the sophisticated Sister Genevieve, hungry for physical consummation. Paoli eludes the pursuit of the Comanche brave Tichimingo of her own race because of her love for the Spanish soldier convalescing at the mission from a wound inflicted by an Indian arrow. Finally Paoli surrenders to the Comanche brave reluctantly in exchange for her Spanish sweetheart's life and returns the faded rose of San José as a symbol of her sacrifice for peace.

In the closing scene in "Tommy Huntress" Clara Driscoll demonstrates further that she is a romanticist: "'Kiss me,' the girl breathed, her mouth close to his. And the Texas moon smiled down upon them out of pure wantonness."

"Phillipa, The Chili Queen" is still another vehicle in which Clara Driscoll projects herself in the character of a different ethnic group. This time she assumes the role of a flirtatious Mexican señorita who employs her charms to entice men to the chili stand. Her lures backfire, however, when an Anglo becomes infatuated with her charms and barely escapes being killed by her Mexican lover who has complete power over her.

But Clara Driscoll tempers her romanticism with a philosophy that was remarkably profound for a writer so young. In "Juana of The Mission De La Concepción," as the visitor departs "through the gathering shadows of the twilight," he "thought out of what small things are woven the great tragedies of life." (101)

In "The Old Priest of San Francisco De La Espada," which focuses on a lonely and senile man of the cloth, who, unable to recover from an earlier love, is led to believe through a hallucination that the woman has returned from the dead, the author rationalizes that

> It is to the deserted abodes of the living that the weary-hearted wend their despairing footsteps in search of their one goal—death. It is not for us, who are but human, to gauge the strength of a temptation or the depth of a passion. For is not the sincerity of the human soul as a fleeting shadow caught from the face of the burning sun by the outspread wings of an eagle in its flight? (108)

Frequently the author is both romanticist and philosopher as she demonstrates in "The Red Rose of San José." For example, when the pursuing Comanche brave Tichimingo outdistances Paoli, he tells her: "You will love me, little Paoli. You will love me much. It is always so with the things that fight the bravest against capture." (184)

Mexicana, the third genre to testify to the author's versatility and prolific output, was written in collaboration with Robert W. Smith and copyrighted by Clara Driscoll on December 20, 1905.[1] Raymond Hubbell, one of America's foremost composers in the early 1900s, who is probably best known for the song "Poor Butterfly," contributed the musical score. Sam S. and Lee Shubert produced the comic opera in New York's Lyric Theatre. Its highly successful run opened on January 29, 1906, and closed on April 17 of that year.

The hit of the season ("Mexicana Leads Them All"), the production not only won higher ratings than other offerings, it was listed by David Ewen as the second of three box office successes in as many years featuring the music of Hubbell.[2] The other two were *Fantana* (1905) and *A Knight for a Day* (1907).[3]

It was said that Miss Driscoll capitalized her play "at a heavy outlay for no stage mounting this season had been more carefully correct regardless of cost."[4] Credits show that artists of Drury Lane, the Royal, and the Princess theatres of England created the sets; costumes were designed by Wilhelm of Paris and Hugo Baruch of Berlin; properties were furnished by Nestore and Company of London and Mandolf of Paris; and electrical effects and floral decorations were also imported. Only the wigs, shoes, and boots were provided by New York firms.

Despite the customary scale of fifteen dollars per week for chorus girls, the twelve selected for the front row in *Mexicana* were paid fifty.[5] One Broadway columnist observed that the advertisement for the performers, all of whom were required to be "superlatively beautiful," was deliberately placed under "Amusements" instead of "Help Wanted" or "Personals" to entice "good lookers" into the theater auditorium rather than beautiful chorus girls onto the stage. He also felt that another reason for the deception was that the show would have to get along without the usual blondes since the chorus girls called for in the script were either "Mexican *señoritas* or Indian squaws." At any rate, he was resigned to the reddish or olive faces "overhung with black hair" and further opined that they were a welcome change from the fulvous-hued beauties of "the light pink, white, and yellow bleachings and paintings" to which New York audiences were accustomed.[6]

Some estimated the original expenditure for the production at $50,000; others placed it at a higher figure. A contract, drawn up between Robert Driscoll, Jr., and the Shuberts, dated November 24, 1905, specified that the producers were to pay the former the sum of $100 per week during the run of the play and 50 percent of net profits and to Clara Driscoll royalties of 1½ percent of gross during the season.[7] The contract did not disclose the amount of the investment.

The Shuberts, like the producer-playwright David Belasco, had a reputation for minute attention to detail, lavish settings, extraordinary mechanical effects, and meticulous casting. Headlined by some of the brightest singing and dancing stars of the first decade of the twentieth century, the lineup of the impressive cast, well supported by the chorus of market people, vaqueros, señoritas, rurales, peons, hacendados, caballeros, cargadores, and revolutionaries, was:

Johnny Rocks, a Wall Street broker . . . . Thomas Q. Seabrooke
Tita, an Indian girl vender of pottery. . . . . Christie MacDonald
Captain Carmona, an officer in the Mexican Army. . . . . Joseph Herbert
Juan Adrian, an Indian pulque seller . . . . Edward Martindell
Señorita Marguerita Juarez, daughter of the governor
 of a Mexican state . . . . Caro Roma
Rodrigo Cortinez, a Mexican of wealth and leader
 of the revolutionaries. . . . . Edmund Stanley
Señora Mendoza, aunt to Tita . . . . Maggie Moore
Ines . . . . Blanche Deyo
Manuel . . . . Harry Wallace
Pedro . . . . Almon Knowles
Dueña to Margarita . . . . Helene St. John[8]

A schedule of the songs as they were presented in sequence by acts shows the variety of the music as well as the wide range of Clara Driscoll's talent.

Although playwright Smith brushed Miss Driscoll's libretto with Broadway glitter and Hubbell composed the excellent music, the author herself painstakingly composed the lyrics of every song.

Synopsis of Music

ACT I.

1 Opening Chorus.
2 "How Do You Account for That?" . . . . Captain Carmona and Chorus
3 "United We Stand". . . . . Rodrigo and Chorus
4 "Take Care, Señor" . . . . .Margarita and Rodrigo
5 (a) "How to Tell the Voice of Your Lover" . . . . Juan Adrian
   (b) "The Fickle Weather Vane" . . . . .Tita
6 (a) "Entrance of Johnny Rocks" . . . . .Chorus
   (b) "The Wizard of Wall Street". . . . . Rocks
7 "Graft" . . . . .Rocks, Tita and Chorus
8 Finale.

ACT II.

9 Opening Chorus.
10 "Lorelei" . . . . Juan Adrian
11 "We've Got a Lot to Learn". . . . . Rocks and Tita
12 "My Double" . . . . Rocks
13 "Major Margery" . . . . .Tita and Chorus
14 "I've Heard So Much About You". . . . . Rodrigo and Tita
15 Finale.

ACT III.

16 Opening Chorus.
17 "When Leap Year Comes Around" . . . .Captain Carmona and Señora Mendoza
18 "The Bolero" . . . . . .Margarita, Rocks, Captain Carmona and Señora Mendoza
19 "I Was Just Supposing". . . . . Tita and Rodrigo
20 Finale.[9]

The plot of the three-act opera was negligible. It concerned a Wall Street speculator who becomes insolvent when he goes to Mexico to take charge of a mining enterprise and then is forced to masquerade as the bandit leader of an insurrection in an attempt to recoup his fortune. Programs carried the following introduction:

> MEXICO—Land of the Montezumas, beyond the Sea of Darkness. A country bathed in a white sunshine under blue skies and radiant with tropical foliage and beautiful flowers. The language of its people has a cadence of music; their indolence is a charm and the spirit of *mañana* their dominating characteristic.[10]

The curtain rises on a scene in the market square of a Mexican village in the morning. It features venders and purchasers of pottery, flowers, pulque and tobacco, and assorted kinds of country produce. Mexicans in colorful costumes and Indians in native apparel reveal the leisurely characteristic inherent in the Latin philosophy of *mañana* so vital to their culture. Act II, with a slightly more accelerated tempo, moves to the patio of the hacienda of Rodrigo Cortinez at noon of the following day. Action of the third act progresses to an evening fiesta at the Borda Gardens ending spectacularly with songs and dances appropriate to the setting of tropical splendor.

In addition to credits and the customary advertising, the novel programs included announcements for the patrons. For instance, they were reminded that carriages arrived at the Forty-second Street entrance and departed from the Forth-third, and they were requested not to fold their carriage call cards but to remember their numbers and present the cards to the uniformed attendant (of the Electric Carriage Call Company) only upon leaving at the end of the performance. Special messengers were furnished at the box office to deliver tickets purchased in advance. Attention of the ladies was directed to hat holders attached to the backs of the seats for their convenience. They were instructed to run the hat pin through the brim and then insert it in the hole of the device. The Aeolian Company of Fifth Avenue announced that all hits of the production were available in the form of perforated music rolls for the Pianola.

Mexicana was later taken on the road with equal success. Despite the favorable reviews and box office receipts of the opera, one columnist wondered if Smith and Hubbell had not given it too much Broadway glamour to the sacrifice of some of Miss Driscoll's artistic intentions and authenticity. The same writer deplored the selection of the actress for the part of Ines. It was his opinion that Ruth Denis of Jersey City—the recent star of *Hindustan*—should have been cast "to vivify the lethargy of the Mexicans" rather than "that familiarly cake-walky little imp—Blanche Deyo."[11]

The work, which reflects the lighter fabric of Clara Driscoll's multi-faceted personality, is further evidence of the author's ability to identify with this minority group for which she professed deep affection. The comic opera was apparently a source of much professional gratification for the twenty-five-year-old author. Among her personal effects after her death were fourteen color sketches of costume designs for the production and carefully preserved press notices and other memorabilia of the extraordinarily successful venture.

4

Romance of the Alamo

WHEN CLARA DRISCOLL WENT BEFORE THE
Texas Legislature to appeal for support for the Alamo in 1903, Hal Sevier was
serving his first term in the House of Representatives. After hearing her plea
he introduced the bill in the Legislature to reimburse her. Despite hotly contested opposition, he forced the bill's passage even though the governor later
vetoed it.[1] Mutual friends introduced the couple and soon they became a
popular twosome at state functions and in the homes of their hospitable
friends. Sevier, a young newspaperman, had succeeded his friend John Nance
Garner as a representative from Uvalde County.

Sevier was descended from an old and distinguished family. Born March 16,
1878, in Columbia, Tennessee, the young statesman was the son of Mary
Benton (Douglas) Sevier and Theodore Francis Sevier. The elder Sevier had
held the rank of colonel in the Confederate Army and served with honor on
the staff of General Albert Sidney Johnston. Hal Sevier's mother had the distinction of having been born under the flag of the Republic of Texas in
1839.[2] The Seviers were married in Texas on November 2, 1855.

Irreparably linked with the American Revolutionary frontier, Sevier's ancestry dated back to the fifteenth-century Spanish kingdom of Navarre. The
manner in which the large family migrated through France and England to
every state in the American Union is in itself a fabulous saga. It includes
figures as diverse and important in world history as the Bourbon rulers of
France, the priest St. Francis Xavier, and Governor John Sevier of Tennessee,
who was a veritable king of the American frontier immediately following the
Revolution. Of Bourbon descent through Charles of Orleans, the Xavier family held close kinship with the reigning family of Navarre. A son, or grandson,
of Philip de Xavier was a close friend of Henry of Navarre, who became Henry
IV of France, and married a close relative of the king. Since Marie de Xavier
was the sole heir to the titles and estates of both her houses—Xavier and Na-

varre and Azpilueta of Spain—Don Jon de Jasse assumed her name and rank when he married her.[3]

Grandsons of Don Jon de Jasse and Marie de Xavier migrated to England in 1685, the year of the revocation of the Edict of Nantes. One of these, Valentine Xavier, married Mary Smith of London in 1700, and Anglicized the name to Sevier.[4] Of this issue two sons, Valentine Sevier, II, and William Sevier, migrated to America between 1730 and 1740. They settled in Baltimore, Maryland, and married American ladies. William Sevier and his wife, whose maiden name was O'Neil, had one son. Their son had four children, only one of whom, William Pierre Sevier, left issue.

In 1820 William Pierre Sevier married Lucretia Weller and the couple lived in Russellville, Kentucky, for a while.[5] Theodore Francis Sevier, one of their twelve children, came to Texas, where, as stated, he married. Sevier died in 1915.

Valentine Sevier, II, died in Tennessee in 1803 at the age of 101.[6] He had married twice. John Sevier was the son of Valentine II and his first wife, Joanna Goade, who had migrated to America by way of the Barbados.[7] When the American Revolution began only a few thousand people lived west of the Appalachian divide. By 1790 their number had increased to one hundred and twenty thousand. Able and far-sighted John Sevier led pioneers from North Carolina to the Watauga settlements in 1770 and later to the Cumberland valley in 1779 thus providing the foundation for the future state of Tennessee.[8]

The dynamic John Sevier, with whom Hal Sevier bore collateral kinship and was said to resemble in handsome physical features, was a famous Indian fighter and the hero of the Battle of King's Mountain. The decisive effect that the outcome of the battle had on the American Revolution is a matter of historic record. John Sevier was twice elected to Congress, and, as noted, when Tennessee achieved statehood, was elevated to the governorship. Sevier was twice reelected to the office. His extension of the American frontier and other valuable contributions to the nation over a period of forty years are recorded in many histories and books of genealogy.[9]

Undoubtedly Hal Sevier's interesting family history left its impact. The fact that his mother was a native of the Republic of Texas must have been a source of pride and incentive for his desire to settle in the state of Texas and begin his career. Educated largely under the supervision of his scholarly father, president of the University of the South, at Sewanee, Tennessee, Sevier began his career as editor of a country newspaper in 1895 at seventeen. By the 1900s he had moved to Sabinal, Texas, in Uvalde County, where he established a weekly newspaper, the Sabinal *Sentinel*. It was from Sabinal that he was elected to the Texas Legislature. He served two terms in the House

Robert (Bob) Driscoll, Sr. When Robert Driscoll and his brother Jeremiah returned home after the Civil War, they owned scarcely more than the ragged Confederate uniforms on their backs and the spent ponies they were riding. As a team the brothers collaborated to explode the Great American Desert myth of the Great Plains (of which Texas was an integral part) and became multi-millionaires.

Above, Jeremiah O. (Jerry) Driscoll. At the outset of their collaboration, Jerry usually handled the land buying while Bob directed the ranching operations. By 1890, when their joint holdings were partitioned, Bob acquired as his share, among other properties, the fabulous 83,000-acre Palo Alto ranch in the vicinity of Corpus Christi in Nueces County and Jerry's heirs retained the Refugio, Bee, and Goliad ranches as their portion. Jerry died before the division was completed. Below, the *Brasada* or brush country and the early Texas longhorn that inhabited it. From 1850 to 1865 the open range industry was spawned in this immense region between the Nueces River and the Rio Grande. Men of stamina and fortitude, like the Driscolls, converted the rattlesnake-infested area of cactus and prairie dogs, of shifting sands, and blinding dust storms, into a teeming paradise of milk and honey.

Above, round-up at the Palo Alto. Much of the uncleared *Brasada* is visible in the background. Below, ranch scene at Palo Alto. Ranch headquarters is in the background. An innovative cattleman, Driscoll replaced the lean and shaggy longhorns with whitefaces and herds of the Brahman strain. All bore the famous Wrench brand.

Above, Palo Alto ranch house at Driscoll, Texas, headquarters of the ranching operations. Trees are the native scrub mesquite. Below, rear view of the ranch house showing additional wing. Note the shelves on the back porch.

Julia Fox Driscoll. An attractive blonde woman with scholarly tendencies, Mrs. Driscoll was educated in the Ursaline Convent of San Antonio. She was the daughter of rancher James Fox. Mrs. Driscoll died in London around the turn of the century and is buried in New York.

Robert Driscoll, Jr., circa 1900. Ten years older than Clara, Robert was born on December 21, 1871. He took a law degree from Princeton in 1893 and was proud to have the signature of Woodrow Wilson on his diploma.

Above, Clara Driscoll: Cowgirl. Proud of her range heritage, Clara Driscoll could do everything that her father's cowhands could do except bulldog a steer. In later years, when friends asked her what she was—banker, businesswoman, or political leader—she had a ready answer: "I tell them I am a cattlewoman." Below, Queen of the San Antonio Fiesta. The Fiesta was introduced in 1896 to commemorate the Battle of San Jacinto, which was won on April 21, 1836. A feature of the events was a mock battle in which the participants pelted each other with flowers. Pictured here as the first queen of the Fiesta, Clara was sixteen years old.

Another view of Clara Driscoll in queenly attire, circa 1900. Clara was queen of the festival at least three times. She graced the festivities as queen for the first two presentations and served again shortly before her marriage to Henry Hulme (Hal) Sevier in 1906.

Above, the Alamo property as it appeared in 1903 when Clara Driscoll began her crusade for its preservation. An Eastern syndicate was interested in purchasing the Hugo and Schmeltzer liquor and grocery business for the site of a hotel to exploit the Alamo chapel as a tourist attraction. Unable to raise the necessary funds by subscription to prevent the transaction by the syndicate, Clara Driscoll acted quickly to buy the property herself.

Below, the Alamo as it appeared in 1960 after the Daughters of the Republic of Texas, for whom Mrs. Driscoll bought it, had had the custodianship of the shrine for over half a century. The state of Texas repaid Clara Driscoll for her original purchase and awarded the custodianship to the Daughters of the Republic of Texas in 1905. Mrs. Driscoll declined reimbursement for interest and tax payments on the property. Later she contributed additional funds for the maintenance and improvement of the relic, including $65,000 to clear the sites on which the shacks were located. (Courtesy, Sam Houston State University Library)

Robert Driscoll,
Palo · Alto · Ranch,
Banquete, Texas.

2

Robert Driscoll,
Palo · Alto · Ranch,
Banquete, Texas.

Clara Driscoll's file of original checks issued in payment for the Alamo property, together with explanatory notes detailing the terms of transaction, appear on this page and the three pages following. Even as a young woman of twenty-two, Clara Driscoll had inherited something of her father's business acumen. Note that she used ordinary pins to attach cancelled checks to sheets of stationery.

Payment 3 April 17th 1903 -

money various $1,021.75 -

San Antonio, Texas, April 17th 1903 No.

National Bank

Pay to P. Allen and Subsistence on Beeves, $1,021.75

One Thousand ___ 75 Dollars

PAID APR 17 1903 SAN ANTONIO TEX.

Persons chief Class Driscoll No. $3,778.25

San Antonio, Texas, 4/16 1903 No.

SAN ANTONIO NATIONAL BANK

Pay to Jaz and Subsistence _____ $3,478.25

Thirty four hundred 1814/003 Seventy ___ Dollars

Standard Dollars.

Chief $1,500.00/100 for that

they get time to this subsistence

fund - This in fair to

Allen Class Driscoll and

Driscoll & the Class Driscoll

Fund -

San Antonio, Texas, 3/17 1903 No.

SAN ANTONIO NATIONAL BANK

Pay to Jaz and Subsistence _____ $500.00

Five Hundred 00/100 ___ Dollars

Standard Dollars.

R. Driscoll

Robert Driscoll,
Palo . Alto . Ranch,
Benquete, Texas.

Bond Feb 10th 1905-

San Antonio, Tex.
City National Bank of San Antonio
FEB 10 1905   190   No.   76
Pay to Chas: Hugo _____ or bearer $4579
Forty five hundred seventy 76/100 _____ Dollars.
Clara Driscoll
Pal. Alto. Tex.

Bond. Feb 10th 1905
$ 5,920.27

Robert Driscoll,
Palo . Alto . Ranch,
Benquete, Texas.

Bond. Feb 10th 1904
$ 5,666.23

San Antonio, Texas. Feb. 10 1904 No.
THE CITY NATIONAL BANK
Pay to Chas Hugo _____ or bearer $4666.23
Five Thousand Six Hundred Sixty Six 23/100 Dollars
Clara Driscoll

Bond. Feb. 10th 1904
$ 14,333.77.

San Antonio, Texas. Feb. 10 1904 No.
SAN ANTONIO NATIONAL BANK
FEB 10 1904
Pay to Clara Driscoll _____ order $1-333 00
Fourteen Thousand Three Hundred Thirty Three Dollars   Standard Dollars
L. Driscoll

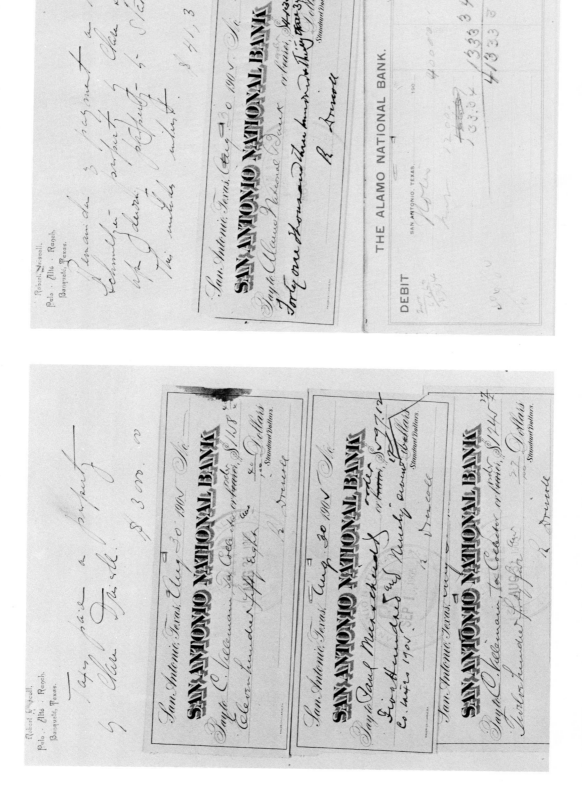

Mission San Antonio de Valero, commonly called the Alamo. (Photograph by Joe Elicson, San Antonio)

Clara Driscoll: author and playwright. This photograph was taken during those early years when the lady was engaged in writing a novel, a book of short stories, and her comic opera—all in three years. There was invariably a certain elegance reflected in Clara Driscoll's dress during her early twenties.

Above, publisher's announcement of *The Girl of La Gloria* released in 1905. On the original card the illustration of the heroine Ilaria was in color. Lower left, Florence (Flo) Eagar Roberts and son. Florence Eagar, Clara Driscoll's closest woman friend, illustrated the author's second book, *In the Shadow of the Alamo.* Lower right, a rare autograph from a copy of *The Girl of La Gloria.* (The latter, courtesy, Library of the University of Texas at Austin)

of Representatives: first in the regular sessions of the Twenty-eighth Legislature, January 13–April, 1903; and in the called session, April 2–May 1, 1903, during the administration of Governor S. W. T. Lanham. In the Twenty-eighth Legislature he served in the regular session, January 1–April 15, 1905; and in the first called session, April 15–May 14, 1905; and in the second called session, March 26–April 3, 1906.[10] During the second called session he had accepted the position of financial editor of the New York *Sun* but returned to Texas to help pass legislation to correct an error in the election law.[11] Sevier had the reputation of being an able legislator but the lure of printer's ink and the routine of meeting deadlines were too strong to resist at this time.

Whether Hal Sevier swept Clara Driscoll off her feet or not is unrecorded. Certainly he campaigned for her hand as he had never electioneered in the political arena and the romance was no whirlwind affair. It took him three years and came as a surprise to some of the bride's friends.

> While it has been a dainty morsel of society gossip for several months that the most favored suitor in Miss Driscoll's eyes was Mr. Sevier, the marriage announcement brought surprise to even many of the young lady's most intimate friends.[12]

After meeting the young statesman in 1903, Clara Driscoll embarked upon a writing career, as noted, and the two were not married until 1906. By that time, as indicated, Sevier had taken the editorial post in New York and she had published two books and had witnessed the production of her comic opera. The New York newspapers lead ran thus:

> Henry Hulme Sevier, for over a year financial editor of the New York *Sun*, and Miss Clara Driscoll, author of "Mexicana," comic opera, which made a hit of the season last winter at the Lyric Theater, were married at St. Patrick's Cathedral, Fifth Avenue, today by Reverend Father Haues . . . in the presence of a party of relatives and professional friends.[13]

So on July 31, 1906, at high noon, these two were wed. The wedding was a small but fashionable affair. The nation's press reported the marriage as "the Romance of the Alamo" and various newspapers hailed the bride as the "Alamo Queen."[14] Some, including the New York *Journal*, repeated the detail involving Sevier's part in getting the bill passed to reimburse Clara Driscoll after she made her appeal to the Texas Legislature for an appropriation to preserve the shrine.

Apparently no photographer was present to take pictures of the bride and groom. The Texas press repeated the photograph of Clara as she appeared the preceding April in the role of "Queen of the Carnival" in San Antonio.[15] In the photograph she is wearing a formal low-cut gown with a chaplet of flowers adorning her hair and around her neck a heart-shaped locket and a rope of pearls extending to her waist. At this time Clara Driscoll appeared to be much younger than her twenty-five years, and portraits of the period reflect the very essence of femininity.

The Texas press further lauded the bride, who had also been acclaimed the toast of Broadway after the successful run of *Mexicana*:

> There is probably no better known young woman in the state today than Mrs. Sevier. Miss Clara Driscoll was recognized, not only as one of Texas' most accomplished belles, but as a woman of literary ability and wealth who had devoted her life to patriotic endeavor in behalf of the state's most historic possession—the war-scarred Alamo.[16]

In addition to crediting Sevier with a successful political career, the press stated:

> The groom is well known in Texas, especially in the Southwestern part, He was formerly editor and publisher of the Sabinal *Sentinel* and earned for himself a distinguished reputation in the field of journalism. He is now on the editorial staff of the New York *Evening Sun*.[17]

Following the simple, unostentatious ceremony, the wedding party repaired to Delmonico's for a sumptuous feast but not before the bride had sent a telegram to her close friend, Florence Eagar, of San Antonio announcing the marriage. Clara's father and brother were both members of the exclusive group. Asked what he thought of his sister's marriage, Robert Jr., himself a bachelor, was reported to have said, laughingly and affectionately, something like this: "Well, I never thought she'd make it, but I'm glad she did. Thank goodness, now I won't have to lug her packages all over town." Sevier took a leave of absence and the couple left for Europe on an extended honeymoon. It was possibly Sevier's first trip abroad, but Clara had not only attended school near Paris, she had made her frist trip around the world by the time she was eighteen.

On August 4, 1906, at three o'clock in the afternoon, the couple embarked on the S.S. *Amerika*. On the ship's log of first class passengers was listed the name Mr. and Mrs. H. H. Sevier. Although the newlyweds visited three countries—England, France, and Italy—they seemed to enjoy the night life of Paris and the London theatrical season above everything else. The bride filled two sizeable scrapbooks with memorabilia of their travels. Evidently she began keeping her record soon after the couple went abroad ship, as she prefaced the first volume with a picture of a passionately kissing couple, above which she wrote the date of the wedding: July 31, 1906, and underneath, the caption "After the ceremony." Next she included souvenirs indicating *bon voyage* gifts: champagne (twelve bottles!), a decorative fruit basket, flowers, etc. On the following page she included a picture of the boat and sailing data.

She filled the pages of her memory books with scenic postcards revealing the couple's itinerary, with such mementos as programs, favors, ticket stubs, itemized hotel receipts, and even pictures clipped from magazines suggesting their various activities. Frequently she added terse diary-style entries across or above the illustrations, along with reminders that revealed how the bride and groom were adjusting to each other and the marital state. For instance, across one color postcard she recorded "First quarrel" and dated it August 7, 1906. On the same page she observed that "Even cross Bobby is always willing to open my trunks." If the disagreement involved opening her luggage, it must have been relatively minor. At this time the couple had been at sea only three days and had been married less than two weeks.

By September the Seviers were registered at Hotel Chatham in Paris. At this point again the bride reveals a slightly facetious domestic situation. The pasted picture of a man shaving bears the inscription: "Hal's early morning occupation." Another pasteup on the same page is a bathroom with the self-explanatory admonition opposite: "Clara, get out of here!"

At the top of a succeeding page with documentation she writes, "Six glasses a day!" Apparently she was becoming concerned about her husband's consumption of liquor. Itemized hotel receipts show frequent orders for whiskey, ginger ale, and other alcoholic beverages. It is only logical to think that the bride and groom were entertaining others at such times.

In Paris the Seviers enjoyed the gay night life for which the city has always been famous: theaters, cabarets, cafes. Souvenir programs include a theater-concert Du Moulin Rouge, the Folies-Bergére (August 31, 1906), the Marigny Theatre, Champs-Elysées, and Café De La Paix, among others. Special favors for the ladies were customary, and the bride mounted each and identified it with date and place. One from the Café De La Paix, dated September 1, 1906, was an elaborate fan featuring a cat holding up a glass of champagne.

A comment inscribed on a scenic postcard, under date of September 11, 1906, reflects the down-to-earth fabric of Clara Driscoll Sevier's character and betrays perhaps something of the intimacy of the couple. "Hal with his nose in the air," she reports cryptically. Then she adds enigmatically below the phrase, "The misery of it is that people go back to the Hill and try to do what they do!!!" Whether she intended Hill to indicate the location of their hotel is problematical. Could she have meant that the two returned to their hotel after an enervating night on the town to try to do what honeymooners do when not dissipating? Anyway, the three exclamation marks are the lady's. At this date the newlyweds had been married less than two months.

Apparently the couple—or at least Hal—had developed an addiction for champagne. One full page dated September 13 and 14, 1906, runs thus:

OH!!!!
WHAT A NIGHT
8:30 Marignlly [*sic*]
11:30 Bal Tabarin
Champagne
1:30 a.m.. Rat Mort, Champagne
5:30 still Rat Mort and more Champagne
6 a.m. Drin[ks]—5—the Halles Market
7 a.m. Filet de Sole Restaurant for breakfast
8 a.m.—back to Champagne—until 5 p.m. next day.

By the end of September the newlyweds had progressed to London, where they checked in at the Savoy. They attended the Palace Theatre Varieties, saw "The Beauty of Bath," at Aldwych Theatre, September 24; "The Bondman" at the Theatre Royal, Drury Lane, September 30; enjoyed a musical extravaganza at the Gaiety Theatre, October 1, entitled "The New Aladdin," which Mrs. Sevier must have compared with her own comic opera *Mexicana*. The next night, October 2, the couple saw "The Earthquake at the London Hippodrome.

From October 2 to October 5 it is presumed that the two rested and caught up with their sleep to be able to enjoy the autumn opera season of 1906, with the Royal Opera productions opening at Covent Garden. In succession the Seviers were present for *Rigoletto*, October 5; *Carmen*, October 8; *La Boheme*, October 9; and *Madame Butterfly*, October 10. What the couple found to amuse themselves between October 5 and 8, Clara fails to record. They enjoyed sightseeing and Clara found old ruins and historic monuments fascinating. Both took pleasure in browsing art galleries.

Additional memorabilia indicate that on October 8 they were staying at the Shakespeare Hotel at Stratford-on-Avon. Before returning by the end of October or a little later, the Seviers visited Italy, where they particularly enjoyed the Renaissance art and architecture of Florence and in Lombardy the scenery of beautiful Lake Como enclosed by magnificent limestone ranges with its shores bordered by splendid villas and resorts.

5

The New York Years

WHEN THE SEVIERS RETURNED TO AMERICA they took an apartment at 37 Madison Avenue, which had been decorated and furnished according to their specifications while they were away in Europe. Meanwhile, as Sevier resumed his editorial duties on the *Sun*, his wife addressed herself to homemaking and social activities. Since she had attended one of the uptown New York finishing schools at twelve and had visited the city frequently, in addition to being present for the production of her play, which had closed its successful run on April 17, only a few months before the wedding, Mrs. Sevier had no difficulty in adjusting to the accelerated tempo of the metropolis.

Her very first, and most important, chore was to confer with architect Charles I. Berg on the construction of a home. The couple selected a site of 160 acres in the Oyster Bay area of Mill Neck on Long Island on which to build. In anticipation of the home Mrs. Sevier had observed architectural features abroad that she found pleasing and had collected pictures of unusual entrances, formal gardens, statuary, courts, etc. Though she was able to have her architect incorporate into the residence the intricate details and refinements she desired, the mansion on Long Island was also designed to harmonize with the unusual landscape.[1]

Berg, who had a reputation for designing effective country houses, planned the residence to conform to the low, sleek lines of Spanish architecture with a picturesque dash of Italian in the courtyard on the main side of the house. The court was set back with the two ends of the main section of the dwelling projecting to form an L. The two wings typified a cloister effect as the entire arrangement was modeled after the Chertosa Monastery outside Florence, which the Seviers had visited and admired.[2] A decorative well flanked by Italian columns centered the court.

Opening onto the patio was a spacious central hall, or foyer, extending the entire length of the residence. On one side was the living room and on the other, the dining room. One end of the cloister wings contained the kitchen; the other housed the conservatory and library. Since both of the Seviers loved music and books—and Mrs. Sevier performed capably upon the violin and piano—they spent much time in these pleasant rooms. The living room opened upon a wide terrace overlooking a ravine, which was converted into a formal garden.

The court side of the house occupied a higher elevation than the other side. The main carriage entrance was at the lower section leading into rooms a floor below the living room and dining area.

The exterior of the residence was of stucco and terra cotta with a tile roof. The stables and gardener's cottage also exemplified the low style Spanish architecture. As it required almost two years to develop the impressive estate, the Seviers had the gardener's cottage completed first and occupied it temporarily while the mansion was being built. This enabled them to observe the stages of construction and make suggestions as they wished.[3]

A model of the Sevier home shown at the Architectural League Exhibit in New York, while the dwelling was under construction, attracted considerable attention because of the originality of the design and the novel courtyard treatment. Situated between exclusive Oyster Bay and East Norwich, with a large frontage on Oyster Bay Road, the estate was adjacent to that of the family of former president Theodore Roosevelt, whom the Seviers had known previously and whose second inauguration in 1904 Mrs. Sevier had attended. The Seviers and the Roosevelts became close friends, as well as good neighbors, and moved in the same circle of dignitaries and the extremely wealthy. As socially-oriented and hospitable as the couple were, they became popular with the elite of the younger set of New York.

As a young housewife, Mrs. Sevier became interested in cooking, collected recipes, developed an avid interest in gardening, and devoted time to occasional writing—all in addition to social activities. She kept a file containing scores of clipped recipes, many with her own marginal notes and underscorings. She preserved others obtained from friends and copied in longhand. Some of these were for simple foods such as cornbread, biscuits, lemon pie, and Irish stew,[4] all somewhat incongruous to the elegant cuisine of the formal dinners and catered banquets for which she became noted.

At the most, the recipes for old-fashioned dishes revealed that the couple themselves enjoyed down-to-earth Texas food, which the young wife no doubt took pleasure in preparing for her husband and herself. It might have been a holdover, too, from the earlier days at Palo Alto when the ranch hands gathered for home-cooked food that would stick to the ribs and provide the cowboys with the energy necessary to discharge their arduous duties on the range. Clara Driscoll Sevier must have remembered frequent menus consisting of Irish stew, hamhock and lima beans, and honest-to-goodness corn pone and turnip greens seasoned with salt pork.

Other favorite recipes of Mrs. Sevier's collection were chicken tamales and potatoes stuffed with lamb hash. Evidently the couple were fond of egg dishes. In Mrs. Sevier's *E* file were recipes for several: goldenrod eggs ("guaranteed to melt the hardest masculine heart when served with its proper accompaniment, a delicious white sauce"), creamed eggs, scrambled eggs, poached eggs with minced chicken and mushrooms, and three varieties of baked eggs, one of which—*bonne femme*—combined onions with the main ingredient.[5]

Mrs. Sevier was a well-organized housewife. Attesting to her efficiency were the notes and memoranda that she kept. For instance, she made lists: articles and stories in the order of their publication, flowers to be planted at the Oyster Bay Estate—"peonies, columbines, astors, and phlox, jonquils and narcissi for the woods, dahlias and cornflowers."[6] Another notation belonging to the New York period, and one that reveals much of the common sense that Mrs. Sevier practiced, despite her vast wealth, was a wardrobe inventory, in which she listed dresses for various occasions. To some it might have appeared strange, and still another incongruity, for a woman who could have anything she wanted—to categorize her wardrobe as "old," "fixed over," and "new."[1]

How she found time for all of these activities and even managed to do some writing is another amazing characteristic of Clara Driscoll Sevier. She submitted many of her stories and articles in longhand and usually kept an extra copy. Often she would write two versions of a particular phrase or sentence so that the editor could exercise a choice. Invariably she wrote notes to the editor right in the middle of the manuscript with spacing to indicate the break in the continuity. At times she explained the meaning of an unusual word or phrase as she had used it. At other times—especially after a paragraph of description, at which she was skilled, and occasionally after a passionate love scene, at which she was equally proficient—she would direct the editor to "Leave this out if you wish," no doubt with tongue in cheek.[8]

It is doubtful, however, that editors deleted many of Clara Driscoll's paragraphs as she possessed a rare affinity for the range and prairie that few writers of her time could match. Such a story belonging to the New York period was "The Angel of Banquete," which carried the byline of Clara Driscoll and identified the author as Mrs. H. H. Sevier of Mill Neck, Long Island, New York. It begins thus:

The sun beat fiercely on the open prairie. There was hardly enough wind to stir the fleecy Gulf clouds that hung here and there in the otherwise clear, blue sky. A buzzard with outstretched wings circled gracefully over the bleaching bones of a steer's carcass. Everywhere was heat and dead silence.[9]

Mrs. Sevier's chief interest outside the home during the New York years was the Texas Club, which she helped to incorporate on June 4, 1909. Invariably an ardent Texan, she found that the organization filled a special need. The Texas Club was unique in that it was the first state society in New York to have women as active members instead of men. Only women could hold office in the organization as men were accepted as honorary or associate members. Thus a precedent was set by the founders in placing men in a subordinate position to women in a state society. Indeed Clara Driscoll may very well have been among the first ladies in the nation to foresee the advent of the American women's liberation movement.

Membership requirements were birth in Texas, residence in Texas for ten years, or that a candidate be the daughter, wife, widow, or mother of a Texan. To become associate members, men had to comply with similar regulations. The purpose of the club was to preserve Texas traditions and history and to study and perpetuate Texas art, literature, and music, as well as to promote friendship and provide entertainment among the membership.

> The objects of the Texas society are to keep ever present in memory the glorious traditions and history of the State of Texas; to honor the memory of those who gave life, fortune, and sacrifice to the end that Texas should become a unit in the galaxy of states; to study and perpetuate its art, literature, and music, and to promote and cherish the ties of friendship among the members . . . and to provide . . . entertainment for its members.[10]

In 1913 prominent male members included Henry H. Sevier, formerly of the staff of the New York *Sun* but at the time engaged as a cotton merchant of New York City; the Honorable Joseph Weldon Bailey of Fort Worth; Mann Trice, formerly assistant attorney general of Houston; David Crockett, desdendant of the Texas patriot and Tennessee frontiersman; the Honorable S. B. Cooper, former congressman from Texas; former judge Robert Lovett, manager of the Harriman railroad properties; B. F. Yoakum, multi-millionaire railroad tycoon; and the Honorable O. B. Colquitt, governor of Texas from 1911 to 1915.[11]

Annual functions on the social calendar were the Lone Star ball and the San Jacinto dinner and dance. A typical affair revealing the ingenuity of Mrs. Sevier's planning was the Carnival Cotillion and dinner celebrating the Battle of San Jacinto and held in New York's Plaza Hotel in 1911 on the anniversary of the battle, April 21. To emphasize the patriotic motif she had arranged for an electrical dance sequence in which figurantes reenacted the scene at the Alamo. She described it as "a slice of the Lone Star State transplanted to New York."[12] The Texas theme was further reflected in both the dinner menu and numbers on the dance program. Of particular interest were the Potatoes San Patricio. According to tradition Clara Driscoll Sevier's forebears from Ireland helped to found the town of San Patricio and named it for one of their patron saints.

MENU

Oysters Port Lavaca
Soup Mexico
Radishes   Olives   Almonds
Turbot Matagorda
Lamb Goliad
Potatoes San Patricio
Lemon Ice Sarita
Chicken Gonzales
Salad San Jacinto
Biscuit Glace Tortoni
Petits Fours
Coffee

G. H. Mumm & Co.'s
Selected Brut a la Carte[13]

The dance program, with its accompanying music, permitted an even better opportunity for innovation in carrying out the Texas theme. The favor cotillions were devoted to the glorification of Texas's rich heritage, beginning with the first dance "San Jacinto" and concluding with the modern role of "The University of Texas" in contributing to the educational culture of the descendants of the Alamo heroes and the sires of San Jacinto. It is interesting to note that the waltz and the two-step were the favorite dancing routines of the Texas Club members.

*1. First Favor Dance "San Jacinto"
The first, the Military, recalling the forcible expulsion of a tyrannical power by the Minute Men of Liberty.
2. Waltz   "Espanita"   Rosey
3. Two-step   "The Hen Pecks"   Sloane
*4. Second Favor Dance "Indian"
The second, the Indian, suggesting the period when the Aztec contested with the Anglo-Saxon the supremacy of the plains.
5. Waltz   "The Balkan Princess"   Rubens

    6. Two-step   "Grizzly Bear"   Botsford

 *7. Third Favor Dance "Wild West"

      The third, the Cowboy, indicative of the reign of the most picturesque figure in the development of the frontier—the Knight of the Rope and Saddle.

    8. Waltz   "My Heart's a Top"   Vaughan

    9. Two-step   "Kiss Me My Honey, Kiss Me"   Snyder

 *10. Fourth Favor Dance "Texas"

      The fourth, the Products of the Trackless Prairie, showing the wealth of the soil; what brains and energy and perseverance have contributed to the necessities and luxury of the peoples of all the world.

   11. Waltz   "The Spring Maid"   Reinhardt

   12. Two-step   "All Alone"   H. Von Tilzer

 *13. Fifth Favor Dance "University of Texas"

      The fifth, the University of Texas, introducing the colors and pastimes of the institution that is equipping the descendants of the heroes of the Alamo and San Jacinto for higher stations in life.

*The five cotillions depict five stages of the evolution of Texas.[14]

Mrs. Sevier served the organization as president and later was awarded an honorary life presidency. After perfecting the organization, she assisted the club in acquiring a large brownstone mansion in the fashionable Murray Hill district, just off Fifth Avenue and three blocks from the Waldorf-Astoria Hotel, for permanent quarters.[15] To mark the opening of the new quarters, Mrs. Sevier entertained the membership and their guests with a Texas plantation supper. The clubhouse provided living accommodations for visiting Texans and included a dining salon, kitchen, recreation rooms, reception room, and other facilities. It maintained all of the conveniences of an ordinary club for men, "excepting, perhaps, one." The ladies had installed a small tearoom in the basement instead of a bar.

The visiting Texan would be made not only to feel at home at the club, but also to find there the latest issues of Texas newspapers and friendly Texans to greet him. If the latter included the president of the club—Mrs. Sevier—the visitor could feel particularly pleased with himself and the world in general. Mrs. Sevier maintained a lifelong interest in the Texas Club of New York.

Business interests had influenced Sevier's resignation from his post on the *Sun* but did not prohibit him from becoming Washington correspondent in 1912. In 1914, after a trip to California, the Seviers went to San Antonio, where Colonel Driscoll had been ill for some time. He died during their visit.

A prominent Mason, Driscoll was interred in the family mausoleum in the Masonic Cemetery in San Antonio.

The Seviers had planned eventually to return to Texas to live but had spent the first six years of their marriage in New York so that Hal could become entrenched in his profession and enter business. Undoubtedly the death of Mrs. Sevier's father, to whom she had been closely attached, was a determining factor in their decision to relocate at this time.

After Colonel Driscoll's demise, the couple arranged to move from Long Island to Austin, where Sevier founded his own newspaper, the Austin *American*, in 1914,[16] and Clara Driscoll Sevier began to plan another dream house.

6

Laguna Gloria

LAGUNA GLORIA WAS TRULY A MONUMENT
to love. The idea for it was conceived in 1906, when the Seviers were honeymooning in Europe. While they were enjoying picturesque Lake Como in Italy as an ideal retreat for lovers, Clara waxed ecstatic. She wished she might
remain there forever—the place was so quiet and peaceful and beautiful, she
told her husband.

Well aware of her predilection for Texas, Hal Sevier was amused at his
wife's effusion. "You wouldn't be satisfied to live anywhere but in Texas,"
he told her. "But don't worry. I know of a place in Texas that has everything Lake Como has—the mountains, the water, the quiet beauty, peaceful
and romantic atmosphere, and the advantage of being at home. I'll take you
there when we get back."[1]

When Mrs. Sevier first saw the exquisite Texas tract at the base of Mount
Bonnell, five miles west of the capital city on Lake Austin, overlooking the
Colorado River, she could hardly believe her eyes. She concurred with her
husband that the scene was almost a replica of peaceful and romantic Lake
Como. On August, 1915, the Seviers bought the 28-½-acre site from Roy H.
and Ellen Collett for $4,750.[2] Originally the land had been purchased on
May 8, 1832 by Stephen F. Austin for a prospective home. A letter in which
Austin authorized his agent, Samuel M. Williams, to purchase the property for
him is extant. Although the purchase was consummated, Austin's death in
1836 prevented him from building on the site, and the property was left va-
cant for the remainder of the nineteenth century.[3] Stephen F. Austin was
not the only historic figure to admire the scenic Colorado at this point. When
Mirabeau B. Lamar discovered the site on a buffalo hunt in 1838 he declared,
"This should be the seat of empire."[4] In 1839, as president of the Republic
of Texas, he made it the permanent capital.

Shortly after obtaining the land, the Seviers engaged architect Harvey L.

Page of San Antonio to design the residence of early twentieth-century Mediterranean style and contracted with builder Jack Johnson to erect it.[5] The property extends southward to form a peninsula, bound by the Colorado River on the west and the lagoon to the south and east. The couple chose the name of Laguna Gloria, which translates roughly into "Heavenly Lagoon," for the lake—actually a sheltered inlet of the Colorado—and for one of the Driscoll ranches in Duval County. Mrs. Sevier's novel published during the year of the marriage had also carried Gloria in the title—*The Girl of La Gloria*. It is also possible that *Gloria* signified a sentiment shared only by the couple.

A pair of wrought-iron gates attached to limestone posts marks the entrance to the property from Mount Bonnell Road. Mrs. Sevier was able to obtain at a public auction two pairs of these gates, which were once used on the state capitol grounds in the halcyon days when stock roamed free. Interestingly, she discovered the lovely old gates (which once stood at the south entrance to the capitol grounds and at the exit) in a pile of junk in the State-house basement. When she asked to be permitted to buy the gates, she was informed that they would be sold at auction by the state board of control and she would have to bid for them along with others. Fortunately, at the advertised public auction, the lady outbid dealers of old scrap iron and prevented the historic gates from the indignity of becoming dismantled as junk.

An enthusiastic gardener, Mrs. Sevier personally supervised the conversion of the hillside of rock and dense undergrowth into one of the most beautiful homesites of the city. Five acres were formally landscaped. Except for sodding, approximately thirteen acres were allowed to remain in their natural wooded state. Here centuries-old live oaks common to the area shaded the grounds. The landscape facing the Colorado River on the west side made the most of natural terraces and magnificent vistas. In conformity with the Mediterranean-style villa, the formal gardens were Italian in design. On the west side facing the river was a formal terraced patio embellished with a fountain and plantings in stone urns. Steps descended to a lower terrace where a balustrade accentuated an abrupt drop to the land at the river level.[6]

Accents of the lovely landscaped grounds included a sculptured birdbath in the sunken garden, a Roman fountain centering the palm-lined circular drive, a sundial, an Italian wishing well imported from Tuscany, a mounted Spanish cannon and an antique mission bell from the Philippines, and statuary from Venice. The four figures of statuary were emblematic of the four seasons. The old mission bell suspended from a decorative arch, a special gift to Mrs. Sevier, was sounded regularly to announce the hours for meals at Laguna Gloria. To the southeast a balustraded footbridge led to a winding path along the ridge of the peninsula that ends at the juncture of the lagoon and the river.

At the termination of the walkway stood the monumental "Temple of Love," a pagoda-shaped structure consisting of marble columns supporting a red-tiled roof. A few yards beyond it a second pair of the historic wrought-iron gates from the capitol grounds of yesteryear separated the garden area from the water's edge.

But the grounds of Laguna Gloria provided only the setting. The fifteen-room mansion itself, situated at the base of the 775-foot elevation of Mount Bonnell and overlooking the winding Colorado, was the real jewel of the extraordinary mounting. Located on the highest of the four terraces, the residence occupied a regal position and commanded magnificent views in several directions. Comprised of 4,500 square feet and with western exposure, the villa was of stuccoed masonry and concrete construction composed of rectilinear blocks grouped asymetrically.[7]

The main unit of the structure, with the principal front and rear entrances, was in the shape of a three-story rectangle. On the west the apertures suggested two stories. On the ground level double doors, accented by fanlights at the second level, opened into a combination two-story ballroom and living room. Above the original entrance was a small square window. Surmounted above this elevation from the southeast corner and projecting slightly was a four-story square tower. The tower dominated this part of the villa and was the most visible feature from a distance. The flat roof of the three-story segment was encircled by a low parapet wall. The tower was identified by a hipped roof of tile with wide bracketed eaves.

On the third-floor pairs of windows, with bracketed grill, embellished the front and a single window identified the side. The fourth-floor level featured a grouping of three narrow windows in the center of the western and southern exposures, which were accentuated by handsome balustraded balconies supported by three brackets. On both the northern and eastern facades, window arrangements varied from coupled and single trabeated patterns with grills to the diminutive square aperture.[8]

An interesting feature of the second entrance of the first floor, and a detail reflecting Mrs. Sevier's devotion to Texas history, was the sculptured limestone opening that was patterned after the legendary rose window of the San José mission in San Antonio. This decorative aperture allowed natural light for the main stairway originating from the entrance hall. It is of parenthetical interest here to note that the San José mission with its celebrated window inspired what is perhaps Clara Driscoll's most forceful short story—"The Red Rose of San José."[9] Another detail of historic memorabilia relating to the interior of the mansion was a framed copy of Austin's letter and map directing his agent to buy the property—a memento that hung in the entrance hall.

A two-story rectangular wing projecting from the main section repeated the wide bracketed eaves of the tower. An end pavilion extended from the southeast corner of the western facade, and also from the ground level four arched double doors opened onto a patio. A stringcourse separated the two floors. The large square windows of the second floor channeled light and sunshine into a solarium. Intimates of the Seviers and friends who had visited them in New York were quick to note similarities of architectural features of the Laguna Gloria residence with the original love nest on Long Island.

Interior arrangements and furnishings consisted of treasures collected from various parts of the world, some of which were acquired during the Seviers' two-month wedding trip to Europe and on subsequent visits to foreign shores. Both were seasoned travelers and avid collectors. Their cherished possessions included an eclectic accumulation of everything from rare books and paintings to art objects of copper and brass from the Orient, along with porcelains, French china, crystal, and old Sheffield silver. Prized Oriental rugs covered some of the floors and elegant Elizabethan furniture graced some of the rooms. A desk, ornate with inlaid gold leaf decoration and enclosed in a heavy chest, was a treasured item Mrs. Sevier found in Florence. Other favorites included a splendid sterling vodka bottle and cups and a handsome samovar picked up in Russia and an assortment of cloisonné and Meissen, from various places, together with exquisite lamps from the Far East. Mrs. Sevier had a penchant for unusual lamps and even had a few made of novel vases and other *objets d'art* that had captured her fancy.

Across from the entrance to the ballroom was an alcove with the fireplace flanked by two rare carved benches. The wall panel above the fireplace consisted of a carving executed especially for Mrs. Sevier by Peter Mansbendel, an artist originally from Switzerland but living more recently in San Antonio. Still another memorial to Texas history, and one especially meaningful to Clara Driscoll Sevier, the carving depicted "The Battle of the Alamo" and was made from an original rafter of the shrine. A balcony above the fireplace, with entrance from the second floor, was a major architectural detail that completed the wall arrangement. Another balcony at the south end of the ballroom provided space for an orchestra. Some of the most popular name bands of the 1920s played for dances at Laguna Gloria. The Seviers were said to have been exceptionally graceful dancers and loved both popular and classical music.

From the south end of the ballroom an arched doorway led into a tearoom. Adjacent to the tearoom was the large formal dining room. Accessible from four arched doorways at the west, the two rooms were separated by an arcade complementing the arched design of the exterior doors. Convenient to these rooms, but privately removed, were the kitchen and butler's pantries.

Floors in the main rooms of the first story consisted of black tile, while an interesting pattern of black, white, and red tile was employed in some of the hallways. In addition to the solarium, the second floor accommodated a guest room. Four bedrooms comprised the third-floor arrangement, and the tower above the fourth story was devoted to a study. Mrs. Sevier set great store by the study and undoubtedly would have spent more time there had life not crowded in on her with time-consuming responsibilities. As one contemporary recalled, "The unrivaled sunsets of Austin, the craggy cliffs of hoary old Mount Bonnell are visible from Mrs. Sevier's study, and her clever word pictures of these poetic surroundings are the delight of her friends and associates."

Laguna Gloria became Austin's showplace and a mecca for international visitors. Inasmuch as the Seviers were fond of entertaining, their home was the scene of many social functions over the years. The two gained a reputation for their graciousness and their faculty for making their guests feel at ease in their luxurious home. What is more, whether the Seviers were hosts to dignitaries-of-state, celebrities of worldwide renown, or just relatives of small groups of intimate friends from one of the Driscoll ranches, they extended to all the same gracious courtesies. Moreover, they spared no expense in making their guests comfortable and happy at Laguna Gloria, regardless of the size of the party or prestige of the guests.

State and national organizations meeting in Austin or towns nearby were frequently entertained at the palatial estate. Even the Legislature had met at Laguna Gloria, as had important Democratic party leaders of both state and national level. One memorable social occasion was the time when the Federation of Women's Clubs of the United States observed its annual convention in San Antonio with a side trip to the state capital. As the climax of their visit, the delegates were invited to be dinner guests of the Seviers at a garden party at sunset on the spacious lawn sloping down to the Colorado. Several hundred people, including the elite of Austin, attended the dramatic affair held at the most beautiful time of day. Many still recall the graciousness of their host and hostess who had not only perfected the art of entertaining large numbers with amazing ease but were themselves a remarkably attractive couple.[10]

Mary Lasswell, the Texas author probably best known for *Suds In Your Eye* and *Wait for The Wagon*, recalls visits to Laguna Gloria in the early twenties and what Mrs. Sevier was like during the Austin years.

> During my university days I was often invited to sing at Laguna Gloria, especially at meetings of the Pan-American Round Table, because both Mr. and Mrs. Sevier were especially fond of Mexican and Spanish songs. I remember liking to sing there because there was a tiny balcony above the drawing room just big enough for me to stand on. The railing was covered with a handsome Spanish shawl and it was an ideal spot to sing from. . . .[11]

As her friendship with Mrs. Sevier developed, Mrs. Lasswell became increasingly aware of Mrs. Sevier's attractiveness and capabilities. "Clara Driscoll was a woman," she said, "who was born to be noticed and all too frequently misunderstood. Her proud, generous, and impetuous nature made her stand out among her more drab sisters like an eagle. . . ." She was "exceedingly outspoken. . . . She could give a good account of herself at the Court of Saint James or in a heated battle with her political opponents. . . . She 'spoke the language' in whatever element she found herself."[12]

According to her friend, Mrs. Sevier had a flair for fashion and ineffable taste in clothes: "She was without exception the most beautifully and becomingly dressed woman I have ever seen, anywhere, any time. Her sense of style and fashion was almost psychic. . . . Mrs. Sevier loved harmony and softness in her dress and often wore hats and shoes of the same color. . . . She was extremely fond of soft fabrics, chiffon and the georgette crepe of the period. One of the most striking outfits I ever saw her wear was of pale shrimp pink chiffon with a picture hat of the same material. . . ."[13]

Mrs. Lasswell also had vivid recollections of what Mrs. Sevier looked like during the Laguna Gloria years:

> Her reddish-black hair and indescribable brown eyes, deep, almost reddish-brown amber eyes, liquid and lovely with friendliness, sometimes lit with flashes of heat-lightning, were like the eyes of a Marie Laurencin painting against her delicate fine-textured white skin colored only by the reflection from her pink hat.[14]

Above all, Mrs. Sevier "was a complete person, fully developed on all sides of her nature; and . . . it seems . . . that she must have been an extremely lonely person because she found so few companions who were anywhere near her own stature. She was not the kind of person to conform to what she considered petty standards. She set her own. . . ." Mrs. Sevier was a magnetic, self-contained woman. "The elegance Clara Driscoll imparted to everything she was connected with is gone with the era in which she lived."[15]

The Seviers occupied Laguna Gloria from 1916, the year of its construction, until 1929. Even after that they frequently wintered there. Only World War I interrupted their residency at the idyllic estate when the couple spent two years in South America. In 1917 President Woodrow Wilson appointed Sevier to head a United States contingent on public information to combat German propaganda in Argentina and Chile.[16] Sevier's campaign against enemy propaganda was so effective that he was placed in control of the committee's work throughout the entire continent including all of the South American republics.[17]

Following his service in South America, Sevier attended the peace conference in Paris as special assistant to his friend E. M. House, personal adviser to President Wilson. Among his extraordinary experiences in the latter assignment, Sevier recalled his trip in an open cockpit airplane from Geneva, Switzerland, to Czechoslovakia, before the creation of that nation, to confer with Eduard Beneš, the leader who later became president of the new republic.[18] On September 3, 1918, the United States recognized the National Council as the supreme body controlling national interest of the country. Then on October 14, 1918, Beneš notified the entente states of the establishment of an interim Czechoslovakian government in Paris with himself as the head. On October 18, 1918, a declaration was issued from Washington, D. C., recognizing the independence of the republic. The conference at Geneva, to which Sevier and House were United States representatives, gave the new nation of Czechoslovakia the form of a democratic republic.[19] Later Sevier engaged in newspaper correspondence for the newly-created Republic of Czechoslovakia and for Poland.[20] These World War I assignments gave the Seviers a welcome opportunity to serve their country and at the same time to satisfy peripatetic interests.

Thus as patriotic citizens, the couple contributed generously to the American war effort. Mrs. Sevier also entertained as canteen hostess and rolled bandages and performed other duties for the Red Cross.[21]

Upon severing his relations with the New York *Sun* in 1912, Sevier contributed articles on political and economic subjects to various newspapers and magazines as the couple traveled before settling down in Texas. Meanwhile, his assignment as Washington correspondent occupied him from 1912 to 1914.[22] He had retired as active publisher of the Austin *American* in 1918 to accept the South American wartime post and sold the newspaper in 1919.

At the end of the war, after the Seviers returned to Austin, they reentered the mainstream of capital social and civic life, as indicated. One of Sevier's favorite projects at the time was the founding of the Austin Public Library Association, of which he was first president. He was also instrumental in building the library in Wooldridge Park.[23] Mrs. Sevier became active in numerous organizations, essentially the Pan-American Round Table, which she founded in 1922 and served as director-general; the Austin Open Forum, and the Austin Garden Club, for both of which she served as president. She never relaxed her interest in the Daughters of the Republic of Texas, for which she was president from 1927 to 1931 and would later serve from 1935 to 1937 and as honorary life president. Both husband and wife were interested in politics, and in 1928 Mrs. Sevier was elected as Democratic national committeewoman from Texas. These years—from 1918, when the war ended, to 1929—were the feast years for Clara Driscoll and her husband, Hal Sevier. Friends who knew them intimately and were frequently guests at Laguna Gloria considered them an ideally happy couple who had everything: love, friends, wealth, fame.

Then in 1929 circumstances made it necessary for the Seviers to give up their paradise in Austin and reestablish themselves in Corpus Christi.

7

Minding the Store

CLARA DRISCOLL SEVIER'S BROTHER DIED
on July 7, 1929, in Santa Rosa Hospital in San Antonio from a blood clot in
his left leg. He had comanaged the Driscoll estate with his father from 1904
to the time of the latter's death in 1914. Since his father's death he had been
the sole administrator of the Driscoll holdings. When Robert Driscoll, Jr., assumed control of the Driscoll empire, he took up where the elder Driscoll had
left off. Not only did he give the development begun by his father new impetus, he—more than any other one man—was responsible for the eventual
conversion of Corpus Christi into a deep-water port[1] and witnessed it operate
as one of the "leading anchorages in the nation"—a project first envisioned
by his father.[2] On June 7, 1930, the first anniversary of his passing, apprecia-
tive Corpus Christians unveiled an engraved boulder of red Texas granite near
the port as a monument to his memory.

Banker, cattleman, financier, and philanthropist, Driscoll led Corpus Christi
and South Texas in many of their most important industrial, commercial, and
civic enterprises for more than two decades.[3] At the time of his death he was
chairman of the Nueces County Navigation Commission, having been the first
named to the office when the deep-water port he espoused became a reality.
Recognized as Corpus Christi's "first citizen," he was also president of the
Corpus Christi National Bank, leading South Texas financial institution. He
founded the Corpus Christi Trust Company, which he later expanded into a
banking firm under the name of Corpus Christi Bank and Trust Company.
Driscoll also followed his father's footsteps in providing excellent hotel and
housing facilities to accommodate the annual Corpus Christi tourist trade.
One of the chain of hotels he financed was the White Plaza in Corpus Christi,
later to be known as the Plaza. Seeing the need for a permanent water supply for the city, he initiated the project to conserve the waters of the Nueces
River and create Lake Corpus Christi at Mathis. Many of these municipal

enterprises Driscoll subisdized personally.

Back in 1926, when he was most actively involved in developing the deep seaport, along with other civic enterprises, he did not neglect Driscoll interests. He had begun the oil development on the Sweden ranch at that time. He had also known of the presence of gas on the Driscoll properties and had undertaken the commercial exploitation of that commodity.[4] In 1928, a year before his death, Driscoll headed a syndicate which paid a consideration of over one million dollars cash for the Taft properties in San Patricio County. The final sale included the towns of Gregory and Taft, 5,000 acres of cultivated land, 3,000 acres of uncultivated land, 100 or more houses in the two towns, plus business buildings.[5] The land purchased was rich and productive and was originally obtained at from a few cents to a few dollars per acre.[6]

Robert Driscoll, Jr.'s performance would be difficult for anybody to follow. Despite the ten years separating the two in age, Clara and Robert had been not only brother and sister but good friends as well. Nor had he hesitated to consult his sister whose ideas he respected and "who was often able to give him good advice."[7] As is so rarely the case, there was positively no sibling rivalry between them. The emotional impact of her brother's death was a severe blow, as they had been members of a closeknit family. Frequently Clara Driscoll Sevier punctuated her conversation with references to her father and her brother. "After all," she explained, "we were a small family and very close. The work they started means everything to me."[8]

Time would heal the wounds of severance. But the demise of Robert Driscoll, Jr., meant eminently more than the loss of a beloved brother and friend. It meant that Clara Driscoll Sevier, as the last survivor of the Driscoll line and sole heir to the fabulous Driscoll fortune, would have to take over the administration of the empire; that the responsibility for the operation of the multiple enterprises would automatically devolve upon her slender shoulders, adding immeasurably to an already crowded schedule of philanthropic, political, and social activities.

It meant more. With the death of Robert Driscoll, Jr., not only did Clara Driscoll Sevier inherit the "minding of the multi-million-dollar store," she also fell heir to the legacy of perpetuating the proud Driscoll tradition of civic enterprise and philanthropy—a tradition that dated roughtly from the Civil War days and had become synonymous with the advancement of South Texas.

But first it was necessary to close Laguna Gloria and move to Corpus Christi, where business interests centered. Consequently, she and her husband moved to the Palo Alto ranch, twenty-five miles from the city. When Clara Driscoll Sevier assumed control of the estate it was a domain comprised of 100,000 acres, with sixteen oil wells drilled to varying depths without a dry hole. It included an incalculable quantity of proven gas with three wells already in production. The Driscoll holdings still included the 53,000-acre Sweden and the La Gloria ranches in Duval County, the 20,000-acre Las Machos south of Alice, the 8,000-acre Clara in Bee County, and the 5,000 acres retained in the Palo Alto spread. Also included were eighteen farms in Nueces and Cameron counties, three cotton gins, and numerous real estate properties in Corpus Christi,[9] in addition to stocks and bonds.

Suddenly Mrs. Sevier found herself wearing an assortment of administrative hats: as president and sole owner of the Corpus Christi Bank and Trust Company; as director and largest stockholder of the Corpus Christi National Bank; as president of the Driscoll Properties Company, which consisted of a chain of hotels; and as president of the Kingsville Produce and Milling Company. Then as if to compound the situation, she held equities in gigantic monopolies. For example, she was one-fifth owner of the Taft Syndicate and one-fourth owner of the Russell Tract Syndicate.[10]

At the outset the Seviers commuted from Palo Alto to her office in downtown Corpus Christi. Located just off the foyer of the Corpus Christi Bank and Trust Company, the office was not pretentious. It reflected an air of efficiency, however, and radiated the warmth of Mrs. Sevier's personality. The couple occupied desks facing each other with only green blotters separating them. The office was a place where a waiting visitor might overhear Mrs. Sevier accept or decline an invitation to make a political speech to endorse a candidate; might catch snatches of a telephone conversation in which she would approve or reject a million-dollar transaction; or advise her ranch foreman at Palo Alto to use no more than five cans of stock dip that afternoon, or remind him to clear the north pasture for the new highway going through.

But if anyone had apprehensions as to the lady's ability to take over the reins of the Driscoll domain, they were soon misplaced. Under Mrs. Sevier's shrewd management the estate almost doubled, and she was later recognized as one of the most astute businesswomen in the nation.

> As her brother had succeeded her father, Mrs. Clara Driscoll [Sevier] followed the footsteps of her brother and was soon recognized as outstanding among the nation's businesswomen. . . .[11]

Not only that, she often turned away from her private interests to devote time to outside activities designed to help others—activities that required initiative and unusual executive ability. Her counsels in Democratic party procedures and policy gained increasing respect.

How she managed her extensive enterprises with equal skill and continued to serve actively in political, social, and civic organizations was her own secret.

Of her varied interests Mrs. Sevier preferred ranching. When friends asked what she was—banker, businesswoman, political leader—Mrs. Sevier had a ready answer: "I tell them I am a cattlewoman."[12]

Clara Driscoll Sevier was indeed a cattlewoman and ranching was in her blood. In resuming occupancy of the comfortable, sprawling ranch house built more than a half century ago of lumber shipped by schooner from Louisiana, she left it unchanged. Naturally she attached sentiment to it. Not only had it been her childhood home, it had provided a base of operations for both her father and her brother as they created the Driscoll empire and built Corpus Christi into an industrial center. While originally the ranch included the land between Robstown south to Bishop, and from Petronilla west to Agua Dulce, it now extended only to Driscoll, which she consistently claimed as her place of residence in Nueces County, Texas.

Furthermore, Clara Driscoll Sevier had always thought of Palo Alto as a haven of rest during hectic days.[13] It was, she said, so quiet and comforting to see the cattle grazing contentedly. Although she maintained her office in downtown Corpus Christi, she spent as much time at the old ranch headquarters as other duties would permit:

> I like to go out there and get away from things. I can always find plenty to do. The ranch hands come in to see me, keep me informed about what is going on. I read a great deal, and then I like to take the assortment of mail which has accumulated at my office in Corpus Christi and open it in a leisurely way.[14]

Mrs. Sevier might well have added that she really loved cattle per se. Sometimes at cattle auctions she bought more animals than she really intended to buy, found it difficult to quit bidding.[15] She had learned early how to appraise different breeds; and fine specimens of animals, including both cattle and horses, fascinated her. She was also a dog lover and kept many canines in the kennels at Palo Alto, including a fine pack of Russian wolfhounds.

In her novel involving the range one character points to a small herd of sleek Herefords. "Do you suppose those pedigreed dandies are too proud to crop Texas grass?" he asks the Corporal.

"Not on your life! I tell you it's those fellows out there—those four-footed bluebloods that have transformed the country."[16]

In the same book the author stresses the personal interest stockmen take in their cattle. She says, with her father in mind, "When a man owning anywhere from five to seven hundred thousand acres of land, can take you over his property and point out among his thousands of head of cattle, the individual ones . . . you can judge how the owners . . . love these dumb creatures."[17] For instance, he might say: "See that linesided two-year-old over there? A year ago I saved his life by feeding him moss"; or "That heifer yon-der, I stood her on her feet one whole day"; or "That yearling on the right with half of her tail gone—I broke off the other half pulling her out of a bog. . . ."[18]

In the fewest years Clara Driscoll Sevier became one of the most important leaders in South Texas as her legend continued to spiral.

8

The Chile Ambassadorship and Divorce

THE TEXAS SENATE AND ALSO THE HOUSE of Representatives submitted resolutions to President-Elect Franklin Delano Roosevelt endorsing Hal H. Sevier for the ambassadorship in Chile. In enumerating his qualifications, they cited him as one of the most distinguished men of Texas—a patriot, statesman, and diplomat—who had traveled extensively in foreign countries for many years and particularly in Latin America.

They reminded the president-elect of Sevier's previous experience as emissary to South America under the appointment of President Woodrow Wilson when the diplomat rendered invaluable service to the Commission on Public Information by compiling pertinent data for the United States government and combating effectively German propaganda.

They pointed out further that Sevier's activities in Argentina, Uruguay, and Paraguay had been so successful that his activities had been expanded to include the whole South American continent. Moreover, his overall service had won him such respect and affection of the people of South American countries that they had petitioned the United States government, after the armistice was signed, to permit Sevier to retain the post indefinitely.

The legislative bodies resolved further that Sevier's "brilliant and distinguished wife, the Honorable Clara Driscoll Sevier, no less a patriot, statesman [sic], and diplomat of magnificent ability and charming grace," would reflect added credit to the appointment.[1] Consequently, the honor came as no surprise to the Seviers' friends. The fact that the couple, as ardent and loyal Democrats, had been liberal contributors to the Roosevelt campaign, also bore weight.

The state press, and members of the Democratic party in particular, applauded the president's action.

Since the diplomatic corps is any country's first line of defense, President Roosevelt has exercised great care and precision in choosing American ambassadors to foreign countries. Since Mr. Sevier is so well equipped to serve his country in Chile, it is no wonder that the President has designated him as ambassador to the country.[2]

From their previous contact during World War I both husband and wife had found life in South America delightful, and much of Sevier's work in the diplomatic corps had been accomplished in Chile. If somewhat retarded by archaic customs, the Chileans were nonetheless charming and adaptable. The Seviers loved the Aconcagua, with its yearlong snowcapped peak reminiscent of the Swiss Alps. The spicy air of the countryside was invigorating and they had adjusted to the imminent threat of earth tremors from the active volcanoes without consuming fear. Mrs. Sevier had enjoyed the social life of Santiago, where the people were renowned for their hospitality; and the experience had inspired her to organize the Pan-American Round Table following the couple's return to America.

The ambassadorship posed one problem, however. Since the death of Robert Driscoll, Jr., Sevier had been actively engaged in assisting his wife in the management of the Driscoll financial empire and the removal of either or both from their home base of Corpus Christi would disrupt this arrangement. At the time of his appointment Sevier was vice-president and a director of the Corpus Christi Bank and Trust Company (as it was called then), while Mrs. Sevier was president and also director[3] Their acceptance of the foreign post, as attractive as it was, would take the direction of the extensive Driscoll interests temporarily out of the control of the family for the first time. Actually acceptance of the ambassadorship and the removal from the United States would mean a sacrifice of business interests to service of country. It was not an easy decision to make, but the Seviers elected to serve America and made arrangements for others to maintain the estate during their absence.

The most important step they took was to place what some people considered to be "the most [nearly] unique oil field in the state—the 53,000-acre Sweden ranch in Duval County—under the control of the Continental Oil Company.[4] The transaction, said to have run into seven figures, allowed the Driscoll estate to retain title to oil and gas production to 3,000 feet and above, while the oil company took over the operation, as well as the oil rights to lower strata.[5] The Driscoll ranch, according to leading geologists, had long been an inviting field for oil development. Efforts, however, to obtain leases on it were unsuccessful until the Seviers decided to accept the South American assignment.

By 1934 Continental Oil Company had drilled one well to a deeper "pay" at 3,448 feet in the south edge of the shallower producing area, and it was averaging 150 barrels a day. The company drilled a second well in the north edge of that area to a depth below 3,500 feet after encountering numerous showings. A part of the sales contract stipulated continuous drilling for a considerable length of time. Production on the older portion retained by the estate ran to 225 barrels daily.[6]

Texas friends were delighted with the honor conferred upon the Seviers and initiated a series of festivities to mark their departure. The Pan-American Round Table led off with a state reception in the E. H. Perry home attended by several hundred Democratic party leaders and Texas officials and their wives. The Daughters of the Republic of Texas, for whom the couple had entertained lavishly the preceding year, toasted the Seviers with a banquet at which Senator Tom Connally, a close friend, and former governor Pat M. Neff, also a good friend, were the principal speakers. Four hundred guests assembled to pay tribute to the Seviers.

(In 1932, the year before their departure, the Seviers had invited the Daughters of the Republic of Texas to hold their annual convention in Corpus Christi as their guests. The invitation, which was extended in 1931, was postponed until the following year because of an automobile accident in which Mrs. Sevier was injured. As part of the schedule of entertainment, the Seviers gave their guests an extended tour through the Rio Grande Valley in chartered buses and private cars. Highlights of the trip were visits to Brownsville and Sharyland. The Brownsville Chamber of Commerce tendered the group a dinner at a famous restaurant in Matamoros, Mexico. At Sharyland, home of Mr. & Mrs. John Shary [parents of Mrs. Allan Shivers], who introduced grapefruit to the valley, the Daughters were royally entertained and each guest picked a tree-ripened grapefruit as a souvenir.)

The most signal event in honor of the Seviers was a banquet given by the Young Democratic Club of Nueces County on the Marine Deck of the Plaza Hotel on the night preceding their departure, October 20, 1933. The gala affair was Texas's official farewell to an illustrious son and daughter.

The Honorable Joseph Weldon Bailey, Jr., one of the state's most prominent Democrats and congressman-at-large from Dallas, was the principal speaker. Outstanding Democrats from all parts of the state, together with national figures, attended the dinner. Members of the James A. Farley–John Nance Garner political aggregation visiting the state at the time added prestige to the affair.[7] Farley was national Democratic chairman and Vice-President elect Garner was Democratic national committeeman from Texas. In the election of 1932 Garner had loomed as a compromise candidate, who rather than deadlock the Democratic convention, threw his strength to Franklin Delano Roosevelt. Garner, whose election as Speaker of the House in 1931 had elevated him to the position of second highest ranking Democrat in the nation, was nominated to run for the vice-presidency by acclamation.[8] Both leaders were special friends of the Seviers.

A motorcade from Corpus Christi escorted the dignitaries from San Antonio to the city limits, where a police motorcycle patrol accompanied them to the Plaza Hotel.

Robert McCracken, president of the club, introduced Ambassador and Mrs. Sevier. Congressman-at-large Bailey, who was noted for his distinctive oratory, lauded the honor guests as two of the nation's outstanding Democrats and patriots. Both responded briefly to the tributes paid them. Dinner music was provided by Joe Hill and his orchestra. The menu for the elaborate affair was as follows:

Fresh Gulf Shrimp Cocktail

Speared Celery Hearts　　　　　　Mixed Olives Varee

Broiled Select Filet Mignon with Fresh
Mushrooms on Toast
Bordelaise Sauce

Rissole Potatoes　　　　　　Green Peas in Butter

Pineapple and Cottage Cheese Salad

Hot Minced Meat Pie
Brandy Sauce

Hot Rolls　　　　　　Coffee[9]

From Corpus Christi Ambassador and Mrs. Sevier proceeded to Washington, New York, and other eastern points, where they were tendered additional courtesies before sailing for Chile around November 1, 1933.[10]

The Seviers observed sweeping changes in the South American republic since their first visit. At the time of their contact with Chile during World War I three decades of oligarchy true to the tradition of Chilean aristocracy—conservative but malleable—were coming to an end. Whereas at the time of their departure in 1918, the country was still experiencing the throes of transition, the new era that had begun in 1920, with the emergence of the middle classes into politics,[11] had been in existence for thirteen years when they returned in 1933.

Before World War I Chilean economy was based primarily on agriculture and mining. However, due to the inadequacy of both, the nation depended upon imports and exports to supplement it. After the war Chile was forced to rely less on trade and turn to the manufacture of foods and beverages for its own consumption. Meanwhile, the country reemphasized agriculture to try to meet the needs of its expanding population and to improve the dietary habits of the underprivileged.[12] However, Chilean agriculture failed to provide sufficient food for the country because of the limited acreage, failure to take advantage of modern farming techniques, and the use of cheap labor instead of machines. It was said that by the introduction of modern farming methods and machines the nation could have produced for a population four times its size.

The country's exports were not varied. Major mining enterprises provided 70 percent, medium and small mining companies furnished another 20 percent, and the remaining 10 percent came from agricultural products and a narrow range of industrial goods. The major agricultural shipments consisted of wine, beans, onions, and garlic, as well as specialty fruits, while the most important industrial products exported were iron and steel goods, newsprint and fish meal.[13] With its industrialization, Chile had been forced to depend upon imports to keep its new plants in production. The steel industry, for example, had to import one-third of its coal requirements. Petroleum derivatives also had to be imported along with quantities of cotton and sugar to keep the mills and sugar refineries in operation.

From the time of the conquest Chile produced wine, but until the middle of the nineteenth century the quality was inferior. The induction of vines and expert wine manufacturers from France and Spain improved the quality so that by 1875 Chilean vintages were exhibited at international expositions. As the quality improved, the industry expanded. Vineyards dominated the central valley but were most numerous in the area of the capital of Santiago. The Chilean custom of drinking wine with meals assured a stable domestic market. More important, the excellence of the present quality, second only to the wines of France, increased its value as an export.[14] By 1933, the year of Sevier's appointment, the exportation of Chilean wine to the United States provided the basis for a very important trade relationship between the two countries.

When the Seviers arrived in Chile in 1933, the South American republic had not recovered from the depression, which had magnified the basic weakness in the economy and fomented social discontent. Unemployment was widespread and international trade was adversely affected. Civil strife ensued.

The political situation in Chile resembled that of France. Under the multiparty system, as many as thirty parties were known to register for one election. Party coalitions were known to organize and at the time of Sevier's appointment as ambassador the influential Popular Front—a political combination of leftist and left-of-center parties—exerted its influence. After unsuccessful attempts of two leaders—one Conservative and the other Socialist—to gain control of the government, Arturo Alessandri Palma was elected to the presidency for a second term in 1932. As champion of the common man, Alessandri had first led a coalition to the presidential victory in 1920 only to be forced to resign and leave the country because of an uncooperative Congress in 1924. Recalled from Rome, Alessandri made a triumphal entry into Santiago in March, 1925, only to be replaced in the forthcoming elections of that year by Carlos Ibañez del Campo, a military dictator.[15]

Finally after Chile's traditional parties succeeded in reorganizing in 1932, Alessandri—as the candidate for the Center-Right—was restored to power. As measured by democratic criteria, Alessandri's political contribution was both praiseworthy and reprehensible. He is generally credited with helping the nation to recover from the effects of the depression. He balanced the national budget, allowed the reorganization of the Chilean Nitrate Company—a monopoly whose control was shared by foreign and domestic capitalists and the Chilean nation; and resumed payment of the national debt. By 1934, the end of Sevier's first year in the embassy, economic recovery seemed assured and a measure of political stability had been established. In addition, Alessandri had reestablished constitutional government.

On the other hand, despite his restoration of democratic principles of government, Alessandri became dictatorial in the face of the political foment of the period that spawned a contingent of Nazis rooted in the republic's influential German population and supported by a powerful group of Fascists. In an abortive coup in 1938 he ordered his national police to liquidate a group of Nazis and, some insisted, to purge Socialist youth who had forcibly occupied several buildings in Santiago. After surrendering to the police, no fewer than sixty-two young persons were killed.[16]

However, by this time the Radical party had withdrawn its support from Alessandri. Moreover, by using the Popular Front as a launching pad to power in 1938, the Radical party assumed a leadership under three presidents. The first was Pedro Aguirre Cerda, a conscious imitator of Franklin Delano Roosevelt.

By this time the Seviers had abandoned Chile. But it would be totally unrealistic to think that the internal dissension in the South American republic had no effect upon their private lives. Despite surface appearances, conditions grew progressively worse. The first year of Sevier's administration, despite that fact, had not been a complete loss. The couple had maintained amicable relations with the current party in power, they had entertained frequently at the American embassy, and were popular with most government officials. Also Mrs. Sevier had had the opportunity to tour Alaska by way of Vancouver.[17] However, to Sevier the duties of the foreign office had become increasingly distasteful; and whether for reasons of political unrest or some more immediate personal difficulty, including ill health—or a combination of several—the envoy applied for sick leave to return home. Thus he and Mrs. Sevier returned to Texas in 1935, two years before the expiration of his term.

Even before his resignation was announced, reports were rampant that Sevier was failing to discharge his duties in a manner commensurate with the dignity and importance of the ambassadorship. It was rumored that Mrs. Sevier was making a special effort to offset his inefficiency. Visitors to South America returned with unsavory tales that undoubtedly gathered moss upon circulation. Criticism of his performance began to appear in national periodicals a year before he resigned. One of the most voluble, if succinct, was *Fortune Magazine*:

> . . . Hal Sevier, Ambassador to Chile, isn't really Ambassador at all. His wife is. Sevier is an active Texas Democrat (Tennessee-born), a protégé of Garner, and an Austin newspaper publisher. He's pretty impressed with the importance and the dignity of being Ambassador but doesn't know quite what to do about it. Mrs. Sevier ("The Woman Who Saved the Alamo") does her best to tell him, does, in fact, just about whatever is done. His Spanish is feeble; hers is fluent. Washington gossip is that when Hull wandered about South America recently, he discovered that in conference Sevier will say "yes" affably enough to anything but doesn't know half the time what he's saying "yes" to. From a business point of view, Sevier's main job is to smooth the way for exports of Chilean wines.[19]

Upon their return to Texas in 1935 the Seviers were separated. Regardless of what had happened in Chile to precipitate the break, both remained silent. Speculations as to the reasons for the domestic discord were advanced. Some people felt that Sevier's occasional flights of infidelity might have contributed. Others were of the opinion that Sevier's immoderation was a factor. Some wondered if Sevier had not tried to wrest full control of the Driscoll empire from his wife's hands. Still others theorized that for Clara Driscoll, Hal Sevier her husband, had lost integrity—a trait upon which she placed exceedingly high value. Since neither of the estranged couple was inclined to confide intimacies to others, none of these probabilities were ever confirmed as fact.

And even though friends accepted the separation, they were not expecting divorce as the two had so much in common: superior minds, talent, interest in history and people, the Democratic party, appreciation of the arts, fondness for travel. For that matter, no mention was made of divorce. For two years after their return, the Seviers withdrew somewhat from the public eye. Their desire for privacy was respected. Friends thought that they may have been trying to reconcile their differences, whatever they were. Though they both visited Palo Alto, they maintained separate suites in downtown hotels in Corpus Christi. They displayed no open hostility, however, and Sevier continued to manifest an interest in the management of the Driscoll estate.

Then, as late as May, 1937, when the two were in San Antonio, where Sevier was attending a banker's meeting, the news of an impending divorce action dropped like a bursting bombshell. On the afternoon of May 19, 1937, newspapers carried the unexpected announcement that Mrs. Sevier had filed suit for divorce in Corpus Christi through her San Antonio attorneys, Bell, Seeligson, and Trueheart. Whether Mrs. Sevier had intended for the news to surface at that time or whether she had discussed its imminence with her husband is not clear. When reporters approached Sevier in the lobby of his hotel and requested a statement, he appeared to be taken by surprise. His reply was unusual: "I am distressed by this information and I want to remonstrate with Mrs. Sevier before I make a statement."[19] Whereupon he contacted Mrs. Sevier in her suite and returned to the hotel foyer to make an additional statement:

> She is ill and nervous and I think we had better not disturb her anymore. You can say for me that regardless of any action my wife wishes to take, my affection and esteem remain as they always have been for her. But nothing, [on] legal or moral grounds, would prompt me to contest the suit."[20]

Later Mrs. Sevier could not be reached for comment. Her attendants explained to reporters that she was confined to her bed as the result of a recent heart attack. Then on May 22 the press announced that Mrs. Sevier was planning to drop the divorce suit and was considering a reconciliation. Informed of the news, Sevier telephoned his wife for a confirmation. She was quoted as admitting that the report was true but requested that Sevier call her the next day for a final answer. When he placed the call, attendants said that Mrs. Sevier could not be disturbed and Sevier was denied further contact.[21]

Clara Driscoll Sevier filed suit in the Twenty-eighth District Court in Corpus Christi, and on July 7, 1937, the thirty-one-year marriage was dissolved. The divorce was granted on grounds of mental cruelty that resulted in a nervous disorder. The petition specified that there was no community property and there were no children.[22]

During the earlier, happier years Clara Driscoll had written: "But I am a woman with all a woman's power of loving and longing to be loved in return."[23] In that same idyllic period she had also declared: " . . . In their kiss the world was forgotten—they had given themselves to each other for eternity."[24] *But eternity had been only thirty-one years!* The joyful life the two had shared through the years was now at an end.

Clara Driscoll, circa 1900. Clara was a Texas belle before she became an American legend and the toast of Broadway. This was thought to have been the first photograph she gave Hal Sevier, whom she married in 1906.

Henry Hulme (Hal) Sevier, circa 1895. This is a photograph of the young journalist and editor made when he came to Texas from Tennessee to seek his fortune at seventeen. It was perhaps the first photograph that Sevier exchanged with Clara for the one on the preceding page.

Above, Clara and Hal honeymooning in Europe. Below, the couple ten or fifteen years after their marriage. Sevier retained his good looks for which he was noted.

The Sevier residence at Mill Creek on Long Island. Fronting on Oyster Bay Road, the estate was adjacent to that of former president Theodore Roosevelt and his family.

Above, balcony of terrace overlooking a ravine which was converted into a formal garden. Below, view of the cloistered patio of the Long Island residence.

Above, the driveway of the residence led to rooms a floor below the living and dining areas. Below, central hall of the Long Island mansion. A special feature of the structure, the great hallway extended the entire length of the residence and connected with the patio at the back.

Facade of Laguna Gloria in the final stages of construction. Situated at the base of Mount Bonnell, the residence in Austin, Texas, overlooked the winding Colorado River.

Above, rear view of Laguna Gloria showing the patio and garden. Opposite above, detail of the entrance to Laguna Gloria after completion. Note the rose window to the right copied from the San José mission in San Antonio. Opposite below, wrought-iron gates were originally used on the Texas capitol grounds in the days when stock roamed free. Mrs. Driscoll acquired two pairs of the gates at a public auction.

Above, formal dining room of Laguna Gloria. Opposite above, formal garden at Laguna
Gloria. The gardens were Italian in design to complement the Mediterranean-style villa.
The statuary was imported from Venice. Opposite below, snow scene at Laguna Gloria.
View is from one of the gardens. The couple found the Austin winters to be delightful.

Members of the Daughters of the Republic of Texas congregated at Laguna Gloria before departing on a tour through the Rio Grande Valley as guests of Mrs. Sevier in 1932. She had extended the invitation for 1931 but had to postpone it because of an automobile accident. Note hats and long dresses were in vogue in the thirties. Although Clara customarily wore a hat, she is the hatless lady in the center of the front row with a flower in her hair and a dress draped at the hips. The Seviers were living in Corpus Christi at this time but returned frequently to entertain their friends at Laguna Gloria.

Above, Robert Driscoll, Jr., Corpus Christi financier and developer, circa 1925. When Driscoll died on July 7, 1929, the responsibility of managing the vast estate descended to his sister Clara, the sole survivor of the family. Below, monument to Robert Driscoll, Jr., at the Port of Corpus Christi. The engraved boulder of red Texas granite was unveiled on the first anniversary of Driscoll's death, July 7, 1930. The inscription reads: "In Grateful Memory/Of/Robert Driscoll/First Chairman Of The/Nueces County/Navigation Commission Whose/Wise And/Unselfish Public Service/Was Essential/To Its Successful Building and Future/Usefulness/The/Port of Corpus Christi/Is Affectionately Dedicated."

Above left, the first oil well on the Driscoll ranch in Duval County was brought in in 1927. In the preceding year Robert Driscoll began the active exploitation of the family's oil and gas interests. Above right, another view of the first well. It was a gasser! Below, waiting for a gasser on the 53,000-acre Sweden ranch in Duval County, Texas. The Seviers' acceptance of the foreign post made it necessary to turn over the direction of the extensive Driscoll interests to others for the first time. The Duval County oil field was placed under the control of the Continental Oil Company. The transaction was said to have run into seven figures.

Clara and Hal visit with their Russian Wolfhounds at the ranch headquarters. Note other dogs in the background. Clara was particularly fond of dogs. When the couple moved to Corpus Christi after Robert's death to assume management of the far-flung Driscoll interests, they lived at Palo Alto for a time and commuted to their offices in town.

Above, United States ambassador to Chile, Hal Sevier and Mrs. Sevier with official embassy staff. Seated with Ambassador and Mrs. Sevier is the Chilean minister of foreign affairs. The photograph was taken in the drawing room of the Ameircan embassy, circa 1934. Below, the United States Embassy, Santiago, Chile, circa 1934. In the two years they stayed they entertained here lavishly.

When the divorce became final and Hal Sevier returned to Chattanooga, Tennessee, to live in the home of his sister, Mrs. Frederick Giddings, the Austin *American*, the paper he founded in 1914, eulogized him:

> Years ago a young man came out of the Southwest to serve as a member of the Texas Legislature. He was of noble appearance, one of the handsomest men Texas has known. His character, his ability, and his qualities of friendship and courage, won him prestige and influence.
>
> When he left the legislature, Hal Sevier remained in Austin. He founded the Austin *American*, and served as its publisher for a number of years, until broadening business interests claimed his time and attention.
>
> His help to President Wilson and President Roosevelt, his assistance to the Democratic party, his contributions to inter-American good will, made him an important figure in the top ranks of democratic statesmen.
>
> His personal qualities endeared him to many. He never made an enemy, he never lost a friend. The personality of this distinguished Texan may be summed up—Hal Sevier: Gentleman.[25]

After her divorce Clara Driscoll took legal action to resume her maiden name. In her petition to Judge W. B. Hopkins in the Twenty-eighth District Court of Corpus Christi, she stated that in view of the fact that she had been separated from the former United States ambassador Hal Sevier for some time and that she had been granted a divorce, the restoration of her maiden name would be "highly advantageous to her."[26] Thereafter she became officially known as Mrs. Clara Driscoll.

Apparently Sevier reversed himself on his earlier decision not to contest his wife's action. In February, 1938, he returned to Texas and instituted litigation to have Mrs. Sevier's divorce action of the previous year set aside, to have a receiver appointed to take over property valued at $5 million and upwards, and to have a divorce granted in his own name, together with a division of the property which he contended was jointly earned.[27]

Nevertheless, upon the joint petition of attorneys for both sides, Judge Cullen W. Briggs of the 117th District Court issued a judgement upholding Mrs. Sevier's divorce granted in July, 1937, and dropping all suits brought by Sevier.[28] According to the Corpus Christi *Caller*,

> It was understood that some settlement was made outside the courtroom which enabled lawyers for both parties to reach an agreement to terminate all court litigation.[29]

No public disclosure of the amount of settlement was made. As a result of the agreement, Sevier withdrew any claim to joint ownership previously made and gave Clara Driscoll full title to all real and personal property over which there had been a dispute. One is inclined to think that Mrs. Driscoll's settlement was generous. She was not a penurious person and had supported the marriage liberally—she had created two estates, had subsidized her husband's founding of the Austin *American* and other projects, and, in addition, had given him administrative offices in her financial empire. However, despite the amount of the settlement, Sevier died a relatively poor man. A copy of his will reveals that his bequests to his two sisters and brother were extremely modest.[30]

Sevier lived scarcely two years following this final action. His death occurred on March 11, 1940.[31] News of his demise was given front page exposure in the state and national press. An account with a dateline from Chattanooga, which appeared in the Dallas *News*, under the headline "Hal Sevier, Former Chile Envoy, Dies," with subtitle "Texas Publisher, Colonel House's Friend, Succumbs to Illness That Closed Career," stated:

> Henry Hulme (Hal) Sevier, former United States Ambassador to the Republic of Chile, died at 8 o'clock Sunday night in his home here. He had been retired from service in the State Department for about four years.[32]

Even though the article carries the phrase "Succumbs to Illness That Closed Career" in the headline, the cause of Sevier's death is not revealed. Other accounts state that, despite Sevier's declining health that became evident in Chile, the diplomat's death was sudden and unexpected. After consulting with his lawyers in San Antonio and making a trip to Havana, Cuba, he returned to Chattanooga only a few days before his death. While the immediate cause of Sevier's death is withheld, friends indicated that his frustration resulting from the breakup of his marriage was a major factor.

The news release from Dallas concludes ironically by identifying Sevier as the "former husband of Mrs. Clara Driscoll, ranchwoman, financier, and present Democratic National Committeewoman from Texas.

9

Clara Driscoll–Philanthropist

Not only did Clara Driscoll show her interest in the commonweal through unflagging public service, she expressed her love and compassion for humanity through acts of generosity. As an avid Democrat and dedicated stateswoman, she was extremely liberal in her support of the party. In addition to her quadrennial gifts and donations to the campaign funds, she was an angel to the Young Democratic Club of Nueces County, which she organized.

As an active clubwoman, she also had been generous in her support of the various activities and projects undertaken by the organizations. Mention has been made of her assistance to the Texas Club of New York. She contributed liberally to the Pan-American Round Table, another of her brainchildren. She was likewise an ardent supporter of the Austin Garden Club, the Big Bend Park Association, the South Texas Division of Authors and Composers, and the Robert E. Lee Memorial Foundation—all in addition to business and civic organizations. Her generous contributions to the "War Chest" of two world wars was well known in Washington.

Not all of Mrs. Driscoll's donations to charity and acts of philanthropy appeared in the press. She made many private gifts in order to avoid publicity. But of the publicized benefactions, three are conspicuous: her gifts for the preservation of the Alamo, the liquidation of the mortgage on the Austin clubhouse of the Texas Federation of Women's Clubs, and the presentation of Laguna Gloria to the Texas Fine Arts Association for use as an art center and permanent gallery.

For sake of chronology, the first—and supreme example of Mrs. Driscoll's philanthropy—has been treated in Chapter Two under the caption of "The Birth of a Legend." Of all of the organizations with which she was affiliated, the Daughters of the Republic of Texas remained closest to her and her interest in the shrine itself was lifelong. Seven meticulously-preserved scrapbooks devoted exclusively to the organization's activities are evidence of the fact. Testifying further to her dedication to the Alamo, as an all-consuming influence of her life, are files of letters received at the time of the crusade to preserve the historic relic. These letters represent a heterogeneous gallery of persons who donated to the fund—the rich, the poor, the articulate, the illiterate, school children who sent their pennies, descendants of Texas heroes— but patriots all who responded to Clara Driscoll's call. She treasured every letter, answered it, then carefully filed it for future reference.

During her residency in New York in the early years of her marriage she maintained close contact with the Daughters of the Republic of Texas and kept abreast of the continued improvements and restoration of the mission-fortress. On many occasions since her original purchase of the landmark for the organization, she gave financial assistance. She reroofed the Alamo chapel at a cost of $1,000. During the controversy between Governor O. B. Colquitt and the Daughters, from 1911 to 1913, she proffered $15,000 toward the restoration, which the governor rejected. In 1914, when it was considered expedient to charge visitors a fee to apply on maintenance costs, she notified the Daughters of the Republic that she would personally assume the obligation of paying the caretaker's salary.[1] So that the shrine might be free to visitors, she assumed this obligation for a number of years.

In 1930 the state made two appropriations—one for $250,000 and another for $150,000—to purchase land around the Alamo property to convert into gardens.[2] Then in 1931 and 1932, when it was found that the second appropriation was insufficient to clear the grounds completely, Clara Driscoll donated the necessary $65,000 to make up the deficit. She would have paid $70,000, but Mr. John Herff, the owner of the two lots to be cleared, reduced the price in the amount of $5,000 upon learning that she was purchasing it as a gift to the state. This second gift to the state of Texas made it possible to remove the shacks facing Alamo Plaza between the mission and Crockett Street and resulted in the beautiful park lying south of the Alamo church and surrounded by a rock wall and arches.[3] As chairman of the Alamo Acquisition Board, Mrs. Driscoll was able to work with others on the continued restoration of the property and contributed both time and funds, the amounts of which she modestly withheld from the public.

She also served the state organization of the Daughters of the Republic of Texas as president from 1927 to 1931 and from 1935 to 1937, and was later awarded an honorary life presidency. She proposed as early as 1929 at the state convention that the organization publish a history of its valuable work to be placed in libraries and schools. The original committee appointed by Mrs. Sevier, as she was then known, for this purpose included Mrs. Charles E. Milby, Mrs. Mattie Austin Hatcher, and Mrs. O. M. Farnsworth.[4] Mrs. Driscoll organized the Corpus Christi chapter of the Daughters of the Republic of Texas in 1932. At the same time she invited the state organization to hold its annual convention in Corpus Christi and feted the visitors with the grand tour of the Rio Grande Valley. The local Corpus organization adopted the name Clara Driscoll Chapter and accorded its founder an honorary life presidency.

In 1938 the mortgage on the clubhouse of the Texas Federation of Women's Clubs, which was built in 1929–1930, was overdue. The total indebtedness was $92,000. The Praetorian Insurance Company held a first lein in the amount of $65,000. Other creditors included the First National Bank of Dallas, $13,994; Smith Construction Company, $2,875; and Mrs. James F. Welder of Victoria, $7,205.64.[5] The First National Bank agreed to reduce its claim to $10,000 and Mrs. Welder hers to $5,000.

In March, 1938, Mrs. H. O. Carlisle, a club member and friend of Mrs. Driscoll, approached her for a loan to pay off the mortgage. It was a routine procedure as Mrs. Driscoll, a banker, was in the business of making loans. Under the most generous conditions, including an interest rate of only 3 percent, Mrs. Driscoll consented to refinance the loan.[6] She proposed that the clubs stay within a budget of $8,000 per year for five years and that each of the 1,080 organizations in the state assess themselves $5 per year to create a sinking fund until the debt was absolved.[7] The greatly relieved ladies adopted all of Mrs. Driscoll's proposals unanimously. The refinancing was consummated on March 5, 1938, and everyone concerned was delighted. Located in Austin at Twenty-third and San Gabriel streets, the two-story brick colonial clubhouse—erected at a cost of $300,000 and containing auditorium, art gallery, library, and many refined features—was, and is, a valuable property well worth saving.

In March, 1939, without any prepublicity or fanfare whatever, when the fifth district of Texas Federation of Women's Clubs met in the financier's hometown of Corpus Christi, Mrs. Driscoll appeared before the group and stated that she was converting the loan granted the previous year into an outright gift.[8] She had already demonstrated a generosity that many cautious bankers would have questioned. Since the donor no longer lived in Austin and the gift of $92,000 would first benefit that city, then the state, even some business associates were surprised.

In recognition of Mrs. Driscoll's gift and other benefactions, Governor W. Lee O'Daniel issued a proclamation declaring October 4, 1939, to be Clara Driscoll Day in Texas. The text of the governor's proclamation follows:

> Whereas, throughout all human history, women have made great sacrifices of time, talent and money for the advancement of the better things in life, including a religious reform, higher morality, true patriotism and loyalty, and advanced civilization, and
>
> Whereas, within the boundaries of this Great State of Texas now lives a native daughter endowed with those unselfish attributes of human service, and financial means with which to carry out her altruistic ambitions, and
>
> Whereas, through the efforts of this distinguished lady, the most sacred, hallowed and cherished shrine of liberty, the Alamo, now peacefully stands in the quiet surroundings of Alamo Park, instead of being shadowed by giant commercial structures as was proposed, and
>
> Whereas, the generous contribution of this lady, gave to the women of Texas a debt-free club building at Austin for the headquarters of the Texas Federation of Women's Clubs, so that they may carry on their great work for the improvement of society in our State, and
>
> Whereas, this daughter of Texas believes explicitly in the principles of Democracy to the extent of devoting much of her time, and ability, and money to the causes of Democracy by serving the Democratic Party unstintingly in a true self-sacrificing manner;
>
> Now therefore, I, W. Lee O'Daniel, Governor of the Great State of Texas, believing that this lady should be publicly honored, and recognizing the desire of the Texas Federation of Women's Clubs, and others to do her honor, do hereby proclaim Wednesday, October 4th, 1939, as
>
> CLARA DRISCOLL DAY
>
> and call upon all Texans to gather in the Capitol City of Austin on that day for the main celebration, or if unable to come to Austin, to arrange such celebrations as are appropriate at other places throughout the State to do honor to this distinguished humanitarian and benefactress.[9]

With appropriate festivities October 4 was officially celebrated in Austin. The day-long schedule of activities began with a coffee in the crystal ballroom of the Driskill Hotel at 11:00 A. M. It was followed by an open house at the Governor's Mansion, from one to five, with Mrs. O'Daniel and Mrs. Driscoll receiving. Simultaneously a formal tea was held at the Federation clubhouse from three to five. Following the two events, Federation officials held a banquet at the Driskill Hotel with Mrs. Driscoll as honor guest. Later a formal reception at the Federation quarters concluded the festivities.[10]

Another feature of the packed schedule was an exhibition of the art of Rio Grande Valley artists in the gallery of the Federation Building, with the artists themselves assuming hostess duties throughout the day. Many of the paintings, including both oils and watercolors, reflected the atmosphere and scenes with which Mrs. Driscoll was familiar as well as other parts of the country. Art groups represented were the Rio Grande Valley Art League, the Upper Rio Grande Valley League, the Lower Rio Grande Valley League, and the Brownsville Art League.[11]

Mrs. Driscoll arrived in Austin Tuesday afternoon to be present for Wednesday's activities. Preceding Wednesday's official observance, Mrs. Harold Abrams of Dallas entertained the state Federation board with a dinner at the headquarters with Mrs. Driscoll guest of honor. At the dinner Mrs. Driscoll explained that she made the gift to the organization because of her faith in it and to assist with the continuation of its work. "If women work together, their field for activity is unlimited," she said. Attorney General Gerald Mann and Clinton King, Fort Worth artist who painted the portrait of Mrs. Driscoll to be unveiled later, paid tribute to the honoree.

Interviewed on the morning of October 4, Mrs. Driscoll stated: "This is a wonderful day for me. My happiness lies in the fact that so many of my Corpus Christi friends have taken the trouble to make the trip to be here with me. . . ."[12] Among the friends from Corpus Christi who accompanied Mrs. Driscoll were Chamber of Commerce manager Jeff Hall, James Spivey, George Gilliam, R. W. Cooper, and prominent Corpus Christi business associate, Roy Miller, who made both major addresses. Among the special guests at all of the events were Governor and Mrs. W. Lee O'Daniel, Representative Richard Kleberg (a close family friend), other state officials, and state and national officers of the Federation of Women's Clubs.

Climaxing the crowded calendar of events was the formal reception held Wednesday evening at the Federation quarters with members of the organization acting as hostesses. More than a thousand persons from Austin and other parts of the state assembled at the Federation Building to honor Clara Driscoll. The elaborate program was divided into two segments. Highlight of the first was the keynote address by Roy Miller on the topic, "Clara Driscoll—Patriot" and the unveiling of the life-size portrait of her painted by artist Clinton King—a gift of Mrs. Harold Abrams of Dallas. A seated composition of Mrs. Driscoll in white satin evening gown against an ice blue background, the portrait was to be hung permanently in the clubhouse.

Declaring Mrs. Driscoll to be "Texas' foremost patriot," Miller portrayed her as " . . . a dreamer and doer who makes dreams come true." With considerable accuracy, he pointed out that

> Clara Driscoll needs no eulogy. Her achievements tell their own story. What she has done and is always doing for Texas and Texans is already written large and in-

delibly on unnumbered pages of history that record the glorious progress of our state for more than a quarter of a century.[13]

Miller outlined the many worthwhile contributions of the guest of honor to the people of Texas as he emphasized her gifts to preserve the Alamo and the Texas Federation of Women's Clubs Building. Later when he sent Mrs. Driscoll a copy of his tribute, he wrote: "Miss Clara, All Texas is proud of you. We honor you for what you have done, but we love you for what you are."[10]

Preceding the keynote address, formal tributes were paid Mrs. Driscoll by the organization's president, Mrs. Joseph M. Perkins, on behalf of the Texas Federation of Women's Clubs; by Mayor Tom Miller, representing the city of Austin; and Governor O'Daniel, for the state of Texas. Mrs. Perkins stressed the indebtedness of the sixty thousand clubwomen in the 1,080 clubs of Texas for the munificent gift made to them by the financier. Mayor Miller assured the guest of honor that people of Austin still thought of "Miss Clara" as a citizen of the capital. He mentioned that her home on the Colorado was situated on the site Stephen F. Austin chose for a home and expressed the belief that Austin "would be well satisfied to see that dream home occupied by Mrs. Driscoll."[15]

Governor O'Daniel declared in his remarks that ". . . when we have great characters such as she, we need not be afraid of the howling of war lords—civilization is secure. . . . Many of the great deeds in Texas have been the brainchild of some good, unselfish, and humanitarian women." He further stated that, "I feel this is the kind of lady Mrs. Driscoll is. She saved the Alamo for the past and the Federation building for the future."[16]

At the unveiling of the oil portrait, to the accompaniment of the music of "The Eyes of Texas," the speaker introduced artist Clinton King and the donor, Mrs. Abrams, both of whom spoke briefly. Following the ceremony, Mrs. Driscoll responded in her own gracious and inimitable manner. In expressing appreciation for the day set aside to honor her, she added: "My love for the women of the state federation will last as long as I live, and I hope I live long enough to be of further service to them."[17] A classical music program concluded this part of the schedule.

The later festivities were devoted to a candle lighting ceremony in which several guests participated. To initiate the ritual Mrs. Driscoll was presented a taper in a handsome holder engraved with her name and symbolizing *understanding*. As a phase of the ceremony, some thirty friends gave individual testimonials to the honor guest. As each person ended his or her remarks, he placed a rose in a bowl before Mrs. Driscoll. Thus a large bouquet was accumulated for the philanthropist. One lady interjected a little humor into her remarks. "When Clara Driscoll gave $92,000 to lift the club debt," she said, "she also lifted the faces of 60,000 women."[18] The evening's festivities were broadcast over a Texas network.

The Texas Federation of Women's Clubs later bought a piano as a memorial to its benefactress, because of Mrs. Driscoll's love for music, and published a bulletin and *History* which they dedicated to her:

> A great Texan, a great scholar, a great philanthropist, a great patriot, whose magnificent gift to the Texas Federation of Women's Clubs was inspired in her own words: "In order that the club women of Texas may go about their splendid work with a lighter heart, I give them the Federation headquarters."[19]

On October 6, 1943—six years after her divorce and three years after the death of Hal Sevier on March 11, 1940—Clara Driscoll gave Laguna Gloria to the Texas Fine Arts Association to be used as a permanent gallery. Since business interests had necessitated her residence in Corpus Christi, she had not occupied the mansion for some time. She had been offered more than one hundred thousand dollars for the property, but selling the home that had held such beautiful memories was to her unthinkable. She had tried leasing the estate, but that, too, had proved unsatisfactory. So Laguna Gloria had remained idle and had begun to deteriorate. Finally it appeared that the Austin property had become a problem. Still Mrs. Driscoll seemed to be parting with Laguna Gloria reluctantly.

She made the formal presentation to Mrs. Roger Robeadeau, president of the Texas Fine Arts Association, at the organization's regular meeting. At the same time she presented a check in the amount of $5,000 for necessary repairs and maintenance, and three objects of art: an authentic Italian chandelier hanging in the living room, the carved Alamo panel by Peter Mansbendel, and an elegant handcarved table.[20] In her presentation remarks, Mrs. Driscoll said:

> I have always felt that Austin being the capital, and a city of great beauty, is the logical place where something of that kind should be established. I have never wanted to sell the home in which I lived. I am happy now its use may bring pleasure in the appreciation of art to the people of Texas. We perhaps forget that founders of Texas were men of education and taste. . . .
>
> Texas has given a number of very good artists to the nation, Wayman Adams is one; Onderdonk of San Antonio, another. . . .
>
> In order to prove my interest in establishing a permanent art gallery here, I am glad to make this gift.[21]

As she acknowledged Mrs. Driscoll's remarks and accepted the gift and check, Mrs. Robeadeau stated: "This and other money will be used to convert the home into a state-wide art center in which all Texas will take pride." [22]

The deed transferring the property to the organization was presented by Mrs. Driscoll on December 4, 1943, at a small dinner at the Driskill Hotel in Austin tendered her by the board of directors of the Texas Fine Arts Association. In addition to the customary vote of thanks and individual expressions of commendation, the group chose for their acquisition the name of Laguna Gloria Art Gallery. In responding to the tributes, Mrs. Driscoll drew a meaningful analogy that revealed a great deal of herself:

> Death prevented Austin from spending the rest of his life here. I also have been prevented. As long as I retained Laguna Gloria, personally, I felt there was some chance of returning here. Half of my heart went out when I gave it. In the future what I once possessed so proudly will be used for the youth of Texas . . . to educate and to preserve the things that are beautiful in life. [23]

Obviously these statements were painful to the philanthropist. The power of the analogy is revealed by inference. Life's exigencies had prevented her continued occupation. One of the acceptors of the gift had pronounced it "a dream come true." [24] The irony of that statement was not dissipated on Clara Driscoll. It was precisely to her the final vestige of a shattered dream—now transformed into a monument to loneliness. *Half of my heart went out when I gave it. . . .*

10

National Democratic Committeewoman

THE EXPERIENCE CLARA DRISCOLL HAD IN preserving the Alamo marked the beginning of her intense interest in politics and gave impetus to a career that catapulted her into the national political limelight. From 1928 to 1944 she served as national Democratic committeewoman from Texas—a span of sixteen years and longer than any other person. First elected to the position in Beaumont in 1928, she was reelected at the Democratic convention in Houston in 1932. In 1936, when the party convened in San Antonio and Mrs. Driscoll was ill and unable to attend, she was prevailed upon by friends to permit the presentation of her name "as a necessity." Immediately five other candidates, who had been nominated, withdrew their names in deference to Mrs. Driscoll's leadership.[1]

An eager, excited crowd estimated at ten thousand milled about the speakers' stand in the athletic field adjacent to the Central Texas oil metropolis of Cisco. The year was 1928 and an event significant in the nation's political history was about to take place. A great Southern Democratic leader by the name of Alfred E. Smith had elected to open his party's campaign for the presidency of the United States in Texas. Already seated on the platform was the candidate for vice-president—Senator Joe Robinson of Arkansas—among other notables.

At the very peak of wild enthusiasm greeting him [Smith], out there on the field a slender woman in a blue tailored gown arose . . . and advanced to the microphones. Only a slight gesture was needed to quiet the cheering and milling of the multitude, and then Mrs. Clara Driscoll, Texas' first Democratic national committeewoman, proceeded to introduce Senator Robinson in a brief, clearly audible speech that is today declared by those who heard it [to be] the best of the considerable number made that day . . . to plunge the nation into the memorable campaign of Alfred E.

Smith for the office of President.[2]

But Clara Driscoll's initial efforts to help elect Al Smith on the Democratic ticket in 1928 went unrewarded. For the first time since the Civil War Texas went Republican and the nation rejected the man who was both "wet" and Catholic. The landslide for Herbert Hoover, who promised to put a chicken in every pot and two cars in every garage, exceeded the wildest expectations.[3]

Four years later in 1932 Mrs. Driscoll campaigned for Franklin Delano Roosevelt and John Nance Garner, the rugged cob pipe-smoking Texan, and tasted the fruits of success. The Roosevelt–Garner team defeated the incumbent Herbert Hoover by a popular vote of 57.3 percent to 39.6 and an electoral college count of 472 to 58, even with Norman Thomas running a poor third on the Socialist ticket.[4] Plainly it was a mandate.

Again in 1936, when Roosevelt made his bid for a second term, Mrs. Driscoll actively supported him. In addition to her customary donation of $25,000 made quadrennially to the Democratic party, she contributed $10,000 to his campaign fund, though it was obvious that Roosevelt had Texas in the palm of his hands regardless of funds. Always a dedicated Texan and a loyal Democrat, she issued the following statement:

> What we do in Texas assuredly will add strength and backing for the party in other states. These other states are watching to see if Texas is interested and active. We will show the other 47 states that Texas again will take the lead for democracy.[5]

Once again the Texas Democratic committeewoman savored the taste of overwhelming victory when the Roosevelt–Garner combination carried every state except Maine and Vermont and swamped Alfred M. Landon, the Republican candidate, by more than ten million votes with an electoral college tally of 523 to 8.[6] It was a tremendous expression of public faith and the president accepted it as a mandate for further reforms. With his personal dynamism and congressional majorities, there seemed to be no obstacles. Consequently, he embarked on his second term with unabated enthusiasm for spending. "Where the First New Deal contemplated government, business, and labor marching hand in hand toward a brave new society," according to historian Arthur M. Schlesinger, Jr., "the Second New Deal proposed to revitalize the tired old society. . . . The First New Deal characteristically told business what it must do. The Second New Deal . . . told business what it must *not* do."[7]

During their first four years in Washington, President Roosevelt and Vice-President Garner maintained an amicable, even affectionate, relationship. Garner called Roosevelt "Captain," and the president called him "Jack." The president was among the few to take such liberties. Reporters had invented the "Cactus Jack" label, and in his hometown of Uvalde, Texas, close friends addressed the vice-president formally as "Mr. Garner" or "Judge Garner." Even his wife called him "Mr. Garner." Roosevelt frequently sought the vice-president's advice and the two customarily lunched informally at the president's desk in the Oval Office. In fact, as legislative technician, Garner accelerated Roosevelt's recovery program and disagreed with only one of his actions. In an effort to stimulate foreign trade, Roosevelt had recognized Russia in November, 1933.[8] Garner felt that in allowing Foreign Minister Maxim Litvinoff to outmaneuver him in winning a soft recognition for Russia, denied by Wilson and succeeding administrations since 1917,[9] the president had made a mistake.

Garner's second term in the vice-presidency was half over before he even thought of Roosevelt or himself being a possible political candidate in 1940. As a matter of fact, Roosevelt had informed Garner immediately after the 1937 inauguration that he never intended to seek any public office again. His reiteration of this intention at the victory dinner of the Democratic party on March 4, 1937, was accepted by Garner as the final word.

In the second administration, however, as Roosevelt leaned further toward the left—after an election that Congress and the country at large had interpreted as a victory for the right—Garner found himself in further disagreement. Particularly in the first two years of the second term did Garner become disenchanted with Roosevelt's policies. The existing legislation had not ended the depression, the national budget remained unbalanced, and the excessive spending, in the vice-president's opinion, threatened the foundation of American freedom. Bones of contention were the automobiles workers' sit-down strike, the Supreme Court enlargement fiasco, and the president's attempted purge of those Democrats who did not go along with his entire program.

The most serious argument the two had involved the automobile strike in Michigan. The strike had begun at a General Motors plant at Flint during the first two months of 1937. Soon workers of seventeen General Motors plants and others employed the sit-down strike as a weapon to gain their demands. While inactive, the workers remained barricaded inside the factories in sitting positions at their machines. When officers and strikebreakers tried to dislodge them, the strikers drove their opponents away with a barrage of bottles, tools, spare automobile parts, and crockery. Apprehensive of the destruction of expensive machinery, a majority of employers met the laborers' demands. Manufacturers thus capitulated to the terms of the United Automotive Workers Union. Henry Ford was a notable standout.

Garner regarded the sit-down tactic as labor leader John L. Lewis's bid for personal and political power. Furthermore, he believed that Lewis was expecting—and getting—the support of the president, whose tolerant attitude inured the strikers against government intervention, as a payoff for the latter's support. Lewis had tossed $500,000 into the Democratic campaign pot. Since the strike was affecting national economy and the morale of United States citizens, Garner confronted Roosevelt and insisted that he take action. At the same time he emphasized that the nation was entitled to know the president's attitude. The two men argued for hours. When President Roosevelt informed the vice-president that he could not interfere without bloodshed, Garner retorted that Lewis was a bigger man than he "if he could not find some way to cope with the situation."[10]

The sit-down strike brought the New Deal into critical focus. It altered the power structure within the economy and gave members of the middle class second thoughts about labor's demands and an administration that stood complacently by as the laws against such acts were flagrantly violated.[11]

While the sit-down strikes were in progress, Roosevelt decided to discipline the Supreme Court. Throughout his first term the Court had opposed his increasing authority and the expansion of general governmental powers, both state as well as national, as a means of coping with the depression. Of the nine justices only three were pro-New Deal. Four others were intransigent reactionaries, while two—Chief Justice Charles Evans Hughes and Justice Owen J. Roberts, though open-minded—voted with the reactionaries on many questions.

As Roosevelt viewed the actions of the reactionaries to "protect" the nation against liberal ideas, they were merely applying a "horse and buggy" interpretation of the Constitution to curtail federal powers. Since to reduce the strength of the Court by amending the Constitution would have been too time-consuming, if indeed feasible, the president made a proposal to Congress to shift the balance on the Court by increasing the number of justices. His proposal stipulated that a justice, upon reaching the age of 70, would have the option of retiring at full pay. If he elected not to step down, the president was to appoint an additional justice, up to a maximum of six, to reduce the work for the aged jurists remaining on the bench.[12]

Undoubtedly the president had hopes that his plan might be construed as part of a general measure to reorganize the judiciary. The amazing thing is that he actually expected Congress to pass it and the American public to accept it. He was banking on the fact that the Supreme Court's decisions had recently come under close scrutiny by liberals and legal theorists alike. Not only did the conservatives denounce the proposed legislation, liberals complained that the principle of "court-packing" might be employed in the future to subvert civil liberties.

Dissent among congressmen was immediate and acute. Many who before had supported New Deal legislation came out strongly against the "court-packing" proposal. The press excoriated it and members of the judiciary were incensed. The upshot of it was that when Roosevelt summoned a special session of Congress in November, 1937, and submitted a program of what he considered emergency legislation, not one of the bills was passed.[13]

While Roosevelt's inflationary measures further alienated conservatives without improving the economy noticeably, he decided to purge the party of dissidents to his policies and try to reenergize his New Deal program. Garner had advised him against this action explaining that the conservative Democrats deserved his support and that it was logical for some to disagree with parts of his proposals and concur on others. Notwithstanding, Roosevelt campaigned against these senators in the primaries of 1938 and urged the support of others who were favorable to his reform measures. Notably among those senators he tried to unseat were Walter F. George of Georgia, Millard F. Tydings of Maryland, and "Cotton Ed" Smith of South Carolina. All three were renominated by their state parties and reelected by their constituents in the November election.[14] The South resented Roosevelt's attempt to interfere in local politics. Thus his purge failed.

During the final years of the second term, the breech between Garner and Roosevelt widened. It transpired that as early as the Christmas holidays in 1937, bar and cocktail pary gossip at the capital had it that Garner was to be among the first in Roosevelt's purge to get the hatchet. On the surface, however, both men appeared cordial and Garner tried to play down the split for the sake of seeming party solidarity. Still Roosevelt's policies offended him: bigger-than-ever spending proposals, the use of relief funds for political purposes, his left-wing swing and its adverse effect on the party, his increasing ambition for personal power, his executive appointments, and the apparent coddling of Communists and fellow-travelers and their infiltration of the government.

Since President Roosevelt had announced as early as 1937 that he would not seek a third term for the office, speculation in the party was that his successor would be chosen from three men: Secretary of State Cordell Hull, Postmaster General James A. Farley, and Vice-President John Nance Garner. Certainly no one watched the current political scene more closely than the Democratic committeewoman Clara Driscoll. All three would make worthy candidates, in her estimation, and would represent the party well. They were also friends and she could support the party's choice of any one without reservation.

The distinguished secretary of state, who had served in the United States House of Representatives continuously from 1907 to 1921 and again from 1923 to 1931 and had gone to the Senate in 1931, would probably be the president's choice. A man of unquestioned integrity and high moral principle, Hull had made a notable contribution to the improvement of United States relations with the Latin American countries and had advanced the Good Neighbor Policy, with both of which Mrs. Driscoll concurred enthusiastically. She also greatly admired Hull's stance on the employment of peaceful methods to settle international differences.

If less qualified, James A. Farley—a person of unusual charm—was a good man. The New Deal tactician, Farley was an organizer and predictor whose assessments usually proved to be accurate. But Farley was moving away from New Deal policy and was in sympathy with the Democrats who challenged Roosevelt's leadership; so he would not likely have the president's support. Although Farley was a Catholic, if he chose to run, he would not have to face the same handicaps that Al Smith had. Prohibition and Tammany Hall would not interfere as they had with Smith's campaign. True, Farley lacked the experience of Hull and Garner, but he was both reliable and reasonable.

Of the three, Mrs. Driscoll's unequivocal choice was Garner. By both seniority and experience, the vice-president was eminently the best qualified. Not only that, she felt that Garner deserved the recognition for his outstanding service to the nation that election to the presidency would bring. His political career had spanned almost half a century. He had been a highly efficient congressman for thirty years; had served successively as Democratic whip and floor leader; was elected Speaker of the House in 1931; had been a candidate for the Democratic nomination for president in 1932, when he released his delegates in favor of Roosevelt; and had served honorably as the vice-president of the United States now in his second term. On top of that, Garner placed loyalty to the party above everything else, and she felt that it was time the party repaid him. Naturally, the fact that Garner was a native Texan like herself, besides being a good friend, were additional points in his favor.

In the hope, then, that President Roosevelt would step down in favor of Garner and convinced that Garner would fill the office admirably, Mrs. Driscoll began early to work for his nomination:

> Mrs. Driscoll, long a personal friend of Garner and a staunch supporter in 1932 when he was presented at the national convention as running mate of Roosevelt, has since that time campaigned wholeheartedly for his nomination and eventual election in 1940, the next presidential year.[16]

She contacted influential Democrats of the state and the nation and together they planned strategy. Although she had supported Roosevelt as the party's choice in the past two elections, she was opposed to a third term and felt that he had had the office long enough.

Mrs. Driscoll's first evidence of success was demonstrated at the State Democratic Convention that met in September, 1938. Following her nominating action, the fourteen hundred delegates unanimously endorsed John Nance Garner as their nominee to succeed the incumbent in the White House.

> Of importance in the political panorama over the entire nation this year was the launching of a campaign designed to bring about the nomination of John Nance Garner, now Vice President of the United States, for President. The launching of the campaign itself was largely due to the nominating action of Mrs. Clara Driscoll, National Democratic Committeewoman.[17]

Almost concurrent with the state party's endorsement, Senator Edward R. Burke of Nebraska, who had been urged to be Roosevelt's running mate in 1936, if Garner retired, announced that Garner was his choice for the presidential nomination for 1940. Another ardent supporter of Garner, who came forward from the outset, was Richard W. Norton, a Texas and Louisiana oil man.

To emphasize the official launching of the campaign in Texas, Mrs. Driscoll and other Democratic leaders held a statewide rally at the log-cabin birthplace of Garner in Blossom, Red River County, the following December. This implied comparison of Garner's lowly American heritage with that of Abraham Lincoln, with whom indeed Garner had other traits in common—humility, philosophical expression, brevity—made excellent copy in the national press. Furthermore, it must have really stung the man who moved painfully by the aid of a cane but whose early life had been one of comparative ease and luxury. The rally was effective as hundreds of letters poured in urging the vice-president to take a stand for the nomination.

As the Garner-in-1940 boom got underway, a number of national events augured favorably for the movement. As noted, Roosevelt's attempt to purge the administration of opponents to his New Deal policies failed miserably. The Democrats had lost strength in the November elections and the Republicans had gained eighty seats in the House and seven in the Senate.[18] Thus with the support of the conservative Democrats the Republicans could now dominate Congress. Consequently, by the end of 1938 the conservative coalition emerged more powerful than ever and the New Deal was facing its ideological limits.

Meanwhile, on the surface there was still the appearance of harmony between Garner and Roosevelt as all pre-congressional activity revolved around the vice-presidential suite. Such a constant stream of executive department administrators waited outside his door that word got noised about the capitol that Garner was the man to see. Anyone with a problem took it to the vice-president's office in the capitol. Garner tried diligently to reconcile conflicting viewpoints.

Otherwise conditions were such that the session of Congress opening on January 3, 1939, gave President Roosevelt "his roughest legislative ride."[19] Before it adjourned eight months later, on August 5, his influence had diminished accordingly. The result was that in his Jackson Day Dinner speech on January 9, 1939, the president expressed himself in favor of party unity. His formula for it, however, was that those who disagreed with his policies should cease their opposition or join the Republicans.[20] He followed this with a series of appointments of New Deal lame ducks to key positions, which excited further dissension.

Then, with his relations with Congress at an all-time low ebb, the president proposed a planned-inflation program of federal lending that was purported to run into $5 billion. At the same time he announced at a press conference that published stories of a rift between himself and the vice-president were pure fabrications. Garner's reaction to the new loan proposal was the release of a statement to the press that he had made earlier to Roosevelt.

"Down in our country," the shaggy-browed sage of Uvalde, Texas, was quoted as saying, "when cattle are grazing and taking on fat we don't bother them too much and we don't scare them. We ought to have as much consideration for human beings as for cattle."[21] The president was infuriated at the publication of the statement criticizing his recovery policies. But he proceeded, nevertheless, to draft his new spending bill, now whittled down to $2,390,000,000, in which no one was left out of the planned-inflation largess. At the time the mounting national debt had reached over thirty billion dollars.[22] The Senate passed a modified version of the lend-spend measure, but the House defeated it by a vote of 193 to 167 and refused to take it up for debate.

The defeat of the loan proposal was a step toward the return of constitutional government and away from one-man rule. Also the bill's failure to pass typified a victory for Garner and other anti-New Dealers. Before leaving for home when Congress recessed, Garner urged, as he had repeatedly, the cessation of shipments of petroleum, scrap metal, and other war materiel to Japan. His quips as sharp and penetrating as ever, the philosopher from the Texas Hill Country observed that he never thought it "wise for white men to sell scalping knives to Indians." Just as he expected, his remarks went unheeded.

As the president's star waned at the capital, Garner's ascended. He remained the man whom the tourists and politicians wanted to see. Although he maintained discreet silence—and would never have conceded the fact—John Nance Garner had become the symbol of opposition to the New Deal and, in the minds of many, the future salvation of the country.

By January, 1939, Garner's chances as a political prospect looked exceedingly bright. All polls showed him in the lead if President Roosevelt did not run. A preview of the situation among fifty leading Washington correspondents, which appeared in *Newsweek*, showed that seventeen thought Garner would be the nominee, ten favored Hull, and eleven, Roosevelt, with the others scattering.[23] By March the campaign gathered momentum. Both houses of the Texas Legislature endorsed Garner. Other expressions of support quickly followed. Governors Ely of Massachusetts and Hodge of Kansas announced for Garner, along with the automobile tycoon, Henry Ford. "Jack Garner would make a mighty fine President," Ford stated in an interview. "He's got a mighty fine record. He's on the spot. He knows what's going on. He's got the experience. As things are, I don't think you could make a better choice."[24]

Spurred by this encouragement, Mrs. Driscoll and other leading Democrats urged Garner to break his silence and come out openly for the nomination. Pressed for a statement, Garner still disclaimed interest. However, he conceded that

> The Presidency is the hardest job in the world and the highest honor and greatest obligation that can come to any American. If you have not connived in or abetted any effort in your behalf; if you really do not care for the office and the nomination comes to you because your party and your country think you fitted for its duties, it is your duty to accept and serve. But I don't think I will be nominated and I don't want to be.[25]

In March, Gallup conducted another poll. Gallup asked the question, "If Roosevelt is not a candidate, whom would you like to see elected in 1940?" The statistical results percentagewise gave Garner, 42; Hull, 10; Farley, 10; Hopkins, 8; and McNutt, 5.[26] Despite opposition by columnist Raymond Clapper, who initiated the Stop Garner campaign, Garner's percentage climbed in two months to 50 percent, a gain of 8. In May the Draft Roosevelt movement was being pushed by left-wing appointees. Hopkins, who had told Garner a few months before that he opposed a third Roosevelt nomination, was directing the movement and Tom Corcoran was second in command. On May 11 it was no surprise when Earl Browder, general secretary and erstwhile presidential candidate from the Communist party, announced for Roosevelt for a third term.

By the end of May the Draft Roosevelt campaign had made little progress. Congress opposed Roosevelt on everything except the appropriations for national defense. Most politicians felt that, barring a war psychology, Roosevelt would be weaker than Garner or Hull. Moreover, many influential Democratic leaders came out openly against a third term. The rule against a third term had the sanction of history and the Democratic party's position against it was traditional principle. The House of Representatives in 1895 had voted 233 to 38 against breaking the two-term tradition; and the Democratic membership in the Senate in 1939, in conformity with the principle, overwhelmingly opposed a third term. A newspaper report a few months after the third-term efforts got underway stated that twenty-nine senators had pledged their support to Garner against a third term.

By June the Garner-for-President movement was making real headway. Leaders Clara Driscoll and State Democratic Chairman Eugene B. Germany had established headquarters in Dallas and announced that they would place Garner's name in nomination regardless of who else ran. Both vowed that theirs was a pro-Garner but not an anti-Roosevelt campaign. They explained that they were not necessarily against Roosevelt but were opposed to a third term.

At this time Garner came out openly against a third term but was still reticent about making a statement. Roosevelt, meanwhile, remained noncommittal about his intentions. As Garner appraised the political picture, there was no public demand for Roosevelt to run at this time, but it could be created by the same unethical methods that were now being used by his supporters.

On Capitol Hill Garner was no longer able to see President Roosevelt alone. He saw him only in the presence of cabinet members or legislative leaders. Roosevelt had stopped inviting the vice-president for the cozy luncheons in the Oval Office after the polls had begun to show Garner high on the list of his possible successors. In the midst of all the political furore, the president confided to Postmaster General Farley that he had no intentions of running for a third term but swore the cabinet member to secrecy. Farley went to Europe convinced that Roosevelt would make a statement removing himself from the race. Before embarking, Farley confided the "secret," however, to the man most like to be interested—John Nance Garner.

At this juncture the Hatch Act became a torrid issue and muddied the political waters somewhat. Authored by senators Hatch of New Mexico, Morris Sheppard of Texas, and Warren Austin of Vermont (future United States representative to the United Nations), the measure was designed to prevent an officerholder's oligarchy from controlling presidential succession by letting the president name his successor-nominee. Garner announced that he would follow the principles of the Hatch Act whether it became law or not. The Senate in a thirteen-hour session passed the bill. President Roosevelt opposed it, but unable to find a good reason to veto it, finally signed the act reluctantly. Between the time Roosevelt assumed office and the passage of the bill, federal employees had increased from 563,487 to 932,654. Of these, 300,00 were outside the Civil Service.[27]

But the Hatch Act failed its purpose. It was apparent that the federal officeholders' machine would select the delegates even if the law prevented them from being delegates themselves. Violations of the law were winked at and third-term advocates on the federal payroll proceeded undeterred with their campaign.[28]

By mid-summer of 1939 general war talk throughout the country began to affect the political scene. At this time there were still no announced candidates for the Democratic nomination. A confirmed pacifist, Garner was convinced that Roosevelt's leadership would be a handicap if the country did become involved in war. As he viewed it, the president's inability to delegate authority would interfere with the conduct of a conflict: "He [Roosevelt] wants to be his own secretary of state, his own secretary of the treasury, his own secretary of war and, especially, his own secretary of the navy now."[29]

Regardless of the imminence of a war in Europe or the Orient, Garner strongly opposed a third term. Though as yet an undeclared candidate, he recognized the gravity of the world situation and pledged that, if Roosevelt ran, he would oppose his nomination in every possible way. Still hoping that Roosevelt would issue a statement eliminating himself from the contest, Garner realized that the political climate was becoming progressively more crucial. He saw that the movement by job holders, to whom the president was a meal ticket, was an attempt to create a situation in which no one else could develop strength until Roosevelt made his wishes known. By that time job holders hoped to "have things sewed up."

Meanwhile, Mrs. Driscoll's efforts for Garner's nomination were seemingly meeting with success in California, where she had personally launched the campaign with the assistance of Bill McNicholson and such crowd attractors as the Hardin-Simmons University Cowboy Band, white horses mounted by pretty girls, and the stellar performances of singing star Cindy Walker. In the California campaign Mrs. Driscoll had exploited such slogans as Preserve Peace and American Ideals and Put America to Work. She had also made a special effort to gain the support of organized women's groups. A poll conducted in the state showed that 60 percent of those taking part favored the election of a Democrat for president in 1940, but 64 percent opposed a third term.

Then on September 3 the anticipated war became a reality when Great Britain and France declared war on Germany. On September 21 the United States Congress met in special session to repeal the embargo clause in the Neutrality Act.[30] Garner, who had opposed the embargo from the start, took a major part in obtaining its repeal.

The war was all the third-term proponents needed. Secretary of Agriculture Henry Wallace came forth immediately with the cry that the war in Europe made it necessary for Roosevelt to run for a third term. Next, the third-term advocates claimed that Roosevelt, more than anyone else, could be depended upon to keep the war in bounds. While the third-term campaign picked up speed with the newly-adopted issue of national defense, its opponents embraced a cautious position of silence for obvious reasons of political self-preservation.

Still Mrs. Driscoll and her coworkers refused to accept the situation as untenable and renewed their efforts to obtain a statement from Garner. Approached at his home in Uvalde, where he was vacationing, Garner finally conceded his willingness to make one because of his love for his fellowman and his desire to serve the best interests of the country. Even so, he still doubted that the Roosevelt machine could be beaten and did not hesitate to tell his supporters so. When the form of the draft was discussed by the delegation who called upon him, Garner took a pencil and wrote a forty-five-word statement:

> I will accept the nomination for President. I will make no effort to control any delegates. The people should decide. A candidate should be selected at the primaries and conventions as provided by law, and I sincerely trust that all Democrats will participate in them.[31]

He declared the statement too long but declined to edit it. Instead, he demonstrated his lack of enthusiasm by loading up his car with gear and heading out for a little old-fashioned Texas fishing. The vice-president's declaration attracted wide and favorable attention in the nation's press. However, Democratic officeholders and politicians, who had volubly opposed a third term earlier, now withheld comment.

In New York, Al Smith was an exception: "I think and always did think that two terms were enough for any man. It's been a sort of unwritten part of our Constitution since the days of Washington . . . Garner's all right . . . He knows what's going on . . . He's been hanging around Washington most of his life and should know . . . and I'm reasonably sure he knows the mistakes of the last seven years."[32]

When Vice-President Garner returned to Washington on January 3, 1940, his declared candidacy was almost a month old. After the announcement, President Roosevelt was asked at a press conference to comment on it and his own third-term aspirations. His answer was predictable. He was too busy with foreign and domestic affairs to talk about potential events a long way off. At the $100-per-plate Jackson Day Dinner, Roosevelt's traditional speech was so vague that it was almost a dead giveaway of his intentions to run. It left no doubt in Garner's mind that the president had been a serious candidate to succeed himself from the outset. An interesting sidelight on the dinner, and also a sort of barometer gauging public opinion, was the fact that Senator Hatch, author of the bill designed to curb political activity by federal employees, was booed.

Despite the turn of events, Garner's popularity in the polls continued to increase. A January Gallup poll revealed that 58 percent of the Democrats favored the nomination of Garner if Roosevelt did not run. As polls showed Garner's big lead over other potential candidates, more and more state political leaders called upon him. One delegation came from Wisconsin, where a poll had shown 65 percent of the Democrats in favor of Garner.[33]

Encouraged by the results of the latest popularity polls, Mrs. Driscoll worked harder to test Garner's strength in various state primaries. On February 7 she bucked the powerful Kelley–Nash machine by testing Garner's following in the Illinois primaries. It was the law in Illinois that a candidate had to make a sworn statement that he was a candidate before his name could be placed on the ticket. Garner abided by the law only to learn that the Illinois officials relaxed the law and placed Roosevelt's name on the ballot. Roosevelt had until February 24 to withdraw his name in Illinois but he did not choose to do so. The president was now at least a passive candidate in Illinois, Wisconsin, and New Hampshire.

As Roosevelt kept the country guessing, ignoring all democratic processes, Garner realized the cogency of the subtle game the president was playing. He knew all too well that Roosevelt could work it so that the nomination would be worthless to anyone but himself. In fact, that was precisely what he was doing as the primaries now began to show his strength. Whereas Garner got only three Wisconsin delegates, Roosevelt got twenty-three. Roosevelt also took Illinois in the primary. Even more disheartening, in California, where Garner's chances had looked favorable at the start and where he had defeated both Roosevelt and Smith in 1932, the president was awarded a unilateral victory.

Regardless of these setbacks, Mrs. Driscoll refused to relax her efforts in her candidate's behalf. Nor were her actions ignored by the party. At the Democratic convention held in Waco on May 28, 1940, when she was re-elected national committeewoman for the fourth time by acclamation, she was also accorded special recognition for her services. Chairman Germany of the Executive Committee appointed former governor Pat M. Neff, J. K. Brim of Sulphur Springs, and Under-Secretary of the Interior A. J. Wirtz to escort the national committeewoman to the speakers' platform.

The body gave Mrs. Driscoll a standing ovation and cheered wildly as she and her escorts mounted the rostrum. Former governor Neff represented the group. In his commendatory remarks, he lauded Mrs. Driscoll as "Patriot, philanthropist, and guiding genius of Democracy in the state and nation."[34] Visibly showing surprise, Mrs. Driscoll acknowledged the tribute in a brief but characteristic response. She said simply that she stood by her state and the democracy of her state.

The Texas national committeewoman also was extolled in the state press for her political leadership. Typical examples were the following:

> . . . in the nation's politics she [Mrs. Driscoll] has brought recognition and fame to the Democratic Party of Texas. Continually striving for the ideals of all Texans, she is a leader in the state and nation. In Democratic activity she has carried the message of South Texas many times into the nation's capital, and has drawn national attention to this great industrial, agricultural and defense center [Corpus Christi] in the strongest nation ever erected in the history of civilization.[35]

> * * * * * * * *

> Today Mrs. Driscoll is active in the pushing of John Nance Garner . . . for the presidency in 1940. Her efforts and acts . . . have been instrumental in the selecting of this, one of Texas' greatest men and leaders for the highest place of honor and responsibility that the greatest nation has to offer.
>
> Political activity is demanding in time, as is well known, but Mrs. Driscoll has seen fit to devote her will and efforts to the assistance in the leadership of this great party in Texas. Her friends and coworkers admire and respect her cooperation and ability. . . . The Texas Democratic party boasts of one of its most able members in Mrs. Clara Driscoll.[36]

> * * * * * * * *

> Her unceasing and successful labors in civic and state and political interests merely give added color to her own loyalty and love for Texas, at the same time pointing out perhaps the foundations for the admiration and esteem in which she is held from border to border in the great empire of the Southwest, and far beyond these limits in the nation at large . . .[37]

By the time the Democratic convention met in Chicago in mid-July, it was well known that Roosevelt would use his authority to control it.[38] Still the

Democratic delegation from Texas headed by Clara Driscoll and Eugene B. Germany had pledged to nominate Garner regardless of other candidates. Moreover, in case of a compromise in which Garner might be renominated for the second spot, they were instructed to decline it summarily. That posed no problem, however. Upon Roosevelt's suggestion, the party reluctantly accepted Secretary of Agriculture Henry A. Wallace for the second place on the ticket.

But from the outset the Texans faced a real difficulty. Roosevelt supporters wanted to name him by acclamation and thus prevent the Texas delegation from demonstrating their loyalty to Garner. Although some of the Texans might have conceded because of the certainty of Roosevelt's nomination, Mrs. Driscoll, Germany, and Bascom N. Timmons, delegate-at-large from the state, insisted upon carrying out their original plans. Other delegates observed that in view of the long and distinguished service of Garner to the party, he should not be subjected to the inevitable ridicule that would ensue. Whereupon Mrs. Driscoll and her entourage felt that a little booing would be a minor matter. Anyway, they pointed out, the vice-president would not hear it since he was not present.

Wright Morrow of Houston had consented to make the nominating address for Garner. Senator Carter Glass had been selected to place Postmaster General Farley's name in nomination. The two groups of supporters had attended the convention out of loyalty to their candidates, and there were at least 125 delegates who wished to be recorded as opposed to a third term.

Feeling mounted against Garner and Farley for allowing their names to be introduced. The opposition even tried to use force to prohibit the Texans from staging their planned parade and making the nominating address. A policeman stopped Morrow at the door and removed a Garner button from his lapel. The officer informed Morrow that he was likely to get hurt wearing the button. Morrow replaced the button and told the officer that if anyone attacked him, he supposed he could depend upon him for protection. The man in uniform replied that he would not be responsible. Morrow told the officer to keep the Garner button for a souvenir. Then he pushed the policeman aside and entered the hall.

When members of the Texas aggregation got inside the hall, intent upon carrying out their plans, every aisle was packed with persons who were not delegates and had been admitted without tickets. Never was Mrs. Driscoll more courageous in the face of steamroller tactics and certain defeat. She protested to Chairman Alben Barkley, informing him that the friends of the vice-president intended to mount a parade for which she had engaged a band and had reinforced it with six white horses and girls to ride them. Such a stance might have gained for her such adjectives as "fiery-eyed" and "saber-tongued," but as one national magazine stated: " . . . politicians soon learned to respect her; she . . . could cuss and connive with the best of them, outspend most of them."[39]

Nonplused, Chairman Barkley, who was partisan and mindful of the role he was later to play, went into a huddle with Sergeant-at-Arms Edward Halsey. When Halsey faced the leaders of the Texas delegation, they refused to be intimidated and told him that they intended to exercise their rights and do what they had come to do. Whereupon the sergeant-at-arms extracted from his pocket a directive stating that he could not allow another person to enter the convention hall. If the Texans started a parade for Garner, he explained, they would incite a riot. Mrs. Driscoll tartly replied that if a riot occurred it would be because of people crowding the hall who had no admission tickets and did not belong there. Then she stated emphatically, "We have delegates at an entrance door with admission tickets and they intend to come in with the members of our band who also have admission tickets." Halsey returned to Barkley for further orders. Barkley capitulated. In a few minutes Halsey told Mrs. Driscoll and her assistants that he would clear the halls sufficiently for the parade but drew the line on the horses. The Texans conceded the omission of the animals since they did not have tickets!

So Clara Driscoll had her parade and the Texans were surprised at the large number of delegates from other states who joined it. Furthermore, Morrow and Glass made their nominating speeches even though the booing exceeded all predictions.

On Wednesday, July 17, a six-hour convention session was held in which a platform was adopted by the Democratic party and Roosevelt was nominated. But the way in which his supporters announced his intention of being a candidate for the nomination descended to the nadir of cheap theatrics. On the second day of the convention Chairman Barkley initiated the histrionics by delivering the overdue statement from the president. President Roosevelt, he said, released all delegates and did not desire the nomination.[40] Barkley had scarcely finished before a parade of men and women led by Mayor Kelly of Chicago got noisily underway. The paraders bore hundreds of banners with the slogan Roosevelt and Humanity emblazoned across them. At the prearranged moment a huge picture of Roosevelt was handed to Barkley, who lifted it high above the rostrum. Finally, and precisely on cue, a high-pitched voice cut through the din: "We want Roosevelt! America wants Roosevelt!" Then one by one the voice went through the states from Alabama to Wyoming, with the cry that each wanted Roosevelt. Texas was conspicuous by its omission.

When members of the press gallery investigated, they discovered that a man named Thomas D. McGarry, who was Chicago superintendent of sewers, had rigged up an apparatus in the basement of the convention hall and attached it to the loudspeaker. McGarry had read from a prepared scrip into the amplifying system. Reporters were later to describe it as "the voice from the sewers."[41]

On July 22 Vice-President Garner, who had remained in Washington during the convention, left for Uvalde. He would return in September to preside over the Senate until Congress adjourned. Garner made no public statement during the campaign between Roosevelt and Republican candidate Wendell Wilkie, and had no regrets. No doubt he got a chuckle out of the president's innovative "announcement" of his desire to run for a third term. Of course the parade that "Miss Clara" had succeeded in putting on for him was no laughing matter, but he had to admire her courage. The abortive effort of Clara Driscoll to put John Nance Garner in the presidential chair was said to have cost her upwards of $250,000.[42]

But the Texas stateswoman's personal disappointment at not succeeding interfered in no way with the discharge of her duties as national Democratic committeewoman. Placing party loyalty above personalities, she swung her support once more to Roosevelt and campaigned as vigorously as before. She sponsored Jackson Day dinners, supported the president's birthday balls, and other fund-raising activities for Roosevelt's campaign and for his and her favorite charity, the Foundation for Infantile Paralysis. At times she participated openly and at others she worked behind the scenes. One of the latter was the president's ball held in 1940 at the Plaza Hotel in Corpus Christi under the sponsorship of the Young Democratic Club of Nueces County. At the affair Mrs. Driscoll was the highest bidder for the birthday cake, which she sent to the Orthopedic Hospital. Frequently she matched the receipts of such affairs without announcement of the fact. In 1939 her check to the committee in charge of the Jackson Day Dinner in Dallas was the largest received.[43]

Popular balloting in the presidential race was relatively close, with Roosevelt polling 27,244,000 votes and Wilkie, 22,305,000. But the electoral tally of 449 for the incumbent and 82 for his Republican opponent was decisive.[44] The president's overwhelming electoral majority included the Texas count largely as a result of Mrs. Driscoll's successful campaign efforts.[45]

Clara Driscoll's loyalty to the Democratic party did not end with Roosevelt's victory. On January 17, 1941, when the Texas delegation of more than sixty went to Washington to witness the inauguration of Franklin Delano Roosevelt for the third term, Clara Driscoll was leading them. She and her entourage traveled on the Missouri–Kansas lines as far as St. Louis, where they changed to another train bearing other members of the Texas aggregation. For her contribution to the inaugural parade Mrs. Driscoll again employed the thirty-eight-piece Cowboy Band of Hardin-Simmons University and embellished it with the six magnificent white horses and six lovely girls to ride them as she had planned to do for Garner. Upon their arrival in Washington, the committeewoman and her party paid official calls to Vice-President Garner, who would help to induct his successor into office, and Speaker of the House Sam Rayburn, another Texan who had brought Lone Star laurels to the national capital.

On January 22, 1941, to conclude postinaugural activities, Mrs. Driscoll gave a reception and ball for the Texas delegation with the Cowboy Band providing the music. Special guests at the event included Speaker Rayburn, National Democratic Chairman Ed Flynn, and Senator Connally of Texas.[46]

The war that helped Roosevelt break the tradition against a third term could very well have lost for him his bid for a fourth. In 1943, when he decided once again to remain in office, there was dissatisfaction over wartime regimentation and smoldering resentment from prewar debate over intervention. In addition, some people charged Washington with the responsibility for the Pearl Harbor attack, and the fact that only in 1940 had the government seen fit to terminate the exportation of oil, scrap metal, and other raw (potential war) materials to Japan rankled.

Not only did this confusion permeate the nation, rival factions developed in the Democratic party as a result. Party bosses and Southern Democrats alike rejected Vice-President Wallace as another of President Roosevelt's lame ducks and a visionary who wished to extend the New Deal to the entire globe at the American taxpayers' expense. The suspense that preceded Roosevelt's third-term nomination was absent. Since his declining health was apparent, however, there was serious speculation over the choice for the vice-presidential nominee. To offset the disastrous effects of the factions and to satisfy those who considered his visible aging a liability, Roosevelt proposed a compromise candidate for the second spot on the 1944 ticket acceptable to most of the dissidents. His choice was piano-playing and plain-speaking Senator Harry S. Truman of Missouri, who had attracted favorable attention as chairman of the Senate War Investigating Committee.[47]

Texans were no exception to the political dissension, and in the state the Democratic party was almost hopelessly split. As champion of President Roosevelt, Mrs. Driscoll appeared before the Nueces County Democratic convention in Corpus Christi in 1944 to oppose an uninstructed delegation. County politicians had met to name delegates to the state convention who, in turn, would appoint representatives to the national convention to meet in Chicago. Indications were that the delegation would be uninstructed—or anti-Roosevelt. "For fully 30 minutes Mrs. Driscoll stood before the convention, arguing, pleading, cajoling, in that insistent manner for which she was famed."[48] She succeeded. The convention instructed the delegation to cast its ballots for Roosevelt candidates.

Conditions worsened at the 1944 state Democratic convention. When the anti-Roosevelt forces took charge, Mrs. Driscoll resigned as national committeewoman and joined the pro-Roosevelt faction. Mrs. H. H. Weinert of Seguin was nominated by the anti-Roosevelt faction to succeed Mrs. Driscoll. Later the pro-Roosevelt group renominated Mrs. Driscoll for national committeewoman. At the national convention held in Chicago, however, she declined to contest the nomination of the other lady and was elected vice-chairman of the Democratic national executive committee.[49]

In resigning the position of national Democratic committeewoman from Texas, Mrs. Driscoll, who was ill but still wielding influence from her sickbed, sent the following statement to the convention by W. A. Wakefield.

> I have long been a member of the Democratic party and for sixteen years I have served as National Committeewoman from this state. I love politics and the Democratic party. This is the first time since I was first called on to serve my party that I have failed it. It is with regret that I must refuse now, but I am ill and do not feel that I would be able to serve my party as it should be served and therefore I must refuse.[50]

When the resignation was read at the state Democratic convention, the membership stood for some minutes in a gesture of appreciation to the woman who had served the party with such loyalty and efficiency. Former governor of Texas Dan Moody, her close friend, proposed the tribute.[51]

Despite her failing health and the political unrest, Mrs. Driscoll worked assiduously for Roosevelt's reelection. Even though the president's opponent, Governor Thomas E. Dewey of New York, had learned that the United States had possessed the Japanese code at the time Pearl Harbor was attacked, he was persuaded not to use the intelligence for fear that it might affect the war in the Pacific.[52] Again Roosevelt controlled the organized labor vote and did not hesitate to campaign strenuously. He defeated Dewey by a margin of 432 electoral votes to 99 and a popular count of 25,602,000 to 22,006,000.[53] Once more Mrs. Driscoll had assured the Democratic party nominee of the Texas electoral count.

In helping to elect Roosevelt to the presidency for the fourth time, Clara

Driscoll had ended one of the most distinguished careers of any American stateswoman—sixteen years of unprecedented and tireless service. The presidential election of 1944 would remain the final victory for both.[54] It was said that Roosevelt had a dialogue with the American people.[55] Clara Driscoll had a dialogue with the Democratic party.

11

Corpus Christi Entrepreneur

 AS DARLING OF THE DEMOCRATIC PARTY,
Clara Driscoll was no less a heroine in her hometown of Corpus Christi. In
the South Texas metropolis she earned a special niche in the civic and social
community through her interest in people and devotion to enterprise.

> Leading the full life that she does, Mrs. Driscoll has seen fit to devote her efforts
> and leadership to Texas. Her friends, her coworkers, all Texans, and the people of
> Corpus Christi admire and respect her cooperation and ability. For Texas boasts one
> of its most able citizens in Mrs. Clara Driscoll.[1]

Following Driscoll tradition, she affiliated herself with every movement and
project designed to advance the port city since she became sole heir to the
family fortune in 1929.

> Mrs. Driscoll has always been more than willing to cooperate in the development
> of South Texas oil and gas resources, which has meant much to the community's
> wealth. She has planned in the traditional Driscoll fashion a program, and the ad-
> vancement of the program to a swift, sure, and complete end, thus realizing the
> dreams of her forefathers . . . men who dreamed of a great South Texas . . . has al-
> ways been uppermost in her thoughts. It is with pride and true recognition that this
> city does honor to the leader from Corpus Christi, for this city feels that it is fortu-
> nate in having as a citizen, one whose fame has spread throughout the land.[2]

In 1939, with her marital difficulties behind her, Mrs. Driscoll addressed
herself to business and political activities with renewed vigor.

> . . . the program of Mrs. Clara Driscoll has been wide and farreaching. Deeds of
> merit have illuminated her course and today she carries on in the creed of one of the
> finest and best known names written across the pages of South Texas history.[3]

Except for the two-year absence in Chile, she had personally directed the Driscoll estate, wide in scope and vital to the agricultural and industrial scene of Texas, with later assistance from her secretary, Philip Howerton. Not only had she led in the exploitation of oil and gas resources in South Texas with the result that oil refineries were introduced and chemical plants to convert oyster shells into various products for industry, she also made other notable contributions that were widespread in their influence. As president in active charge of the Corpus Christi Bank and Trust Company and a director of Corpus Christi National Bank, she had pumped into the economy of the city and surrounding territory the sorely needed capital essential to civic improvements and industrial development. This economic aid made possible the erection of a giant zinc smelter plant which used ore shipped in from the outside and other industries that manufactured such commodities as onion seeds and food products as starch, dextrose, and animal fodder produced from milo maize, a new variety of corn introduced during World War II.

In 1939—Corpus Christi's centennial year—Mrs. Driscoll remodeled the Corpus Christi Bank and Trust Company, from where she conducted her business affairs under the name of Clara Driscoll Properties, converting it into one of the most modern institutions of its size in the state. When she assumed active operation of the bank in 1929, it was but two years old. In 1939, in its twelfth year, the bank's resources under her direction had increased in excess of $3 million.[4]

Another outstanding example of Mrs. Driscoll's interest in civic progress was demonstrated in 1939 when she pledged to match—two for one—any funds donated to establish on Corpus Christi Bay a naval training base the size and importance of the installation at Pensacola. When the Corpus Christi Chamber of Commerce voted to underwrite a fund of $50,000 toward the purchase of a site for the proposed training base, Mrs. Driscoll was advised of the action, as an interested citizen.

Immediately, unsolicited, she wired from California, where she was visiting: "Citizens of Corpus Christi must realize that establishment of a naval training school is too great an opportunity for the future growth of our town to lose. Will match any donation two to one."[5]

The large United States Naval Air Station became a reality in 1942, and today the base at the south end of the bay in Corpus Christi is the largest in America.

But Clara Driscoll's most memorable contribution, as a Corpus Christi entrepreneur, in conformity with tradition, was not to industry—as valuable as that was. From the time that Robert Driscoll, Jr., had built the White Plaza

Above, Clara Driscoll—financier and philanthropist, circa 1939. (Courtesy, Corpus Christi Public Libraries) Below, headquarters for the Texas Federation of Women's Clubs in Austin. Mrs. Driscoll granted the organization a loan of $92,000 in 1938, then in 1939 converted the loan into an outright gift. (Courtesy, Sam Houston State University)

Above, First World War president Woodrow Wilson. Clara Driscoll's friendship with Wilson dated from her brother's university days at Princeton in the nineties when Wilson was his favorite professor. Wilson was among the first to discover Mrs. Driscoll's foreign relations capability and flair for politics. Opposite, an invitation to the inaugural ceremonies for the first term of Roosevelt and Garner.

The Inaugural Committee

requests the honor of the presence of

Mrs. Clara D. Sevier

to attend and participate in the Inauguration of

Franklin Delano Roosevelt

as President of the United States of America

and

John Nance Garner

as Vice President of the United States of America
on Saturday the fourth of March
one thousand nine hundred and thirty-three
in the City of Washington

Please reply to Ray Baker
Chairman, Committee on Reception of Governors of States
and
Special Distinguished Guests
Washington Building, Washington, D.C.

Cary T. Grayson
Chairman, Inaugural Committee

To Mrs Clara Driscoll Sevier – a true Texan
and good friend – with warm regards
Aug - 4 - 34
Jno. N. Garner

Above, Vice-President John Nance Garner. Garner was Clara Driscoll's closest friend in the Democratic hierarchy. She tried to win the presidential nomination for him in 1940, when Roosevelt remained noncommittal about running for a third term. Opposite, Franklin Delano Roosevelt. This rare photograph was presented to the Seviers when they accepted the diplomatic post to Chile during Roosevelt's first administration.

For Ambassador and Mrs. Davies
from their friend Franklin D. Roosevelt

Secretary of State Cordell Hull. Mrs. Driscoll admired Hull particularly for his views on foreign affairs and his Good Neighbor Policy. He recognized her superior talent for diplomacy.

Right, Jesse H. Jones. As chairman of the Reconstruction Finance Corporation, the Houston businessman was exceedingly efficient. Between the establishment of the Corporation in 1932 and the defense crisis in 1941, the Corporation poured $15 billion into the American economy. Below, launching the Garner campaign on the West Coast. Mrs. Driscoll, second from right, plans campaign strategy with assistants. To her left is Bill McNichols, her campaign manager.

Opposite, a kiss for Clara. As the campaign gets underway in California, entertainer Cindy Walker greets Mrs. Driscoll with a kiss. Above, red roses for Mrs. Driscoll. California supporters present Mrs. Driscoll flowers at the opening of the rally. Below, a salute in song for Clara. On the Garner campaign trail in California. Bill McNichols, left; Cindy Walker, center; and Mrs. Driscoll seated at right.

Opposite, Mrs. Driscoll greets Marine hero Sergeant Al Schmid with a kiss. Left, the Robert Driscoll Hotel, circa 1950. View is from the side on Antelope Street. Mrs. Driscoll built the hotel as a memorial to her brother and lived in a penthouse apartment on the twentieth floor. It was in her apartment atop the ediface that she died in 1945. Below, on deck of the U.S.S. *Corpus Christi*. After the launching ceremonies sponsored by Mrs. Driscoll August 17, 1943, she was presented flowers by other participants in the event.

KISS FOR A HERO—Sgt. Al Schmid, the Marines' No. 1 hero who was blinded in a machinegun nest at Guadalcanal from which he killed 200 Japanese, received a kiss from Mrs. Clara Driscoll, national Democratic committeewoman, when he and Mrs. Schmid were her guests at Austin during a recent special rally. After one of his two buddies was killed and the other wounded, Schmid continued to fire the 30-calibre machine gun until a hand grenade struck the flange of the gun and exploded in his face, blinding him. The story is officially told that Schmid then whipped out his 45-calibre automatic pistol and said to his injured comrade, "I can't see now; tell me which way they're coming and I'll shoot. He wears the Navy Cross, the Pennsylvania Medal of Valor, and the Purple Heart "loaned" him by World War Hero No. 1, Marine Sergeant Bill Feigle of Houston, who presented it to him on the floor of the Texas Legislature May 1. (Official U. S. Marine Corps Photograph.)

Above, Corpus Christi Bank & Trust Tower. Originally the Robert Driscoll Hotel, the building was a part of the Driscoll Foundation properties until 1970. In that year it was sold to a group of Corpus Christi business executives and converted into the present Bank & Trust Tower. The Driscoll Foundation and archives occupy a great portion of the sixteenth floor of the building. The handsome structure still dominates the Corpus Christi skyline as it overlooks the waterfront. Right, Mrs. Driscoll's pet fox terrier, Spots. The little dog was a constant companion to the lady in her declining years. The pet survived his mistress by five or six years. Before her death in 1945 she made special arrangements with Phil L. Highshew, her chauffeur, to take care of Spots.

Above, the Driscoll mausoleum in the Masonic Cemetery in San Antonio. The mausoleum was built by Robert Driscoll, Sr., in 1900. It serves as the final resting place for Robert Driscoll, Sr., Robert Driscoll, Jr., and Clara Driscoll. Below, Driscoll Foundation Children's Hospital, Corpus Christi, Texas.

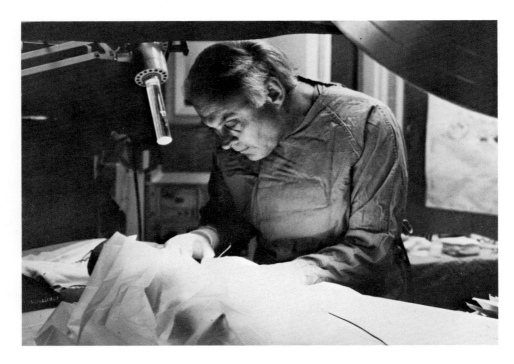

Opposite, Dr. Alfonso Prado, neonatologist, examines a newborn. Above, Dr. Simpson performing cardiac catheterization. Below, residents and physicians engaged in a discussion involving a perplexing case.

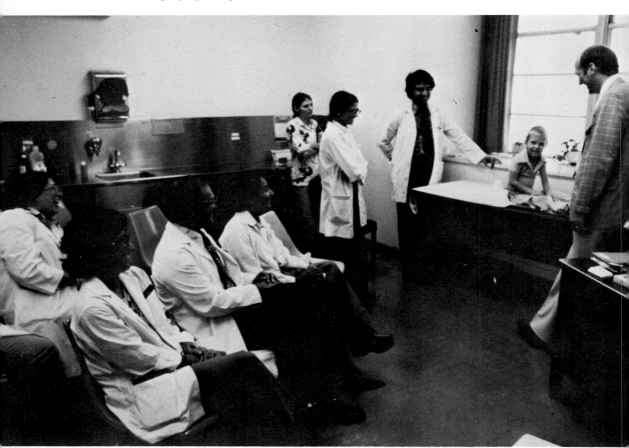

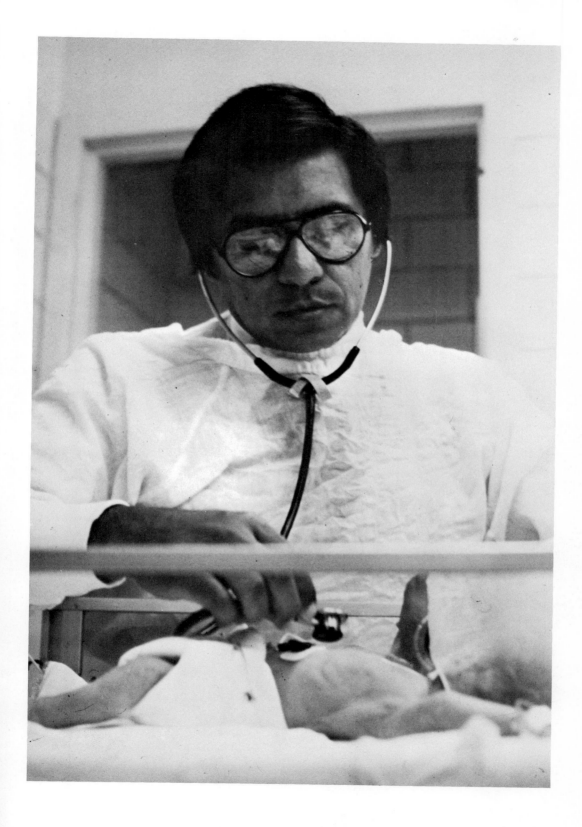

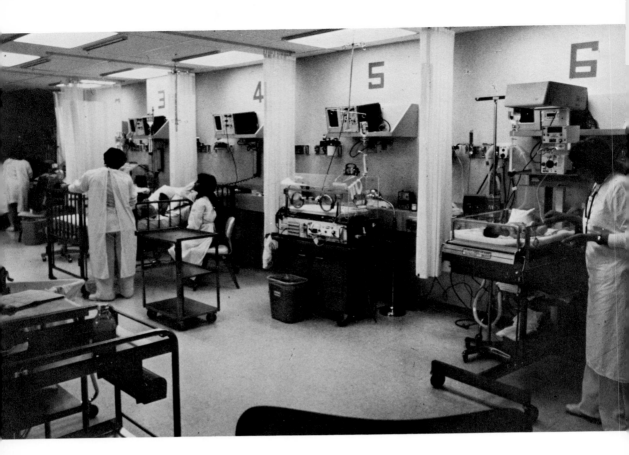

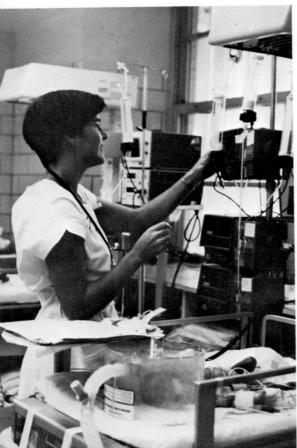

Above, view of lifesaving intensive care unit. Left, a nurse adjusts monitoring equipment in the Neonate Nursery.

(then known as the Plaza) in the 1920s, Corpus Christi's main thrust had been directed toward tourist attraction and the entertainment of visitors. Moreover, Clara Driscoll, like other benefactors intent upon converting the sterile length of Padre Island into a coastal playground—a South Texas Riviera—gave to the port city, as an opener, the most fabulous hotel in the Southwest up to that time.

An esplanade on a bluff above the downtown business district dominates the Corpus Christi skyline. The most significant private enterprise Mrs. Driscoll undertook during her later years was the erection of a luxurious hotel on this natural terrace at the corner of Upper Broadway and Antelope streets overlooking the bay. With a frontage of 160 feet on Broadway and 90 on Antelope, the building consisted of twenty stories. She had conceived the idea of erecting the hotel as early as 1937, probably at the time her divorce became final. But unsettled world conditions and the advent of World War II delayed the construction since the United States government had a monopoly on materials. Although Mrs. Driscoll's campaign duties consumed much of her time, she was able to begin actual construction in 1939.[6]

A memorial designed to honor her late brother, the hotel—the largest and most modern of its type in the Southwest—was completed in 1941. Mrs. Driscoll was warmly applauded for giving the city its finest hotel facility, and the fact that she named it for one of Corpus Christi's best beloved financiers and the first chairman of the Nueces County Navigation District—the Robert Driscoll—won added plaudits.

> . . . the newest and largest hotel and building project ever to be attempted here will carry the name of the late Robert Driscoll, brother of Mrs. Driscoll, who recently let the contracts and directed that construction get under way immediately.
>
> The realization of the actual building of this magnificent office and hotel building is reminiscent of the tradition of enterprise and civic improvement for which Robert Driscoll and the late Bob Driscoll were known.[7]

Architects for the structure were Hedrick and Fox, and McKenzie Construction Company of San Antonio had charge of the erection. Of modified Spanish architecture, with a patio of pure colonial Spanish design, the structure was of reinforced concrete, brick, and tile with polychrome terra-cotta trimming. The first three stories were of black granite and limestone. Mr. Wyatt C. Hedrick of the architectural firm said that the building "was the biggest private building project let in Texas in the past 10 years."[8] Cost of the structure was estimated at $2 million. However, various changes and interior improvements, plus fluctuating market conditions, boosted the cost to a much higher figure, said to have been upwards of $3.5 million.[9]

Built to cater to both tourists and commercial travelers and to provide office space for local businessmen, the edifice was the first of its category in the
section.[10]   Upon completion, the facility contained 322 guest rooms and
apartments and 164 commercial office suites. A special feature was a combination ballroom and auditorium, two stories high, with a seating capacity of
900 to accommodate conventions.[11]   The Robert Driscoll was the first hotel
in Texas with complete air-conditioning specified in the original plans.

Undoubtedly other factors involved in the building of the hotel were that
Mrs. Driscoll's business interests were concentrated in Corpus Christi and she
had been unable to find suitable living quarters after deciding to move from
the Palo Alto ranch into the city. Consequently, she surmounted the twenty-
story edifice with a palatial penthouse designed to meet her own individual
requirements.

Despite the fact that Clara Driscoll was a figure of national prominence and
exceedingly popular in Corpus Christi—even the object of adulation—or because of it, myths evolved as sidewalk philosophers and local citizens watched
the gleaming skyscraper mount to the sky. Over the years the myths have
gathered moss and so have become a part of the Driscoll legend.

Rising from the site at Upper Broadway and Antelope, the Robert Driscoll
stood next to the White Plaza. For many years on the strip overlooking the
city and bay the two hotels stood side by side with only a narrow alley separating them. Why they were thus situated constitutes one of Corpus Christi's
most fantastic stories.

The story attaches to a slender framework of fact. When the administration of the estate fell to Mrs. Driscoll in 1929, the White Plaza was a part of
the inheritance. From 1933 to 1935, when she was out of the country with
her husband, Hal Sevier (American ambassador to Chile), Jack White, erstwhile vaudeville performer and later San Antonio mayor, of whom Mrs. Driscoll disapproved, gained control of the hotel, along with one in Dallas and
another in San Antonio. When the couple returned to Texas, Mrs. Driscoll
brought suit against White to regain control. The federal court, in which the
case was tried, however, decided in favor of the defendant.[12]   At this juncture
fact and fiction part company.

The yarn goes that when the lady lost her case she "swore a mighty oath
that she would build a hotel next to the White Plaza, so tall that she could
stand at a window and vent her displeasure on it in the most suitable way that
occurred to her. And so she did."[13]   The proximity of the hotels with only
an alley between and the fact that the Robert Driscoll was at least four stories
higher lent credence to the yarn.

Even though the tale gained national circulation, it is fabricated from whole cloth without a scintilla of truth in it. Mrs. Driscoll was a spirited person who would not hesitate to stand up for what she felt to be right. But she was neither petty nor crude and—as has been shown—could accept defeat with equanimity. As indicated, she erected the hotel as a monument to her late brother and as a civic enterprise. She chose the site as the most desirable location for such a building.

The "mighty oath" was likewise a part of the fabrication. The same writer states further that "Clara Driscoll was *mucha mujer*, even by Texas standards. A fiery redhead, she could ride, fight, drink, and swear with the gusto of a cowpuncher."[14] Granted the lady was *mucha mujer*. Also she was redheaded. True, she could ride and could indeed fight, especially for the little fellow and the underprivileged. But that she could drink and swear "with the gusto of a cowpuncher" is simply not true. Close friends insisted that in spite of the fact that she was independent and outspoken on occasion, she was not given to profanity. Her vocabulary contained a few innocuous bywords, but obscenities and the use of the Lord's name in vain were beneath her and extrinsic to her personality. Though she was not a religious fanatic, Mrs. Driscoll was a sincere Christian with a profound knowledge of the Bible and forthright respect for high principles. The use of invective was against her religious convictions.

As for the remainder of the accusation, Clara Driscoll was "a controlled drinker."[15] She had to be for the monumental achievements with which history credits her. For that matter, excessive drinking offended her and she avoided the bibulous acquaintance especially in her later years. Her favorite drink was a mild milk punch.[16]

Another version of the myth published in a national magazine and even more widely circulated is equally unfounded.

> Having given away her mansion and large chunks of her fortune, Clara Driscoll established herself in a giant (twelve bathrooms) penthouse atop Corpus Christi's luxurious Driscoll Hotel. She had built the place in a typically willful gesture, after dressing down the manager of another house where she didn't like the service, and promising him she would put up a hotel of her own, tall enough for her to spit on his.[17]

Here again the writer begins with facts and proceeds all too obviously to fiction. Mrs. Driscoll had dispossessed herself of Laguna Gloria, but had won national fame as a liberal philanthropist, and she was a resident of the penthouse atop the Driscoll Hotel. Although parenthesized, the twelve-bathroom fallacy, often repeated, does not escape notice. Intimates laugh at such a gross exaggeration. Naturally the number of bathrooms was determined by the size and architectural arrangement of the apartment, but friends insist that twelve were more than twice the number.

Once more the writer is ignorant of the facts when he credits the manager with ownership and states that Mrs. Driscoll "would put up a hotel of her own." When she erected the Robert Driscoll Hotel, her estate still held the mortgage on the White Plaza, along with two or three other hotels "of her own." It was not until sometime later that the Jack White Interests were able to absolve the indebtedness and gain a title to the property. That Mrs. Driscoll—a woman of impeccable character and one of the nation's most successful businesswomen—"had built the place in a typically willful gesture," is too preposterous for rebuttal.

Mrs. Driscoll occupied her quarters in the Robert Driscoll scarcely four years, a brief period that typified for her both a new beginning and an end. It was the close of a decade of the most productive period of her life as patriot, philanthropist, stateswoman, and entrepreneur. As Women's War Bond chairman of Texas, Mrs. Driscoll—a confirmed pacifist—made a notable contribution to World War II. Giving generously of her time and money, she also traveled and lectured for the cause at her own expense and entertained visitors who came to assist with bond rallies and fund drives. In recognition of her unrivalled demonstration of patriotism, the Veterans of Foreign Wars presented her with the Distinguished Citizenship Medal at a Heroes' Day Ceremony held in Corpus Christi, June 17, 1943. Special guests for the event were Harry Philwin of Memphis, Tennessee, who lost his sight in World War I, and Sergeant William Feigle, the most decorated marine of World War I. Philwin, also a musician, composed a song entitled "Miss Clara," in her honor and sang it at the ceremony.[18]

On June 18 she received the following expression of commendation:

My dear Mrs. Driscoll:

   I wish to offer my very sincere congratulations at your having been awarded the Distinguished Citizenship Medal of the Veterans of Foreign Wars at the impressive ceremonies last evening.

   You have deservedly been awarded this medal as a sincere gesture of appreciation from a community which is aware of the many services you have rendered it.

   With every good wish, I am

                              Sincerely,

                              A. C. McCaughan, Mayor[19]

Only a month before, Mrs. Driscoll had had as her guests in Austin Sergeant Al Schmidt and Mrs. Schmidt at a special rally at the state capital. Sergeant Schmidt, the Marine Corps's number one hero of World War II, was blinded in a machine gun nest on Guadalcanal.

It is thought (from an examination of her personal effects) that Mrs. Driscoll planned to enjoy her new apartment overlooking the city she loved and served, to live leisurely after the close of the war and return to writing. Notes and material among her carefully filed private papers and memorabilia indicate that she was seriously considering the writing of three books: her memoirs with focus on her sixteen-year career as national Democratic committeewoman, a volume based on her travels, in which she would combine the numerous articles she published under the pseudonym of "A Texas Girl" in various state newspapers, and her own individual saga of the Alamo.

What an enrichment these three projected books would have brought to the American tradition! And what a loss to both history and letters that Clara Driscoll did not live to write them! There is probably no more voluminous collection of papers, documents, newspaper clippings and other archival materials dealing with the Alamo and the Daughters of the Republic of Texas extant today than the accumulation preserved by Clara Driscoll. Interestingly, but not surprisingly, the material represents a wide range and scope and is not limited to Clara Driscoll and the Alamo per se.

Before settling down in her apartment, Mrs. Driscoll had placed in storage many of her cherished possessions assembled from various parts of the world and formerly housed at Laguna Gloria. Many of these treasures she removed to the apartment: books, paintings, tapestries, rugs, furnishings, art objects, china, silver, etc., along with her massive collection of private papers, scrapbooks, personal notes, and memorabilia referred to above. Indeed the spacious and elegant apartment had been designed to accommodate the items to which she had attached sentiment over the years.

But what gave Clara Driscoll the most personal pleasure during these years was her little black- and white-spotted fox terrier, appropriately named Spots. The pet, to which she was unabashedly devoted, frequently accompanied her on short trips. Mrs. Driscoll's chauffeur, Phil L. Highshew (truncated to High) helped to take care of Spots. Mrs. Driscoll made private arrangements with High, whom she trusted implicitly and who measured up to her trust, to continue the care of Spots after her death. The adored little terrier survived his mistress by five or six years. It was said that Spots was exceedingly intelligent and returned his mistress' affection.

12

World Traveler

CLARA DRISCOLL WAS RECOGNIZED AS AN inveterate traveler. Attention has been given to her schooling in Paris and travel abroad in the company of her mother, to her European honeymoon, her journeys in South America as the wife of diplomat Hal Sevier, during World War I, and in Europe for the peace negotiations afterward, then again in 1933, when her husband served as United States ambassador to Chile.

She circled the globe three times, once by her eighteenth birthday. Notebooks indicate that she made her third world tour with her husband in the 1920s.[1] Sailing from Los Angeles, she disembarked first at Rio de Janeiro, thence she sailed to Honolulu, then on to the Orient. The Far East held fascination for her. In her travel notes she often resorted to illustrations with freehand sketches of such places as Batavia, Singapore, Calcutta, Hong Kong, Canton, Shanghai, and Delphi.[2] Hong Kong especially impressed Clara Driscoll. It was, she said, the most attractive harbor next to Rio de Janeiro that she had visited.[3]

She made at least fourteen crossings to Europe, including junkets both before and after her marriage.[4] Wherever she went the Alamo story followed her. In many places over the world her relationship to the shrine became known. But her chronicle of the sacred relic of Texas history was the story of the sacrifice of the patriots Travis, Bowie, Bonham, and Crockett during the thirteen-day siege. Those who heard it imparted it to others thus keeping the beautiful saga in circulation among the nations of the world. In Japan, children knew of the Alamo. When Dr. McIver Furman and Mrs. Furman visited the Orient a few years ago, they felt the impact of Clara Driscoll's influence. When the doctor, who has a professional interest in children, engaged some in conversation in the streets and told them he was from Texas, they echoed in delightful chorus: "Al–e–mo, Al–e–mo, Al–e–mo!" To the slant-eyed children of the Orient the Alamo was synonymous with Texas.

Before settling down permanently in Texas, after finishing her education abroad, Clara visited various countries throughout the world with her contemporary and close friend, Florence (Flo) Eagar, who later illustrated *In The Shadow of the Alamo*. Though she enjoyed the scintillating capitals of the world, the young traveler also found the remote and rarely traveled places exhilarating. Historic and literary significance of the countries she visited interested her, together with their legendry and romance. In addition, religion played an integral role in her travels. She collected Bibles in various languages over the world and unusual religious curios and made a study of religious customs of the different countries she visited.

Travel articles appearing in Texas newspapers under the pseudonym of "A Texas Girl" yield penetrating insight into Clara Driscoll, the person. She had a flair for portraying atmosphere and recapturing emotional and spiritual response, along with the ability to pull her reader into the scene. Frequently the immediacy of the locale inspired reflections and philosophical commentaries that were an index to her character. As stated in a preceding chapter, she meticulously preserved printed copies of these articles, annotated with additional handwritten notes, with the intention of incorporating them into a book in her later years.

One of the less frequently traveled places Clara Driscoll remembered with mixed, but lasting, emotions was the ancient town of Funchal, capital of the Portuguese island of Madeira. With her infallible sense of history, she recalled that another of the islands of the archipelago—Porto Santo—had been a favorite haunt of Columbus, who had married the governor's daughter, and that the British had brought Napoleon to the island of Madeira in 1815 en route to his place of detention at St. Helena.

As the ship cruised along the coast for two hours, the traveler got an accurate glimpse of what awaited her:

> It is a veritable paradise, and one of the quaintest, most picturesque spots among the out-of-the-way corners of the globe. From the ship we could see the town nestling in the great amphitheater of mountains towering up some 2,000 feet [actually 4,000 feet], and in the brilliant sunlight the white walls of the houses gleamed out like blocks of chalk against the verdant and gorgeously colored background of luxuriant tropical foliage, flowers, and vineyards.

Though some records credit Joao Goncalves Zarco, one of Prince Henry's navigators, with the discovery of Madeira in 1418, legend points to an earlier time and to two lovers. The sweethearts, an Englishman by the name of

Robert Mackim and Anne d'Arfet, daughter of a nobleman of high birth, were in flight from England bound for Brittany in 1345, when a gale blew their vessel off course. The ship landed on the shores of the island of Madeira. As the crew extricated the craft, the lovers investigated the beauties of the island. Meanwhile, the captain and his men, in order to take advantage of a favorable wind, set sail and abandoned the lovers. The couple inhabited the island for the remainder of their lives and their gravesites mark the location of the Santa Clara Church, the oldest in Madeira, and its adjoining convent.

No sooner was Clara's ship moored in the bay than it was surrounded by a fleet of small craft that displayed the products on which the island's economy depended: wickerwork, laces, linens, fruits, flowers. Small Portuguese boys dived for coins thrown to them by the spectators on deck of the vessel. So expert were the divers that one seldom missed and the passengers found the sport to be highly diverting.

Many surprises were in store for the young travelers when Clara and the other passengers were rowed ashore. The very first was the unique means of locomotion designed to transport the visitors around the town. There were no conventional means of transportation, no carriages or other wheeled conveyances. Vehicles had to operate on runners since all of the streets, except those along the water's edge, were exceedingly steep and paved with sharp cobblestones, too difficult to manipulate on foot or by wheels. The most common type of transportation was the bullock-drawn *carro*, a low two-seated sledge topped by a canopy and guided by a man at the side with a pole. To insure smoothness of operation on the stones, the men in charge placed greased cloths under the runners. As a result the streets became as slick as glass. Another means of conveyance, and much more luxurious, was the *rede*, a linen hammock covered with a gaily striped awning and swung from a pole carried on the shoulders of two Portuguese. The motion of the *rede* was soothing and restful and one lay "back among the cushions drinking in the soft, warm air filled with the delicious aroma of shrubs and flowers . . . a perfume as subtle and seductive as the wine of the vineyards."

The actual descent down the mountains was breathtaking. It involved the use of "snowless" wickerwork toboggans. Clara's description merits attention:

> This was accomplished in sledges made of baskets started at the top of the mountains and allowed to slide down a passageway like a chute to the bottom. The sledges are steered by two men. They perch themselves on either and with a touch of the foot keep the sledge on its course at the turnings. To say this was exciting expresses it but mildly. One sat in momentary expectation of being dashed to pieces.[1]

Everywhere Clara found the high walls overhung with great vines and fuchsias, heliotrope, and clematis, along with the red-tiled roofs of blue-, pink-, and yellow-tinted houses, mellowed by time, intriguing. Even though it was mid-winter, the climate was so mild that visitors reveled in tropical sunshine and weather like spring. The terrace at the hotel where food was served was scenic. "Around us were the vine-covered hills, above us a sky as blue as sapphire, and below lay one of the prettiest harbors in all Europe."

But it was the old church of Santa Clara and its adjoining convent that provided Clara Driscoll with her richest experience at Funchal. She had heard of the Order of the Poor Clares that centuries before had inhabited the convent. The members had been forced by parental authority to become cloistered nuns. Later, laws prohibiting this subjugation were passed and the order became extinct. A carved, highbacked chair in the choir, bearing the date 1736, was said to have been the one in which the last mother superior of the order died. Still there lingered stories that the nuns of this early order were so lovely that tourists visited the island just to see them.

As these thoughts were racing through Clara's mind, she stood across the narrow street before the entrance. Suddenly the huge oaken doors swung open and framed the slight figure of a nun. The woman wore an immaculate white habit and her face was "as fair . . . as if cut from a cameo." Then just as suddenly the door swung shut.

Clara crossed the street and lifted the knocker. Again the door opened and the nun stood waiting for her visitor to speak. Hesitating, "Do you speak English?" Clara asked.

"I am English," the nun answered in one of the sweetest voices Clara had ever heard. Clara's surprise was obvious. It had occurred to her that only a native woman would bury herself in such an isolated place. The nun asked if her visitor would like to be shown over the convent and the church. Clara answered in the affirmative and the white-habited English woman led the way through dim and musty corridors, damp enough to chill the blood, and across ill-paved courtyards, as she recounted the history of the convent and recalled its traditions.

The two entered the church of Santa Clara. Had the visitor heard of the eloping couple who discovered Madeira? They were buried there, the nun told Clara. A lowly cross identified the graves. Then the nun directed her guest to an altar behind which was a prone statue of the Saviour. This, she remarked, was the church's greatest curiosity. She explained that on each Sunday in Lent the statue was carried out among the people and was received with extreme reverence. The original was in Lisbon. The one in Santa Clara was only a copy. The nun told the story of how a beggar appeared at the monastery in Lisbon and requested food and lodging for the night The monks granted his request but, doubtful of his motives, locked the door to his room. The next morning when they unlocked the door, the beggar was gone and in his place was the wooden statue of the Saviour.

Unable to contain herself any longer, Clara asked: "How is it that you are out here on this island, so far away from your home?" The nun informed her visitor that the convent belonged to the Franciscan Order of the Miserrairri of Mary with which she was affiliated.

"We go where we are sent. A nun's home is wherever her order places her."

"But are you contented here?"

"No, we are not contented here because our work is going badly." The governor of the island was trying to drive the members of the order away, and many had already been forced to leave Portugal, the nun explained. "But we are determined to fight it out to the end," she protested.

Although the governor lacked the authority to remove the order by force, he had influenced the people of the island against sending their children to the convent school, thus cutting off their main source of revenue.

"That makes it hard for you," Clara observed.

A painful expression came over the nun's face. "We manage to get along," she replied. Whereupon Clara took a gold coin from her purse and forced it into the woman's hand.

The nun looked down at the gold piece. "For the poor?" she asked.

"For any that need it."

"You are very good and I shall pray for you."

"I hope you will." Clara felt that she would like to have the nun's prayers. The two had returned to the door and the nun politely opened it for her visitor to depart.

But Clara hesitated. She looked at her guide intently. "You are very pretty"—she felt a compulsion to say this—"far too pretty to be shut up in this gloomy old convent. You are so pretty that I came in here to see you again after the first glimpse I caught of you at the convent door."

The nun flushed a little and smiled. But Clara did not feel that she was annoyed by the compliment. The nun opened the palm of her hand in which she held the shining coin. "You see," she said, her smile deepening, "this proves that you are mistaken about my being out of place here. You said you came to see me, and through your visit I have received this help for our cause." As Clara said goodbye, she felt sad in her heart. She repeated to herself that *the nun was too pretty to be there!*

On the evening that Clara's ship steamed slowly out of the harbor, she stood on the deck and watched the lights of Funchal grow dim. She did not think of the miracle of the Lisbon beggar. She thought first of the lovers whose graves were marked by the crude wooden cross and whose pall was the vivid green of the island's foliage and the varied colors of its flowers. Then she thought of the little English nun—"and of her beautiful face and her great sad eyes, in which there was a look," Clara Driscoll would "always remember, and of her soft sweet voice" Clara Driscoll would "never forget."

Clara Driscoll had toured Spain earlier, accompanied by her mother, before she finished her studies in the convent near Paris. Her last visit had been in the spring, the ideal time to visit the country when the sunshine entices people out-of-doors and orange blossoms scent the air.

The midwinter visit in the early 1900s was for the express purpose of introducing the country she had found so delightful to her close friend and traveling companion, Flo Eagar. Entering the Strait of Gibraltar, the steamer on which the ladies were traveling passed under the forbidding British fortress—the Rock of Gibraltar, once thought by the Phoenicians to be one of the Pillars of Hercules, the other ostensibly standing opposite on the African coast. The vessel glided into the bay of Algeciras, where it moored to permit passengers to take a small steamer ashore.

From Algeciras, their first point of disembarkation, the girls boarded a train for Granada—a province of Andalusia in the Sierra Nevada. It was a part of Spain in which history read like romance and whose beauty cast a spell. "Andalusia—the very name has music in it." Upon arrival, the travelers took accommodations at the Washington Irving Hotel and prepared for the exciting days of sight-seeing ahead.

In the streets of the old Moorish city on a typical day one could see various types of the Spaniard from the aristocrat in his "elaborate turnout" to the threadbare mendicant with his grubby hands outstretched, "imploring [a person] for the love of God to give him *cinco centavos*." Frequently the beggars were brown-eyed, bespangled gypsies wearing gaily-colored shawls and dancing in the street or road as they begged for alms. They went in droves and seemed to spring up out of the ground, ubiquitous. Wherever one's carriage stopped, they immediately surrounded it, clamoring for money. The stranger was the beggars' mark. Natives looked upon them with disdain, turned them away with a haughty *"Perdóneme usted, por Dios!"*

Had the gypsies been less peripatetic, color still would have dominated the scene. Invariably one observed slender *torreros* in blue and gold costume, their scarlet-embroidered capes over an arm, engaged in animated conversation; Spanish *señoritas* proudly wearing the headdress of their country—the graceful *mantilla*; the Spanish gentlemen strolling leisurely by draped in their inevitable black capes, one corner thrown back over the shoulder to reveal the rich lining of red velvet or yellow silk; the young flower girl displaying her blossoms of veriegated hues, entreating the pedestrian in her most dulcet tones to purchase her nosegays.

Spanish gentlemen had a custom to which Clara found difficulty in becoming accustomed. They called out to a lady in the street, not from insolence, but simply to express their appreciation, almost as if it were expected. Such expressions as *¡Qué guapo!* ("how goodlooking!"), *¡Qué bonito!* ("how beautiful!"), and *¡Qué gracia!* ("how gracious!") were common. The gentlemen would even walk beside a lady and comment on her beauty or her dress.

But the predominating characteristic of the Spanish people, according to Clara Driscoll, was their utter disregard of time. Closely allied to this trait was their belief that tomorrow would take care of itself and their resignation and acceptance of what is to be will be. Nothing could be more applicable to the Spaniard than the admonition of the Saviour in Matthew 6:34:

> Take therefore no thought for the morrow; for the morrow will take thought for the things of itself. Sufficient unto the day is the evil thereof.

Clara states further that " . . . this acceptance of the inevitable without a cry of protest . . . is . . . his [the Spaniard's] chief charm and at the same time his greatest fault. With the Spaniard, as with the Mohammedan, all is left to kismet, and perhaps, after all, they have learned the true philosophy of life."

Clara and Miss Eagar had chosen Granada not only because of the exquisite scenery but for the location of the Alhambra, the ancient palace and fortress of the Moorish monarchs. Before concentrating on it, however, they visited the cathedral of Santa Maria de la Encarnación—magnificently ornamented with jasper and colored marbles—where in one of its numerous chapels, the *Capella Real* ("Royal Chapel") were the tombs of Ferdinand and Isabella.

Since their hotel was within walking distance of the old Moorish palace, from which Boabdil, the last sovereign of Granada, had been expelled in 1492, the travelers set out on foot to reach it. As they walked to the Alhambra on that leafless February day, when the winter sun failed to discourage the chilly air, Clara kept thinking of how different the very roadway had been upon her first visit. Then those same trees from either side, tall and full-foliaged, formed a thick verdant arch overhead under which deep shadows played and, in places where the sun penetrated the green canopy, flecks of gold etched the shadows and danced across the pathway.

The girls entered the Alhambra through *El Patio de los Arrayanes* ("Court of the Myrtles"), which derived its name from a pond in the center bordered on the sides by hedges of the shrubs. From this impressive entrance court they proceeded to the *Sala de los Embajadores* ("Hall of the Ambassadors")— a two-story-high reception and throne room. There the decorations of arabesque figures and the inscriptions of Cufic (Kufic) character were perhaps the most lavish ornamentations in the entire palace. In these decorations the human face was not shown as that was forbidden by the Koran. Opposite to the entrance was the site of the throne.

Next the girls were charmed by the *Patio de los Leones* ("Court of the Lions"), in the center of which was the fountain, whose alabaster basin was supported by white marble figures of twelve Assyrian lions—the symbols of strength and courage. Opening onto this court were three major salons. One of these was the *Sala de las Frutas* ("Salon of the Fruits"), where the American writer Washington Irving was supposed to have written *Conquest of Granada* (1829) and *The Alhambra* (1832), his Spanish counterpart of *The Sketch Book*.

Another was the Hall of the Abencerrages, which held special interest because of the history attached to it. It was the room in which Boabdil, Granada's last monarch, massacred three chiefs of the Abencerrage line because Chief Hamet of the illustrious family was engaged in an intrigue with the sovereign's wife. The reddish stain around the fountain was from the blood of the victims. Square in shape and with a lofty dome and trellised windows at its base, the room was richly decorated in blue, brown, red, and gold.

The visitors devoted an entire morning to the exploration of the Moorish palace. In the afternoon they visited the outlying building of foremost significance—the *Generalife*. Called the "Garden of the Builder" and possibly dating from the late thirteenth century, the structure served as a summer palace of the Moslem kings. The courts and gardens of the *Generalife* were equally as elegant as those of the Alhambra. There was also an intriguing link of one of the principal gardens with the Hall of the Abencerrages. In it a 600-year-old tree, designated the *Cipres de la Sultana* ("Cypress of the Queen"), had the distinction of being the trysting place of the lovers.

To climax their day of sight-seeing, an hour before sunset the girls ascended the *Torre de la Vela* ("Watch Tower") to get a view of the old Moorish capital below and to observe the constantly changing shadows on the snow-capped peaks of the Sierras. As she reveled in the splendor of "the white summits reflecting the opalescent tints of the declining sun," Clara was reminded of the story of the conquered Boabdil in retreat across the Sierra Nevadas, driven from his beloved city:

He turned and stood on the spot which is now called *El Ultimo Suspiro del Moro*

("The Last Sigh of the Moor") and with tears in his eyes gazed at the fair city he had lost.

His mother, Aisha, noting his grief, taunted him with the words, "Weep not like a woman for what you could not defend like a man."

Clara concludes the story with the translation of a Spanish ballad on the surrender of Granada:

> There was crying in Granada when the sun was going down,
> Some calling on the Trinity, some calling on Mahoun.
> Here passed away the Koran, therein the cross was borne,
> And here was heard the Christian bell and there the Moorish horn;
> 'Te Deum laudamus' was of the Alcala sung,
> Down from the Alhambra's minarets, were all the crescents flung,
> The arms thereon of Aragon and Castile they display,
> One king comes in triumph, one weeping goes away.

But as her train whirled through the magnificent Sierra Nevada to Malaga, where the two ladies would board ship, Clara Driscoll remembered the Spain of happier memories and warmer days. She recalled the Alhambra—the enchanted palace—in the spring when she had read Washington Irving's delightful stories in the environs of the ruins, and her thoughts reverted to the time

> When everywhere you looked the black eyes of the people of Andalusia flashed out at you. When the weird haunting melody of a *Seguidilla* floated through one's brain and caused a feeling of rest to steal over one because of its very sadness, or when the twang of a guitar and the sound of castanets sent the blood quicker through one's veins and when the perfumed air of Seville with its groves of orange trees filled your nostrils and, stealing over your senses, soothed you like a narcotic.

From childhood Clara Driscoll had associated the Orient with the mysteries of magic carpets and open sesame treasures of the tales of *Arabian Nights Entertainment*. Then by the time she was eighteen or nineteen

> The East with its . . . white mosques and gilded minarets, its bazaars with rare silks and fragrant perfumes, its veiled women and turbaned men. . . . The East, whose centuries of history stand written on the crumbling walls of its ruined temples, obelisks, and pyramids, and buried under the trackless vasts of its silent desert . . .

became for her a startling reality.

Her introduction to the Orient was through the city of Algiers, the capital and main seaport of Algeria in North Africa. Under French influence since 1830, the lower portion of the city—or the foreign part—was reminiscent of the broad boulevards, flowering squares, and the Parisian architecture with which Clara was familiar from her schooldays.

But the chief section of Algiers was the Old Arab Quarter. Moreover, its source of enchantment for the visitor was the life and color of the people who milled about its streets—a people seemingly misplaced in a city where the architecture of an alien race had supplanted much of their own, but a race who walked arrogantly, almost defiantly, in the atmosphere of their conquerors, with the unmistakeable dignity born of native heritage. Later Clara would compare the tall Arabs of Algiers with other Orientals, as she visited other countries of the East, but in none would she find a similar royalty of bearing and eyes reflecting such untameness and smoldering fire as these bronzed descendants of the Moors.

The base of the quarter and center around which Arabian life revolved was the Place du Gouverement, which served as a traffic reference point and from which several important roads radiated. Near the Place du Gouverement was the mosque of *El Tiber* ("The Great")—an excellent example of Moorish design that had been left undisturbed.

Since the religious culture of every country she visited played an important part in her enjoyment, Clara and her friend chose the mosque as their first place of inspection. Whether they were aware of it or not, the time they chose was when the Mohammedans were engaged in worship. In an open court before the entrance stood the ablution fountain where the "faithful" washed their feet before entering the sacred edifice.

Not knowing that strangers were expected to follow the custom, the girls entered without complying. To their amazement, they were stopped summarily on the threshold by "fanatical looking Arabs," who tied large flapping slippers over their shoes, ostensibly to prevent the dirt of the street from defiling the holy carpets.

Inside the immense structure, the ladies discovered a "wilderness of space" intersected by marble columns arising from a floor covered by the richest and rarest of carpets from the looms of the East. With their faces turned toward Mecca, several Mohammedans were engaged in prayer. Intermittently the worshippers interrupted their low monotonous chanting to bow and touch their heads three times to the floor in front of them. So engrossed were they in their rituals that they paid no attention whatsoever to the unbelievers who had invaded their sanctuary.

Outside the mosque the travelers joined the throng glutting the streets. It was a diverse panorama of movement and color but totally absorbing. There were women arrayed in white, their legs enveloped in voluminous baggy trousers and their faces concealed behind thick veils. Only their dreamy and melancholy eyes were visible above the folds of the masks—eyes that appeared grotesque by the blacking of the lids with khol, a dark preparation used cosmetically.

In contrast there were female gypsies, wilder and fiercer than their veiled counterparts—women whose darker faces and aggressive manners were emphasized by massive rings and baubles of barbaric design jangling noisily from brow, ears, arms, and ankles.

(Absent from the group were the inmates of houses aligning the dim narrow alleys and almost touching each other from the tops—seraglios whose closely latticed windows hid the curious gaze of women of the harems.)

Among the men walked a fierce black-browed, swarthy-faced band of turbaned Bedouins from the great Sahara stretching its sterile sand wastes south to the sea. Holding themselves aloof from the rest, their eagle eyes appraising the scene critically, was another group—the lighter-faced Moors, their flowing snow-white burnooses wrapped about them. Nearby stood still other representatives of the motley population of the Orient—flat-nosed, thick-lipped aborigines, their bodies black as ebony and with ages of degeneracy mirrored in their faces.

Everywhere one looked business in the square was brisk. Bazaars and shops offered everything the Western imagination could conjure: curios from every corner of the globe, prayer rugs from Persia, carved ivories from India, perfumes, articles of scented sandalwood, intricately wrought necklaces, headpieces of beaten silver set with flashing gems, embroidered fabrics interwoven with threads of gold. In the midst of it all snake charmers plied their art with writhing reptiles before them. In stalls some men sat cross-legged making shoes, while others busied themselves at light carpentry work. Gambling was engaged in openly, and smokers of the *narghile* ("water pipe")—called by foreigners "bubble bubble"—were much in evidence. Just as often were seen men smoking the long slender-stemmed pipes with small bowls. These were the addicts of the lethal narcotic common to the Orient and known as hashish, which brought sensational dreams to the smoker as it destroyed him.

Meanwhile, from time to time strings of camels approached the square bearing loads of grain and other products from the outlying farms. Although obedient and submissive to their drivers, these beasts of burden—noted for their endurance and stamina and rightly termed "ships of the desert"—moved proudly, their heads held high, invariably disdainful of strangers.

It was a familiar scene that would be repeated many times, with but slight variations, and to which the two travelers would grow accustomed as they toured other parts of the Orient. But it was one that never lost its appeal.

One of the strangest places on the itinerary of Clara and her friend was the island of Malta in the Mediterranean. When the island was associated with the Apostle Paul in Biblical times it was known as Melita. The pawn of many warring groups over the centuries—the Greeks, Romans, Carthaginians, and Saracens, and in modern times, the French and English—the island, though it seemed austere, later proved to be rich in religious and historic lore. From the sea Malta appeared to be a dreary study in monochromatic tones of faded yellow. Neither a single tree nor a flowering shrub, nor even a tinted roof, relieved the dull monotony.

Still the little port was teeming with activity as the passenger ship bringing the girls dropped anchor. Several British warships were in the harbor, along with an American military transport with the Stars and Stripes fluttering from its masthead, and other craft from various parts of the world. Soon converging at the gangway were small rowboats to transfer the passengers ashore.

The erstwhile fortress of the soldier-priests known as the Knights of Saint John, an order of hospitalers founded in Jerusalem in the Middle Ages, the island reflected their influence. After their expulsion from Rhodes, Charles V gave the knights a grant to settle on the Maltese archipelago in 1530. In exchange they were to make an annual tribute of a falcon as a symbol of the island's suzerainty to Spain and to defend Tripoli in Libya against the encroachment of the Muslims.

Although the islanders resented the knights at the outset, they eventually accepted them. Depending upon a separate economy, the knights drew their revenue from estates owned by the order in the richest countries of Europe and from privateering against the Turks and their allies. Through the sixteenth, seventeenth, and eighteenth centuries they harassed Turkish commerce and participated as an allied Christian power in the Battle of Lepanto in 1571, which practically destroyed the Turkish navy.

After this strategic victory, the knights proceeded with the building of their capital of Valletta and their hospital. But with their acquisition of wealth and security, the priests became less martial and their rule of the island ended in June, 1798, when Napoleon occupied Malta six days en route to Egypt. After his defeat on the Nile, Napoleon attempted to convert Malta into a center of French trade. He tried to implement his program by despoiling the churches and interfering with religious and local customs. Led by the knights, the Maltese openly rebelled on September 2, 1798. Finally, after two years of warfare, with the aid of the British, the Portuguese, and their Neapolitan allies, the Maltese forced the French to surrender. By the Treaty of Paris in 1814, England acknowledged the Maltese as British subjects and guaranteed them freedom of religion and the rights of representative government.

Upon approaching the island, Clara noted the spot on the coast where in A. D. 60, the Apostle Paul was shipwrecked on his way to preach to the Romans. In Citta Vecchia, the ancient capital of Malta, she visited the cathedral built upon the site of the house of Publius, chief of the island, where St. Paul was entertained as a guest after his rescue and where he healed Publius's father, together with many others, before departing three months later. Publius was said to have been Paul's first convert of the island.

The drive to the ancient capital was eventful as it meandered through miles of fields, to the right and left, enclosed by stone walls. It was here along this route that the visitors encountered the first evidence of color on the island. Interspersing the golden stalks of waving grain were myriads of scarlet poppies.

In Valletta, the capital established by the knights, however, much color was apparent in the Church of St. John, which had been created by the order and in which the tombs of the hospitalers were ornamented with multi-hued marbles. Additional color was reflected in the walls of the cathedral faced with green marble and the floor paved with slabs memorializing the knights. Also in Valletta the visitors found the Governor's Palace, which in the old days had been the official residence of the grand master of the knights, both colorful and imposing. Not surprisingly, its most interesting room was the armory in which were displayed innumerable relics of warfare. The shops in Valletta attracted the tourists with their fine Maltese lace and intricate gold and silver filigree work.

The Maltese people, on the whole, resembled the Portuguese. Women played a less prominent role in the social life than men. At the time of this visit, the women still wore a uniform black costume, with a voluminous hood and cape and long veil in front which particlly concealed their faces. Called the *faldetta*, the severe attire was said to be the women's payment of penance for the dalliance of their sex with the French, who had harassed and abused the Maltese during their occupation.

Shortly before their departure, the girls visited the Maltese catacombs and an old catacomb chapel, outside the walls of Mdina. Another monument to the departed knights and a stark one, the chapel was decorated with human bones. The ghastly ornamentations were arranged in fantastic design on the walls and above the altar "and everywhere the empty sockets of skulls looked down." Over the altar was the following inscription:

> The world is a theater and human life is really a tragedy.
> Every earthly thing is a personification of vanity.
> Death breaks and discolors the illusions and is the boundary
>   of all wordly things.
> Let those who visit this place ponder with these maxims,

pray for perpetual rest to the dead lying herein.
And carry with them a lively remembrance of death.
Peace be with you.

As they hastened to leave the depressing scene, the girls certainly concurred that the Knights of St. John, like Paul himself, *had fought a good fight—finished their course—kept the faith*, and so earned *perpetual rest*.

In Egypt Clara Driscoll spent the day on the Nile and imagined how Cleopatra felt in the royal barge with Mark Anthony beside her. She paid a brief call to Ramses II and marvelled at how well preserved "the Pharaoh of captivity" was. As she noted Ramses II and others whose centuries-old mummified bodies were entombed with his, but in separate sarcophagi, she could not resist conjecture:

Was it for this they [the kings] built their great time-effacing tombs? Was it for the idle gaze of strange people from strange countries that they took such care that their bodies should be preserved? Was it that they had a premonition that through the dim centuries . . . the remains of all that had been mortal of these soulless bodies would be . . . laid under glass in a museum?

She devoted a day to the pyramids of Giza and acquired new dimensions of time and space.

Clara and her traveling companion chose to traverse the short distance between Cairo and Giza in a horse-drawn vehicle instead of taking the trolley. An open carriage permitted them to enjoy the scenery and the movement along the road. The trolley line was to their left, and the girls "shuddered" as the "Western innovation" rushed by. The eight-mile drive on the cool, acacia-bordered road, begun in early morning, was refreshing, and the sight-seers were spared the scorching rays of the African sun that would beat down mercilessly a few hours hence. It was a busy time:

Fellahin from the mud villages along the Nile, their blue and white cotton robes floating in the early morning breeze; soft-gliding, silent, veiled women with great earthenware pitchers poised on their shoulders and dreamy, melancholy eyes looking at one over their purdahs; strings of camels carrying their burdens with proud, up-lifted noses sniffing the cool air; little donkeys trotting briskly along, kept to a lively gait by the shrill cries and incessant prodding of the drivers; little Arab children weighted down by the great loads of grass, rice, sticks, and cane they carried on their shoulders.

En route the ladies rented a basket conveyance equipped with exceedingly large tires to cope with the desert sand and arranged for the services of a tall, graceful Arab to act as dragoman. He was knowledgeable and especially efficient at discouraging the turbaned Bedouins eager to commercialize their services.

As the girls and their escorts approached the rocky plateau of the desert, the ancient monuments loomed from a distance in sharp outline against the blue Egyptian sky. But it was only when they stood at the base of the three Great Pyramids of Giza erected by the fourth-dynasty pharaohs—Khufu (Cheops), Khafri, and Mycerenus—that Clara felt the tremendous impact of the ancient tombs. There, covering an expanse of thirteen acres, the Great Pyramid—that erected by Khufu—measured (according to Clara's statistics) over 700 feet at each of the four sides of the base with a height of 451 feet. Approximately two and one-half million stones, each averaging two and one-half tons, comprised the immense structure. When Clara pondered these dimensions seriously, together with the fact that it required the labor of one hundred thousand men twenty years to build the monument, she reflected:

> What mechanical device aided human labour in lifting those heavy weights?
> What endless suffering, drudgery, and death attended their erection!
> What lives of toil for those hundreds of souls who were said to have worked twenty years on the great pyramid . . . the mausoleum of Khufu! . . .

But these somber reflections did not deter the Texas girl from the temptation of adventure. She climbed up the side of the Great Pyramid and looked through the narrow opening that led into the funerary chambers, long since vandalized. Then "with the assistance of two strong Arabs . . . went to the top." *There from the pyramids of Giza Clara Driscoll looked down the ages*:

> To one who likes to look down on the earth from any great height the view below was superbly magnificent. At the first glance . . . you are made forcibly conscious of the burying ground of Egypt's kings. Tombs rise out of the sands of the desert like spectral shapes. . . . The great Nile, stern, sinister, winds its sluggish course through the green fields that are dependent for existence on its bounty.
> To the east lies Cairo with its mazes of roofs and domes, out of which rise tall and graceful the minarets of three hundred and sixty mosques. To the west stretches the undulating desert, rolling to the horizon. Southward lies the site of the buried city of Memphis and the pyramids of Sakkara. To the southwest, apparently no more than half a mile distant, is an object the shape of which differs from all the rest of the tombs. It is one at which we gaze earnestly—it is the Sphinx.

Although Clara admitted the ascent was difficult and very tiring, she said that going up was just a matter of "being pulled and pushed" and that she had faith in her assistants, "... these Arabs with the agility of cats and the strength of steel in their muscular bodies give an absolute feeling of confidence and security...."

But the descent was extremely hazardous. After discovering the Sphinx, Clara could hardly wait to come down, so eager was she to scrutinize the enigmatic monument with the head of a man on the recumbent figure of a lion.

> My one vivid recollection of coming down the pyramid is of a long tumble through space, interrupted now and then, by the clutches of strong brown hands. That my feet ever touched the stones I cannot remember.

At this point the dragoman brought up a wiry young Bedouin, who proposed to climb the Great Pyramid and return in seven minutes flat for six shillings! Clara told the man he could have the money, and the feat was accomplished. "It was marvelous with what rapidity he climbed up the rough surface. It frightened us to look at his descent. Each moment it seemed as if he would fall." After Clara paid the Bedouin, her interpreter informed her, with almost studied indifference, that several of these men were killed every year in attempting this feat. Then Clara was less than pleased with herself for having encouraged a man to endanger his life for money.

The travelers spent an hour with the Sphinx, viewing the monstrosity from all possible angles. Tradition has it that the immense figure carved from a single block of stone and whose huge paws once held a small temple was placed at the edge of the desert as a propitiatory offering to the gods to keep the sands back from the Nile. Ironically, the problem at the time was to prevent the sands from engulfing the monument.

Venice, with its fresh breeze from the Adriatic Sea, narrow canals, and low-arched bridges; Venice, with its impassioned music, gondolas, and gondoliers, its doges' castles and haunted palaces rising out of the water, was for Clara Driscoll the source of combined romance and literary reminiscence. Arriving at the stroke of twelve midnight, the girls felt themselves under a spell of enchantment from the start. "From that moment on we were under the irresistible spell that Venice holds for all who enter her quiet mysterious waterways."

Almost immediately, after entering the gondola at the station, to be taxied to the hotel, Clara was reminded of Othello, the dusky Moor of Venice, who won the blonde Desdemona with heroic tales of his military prowess, only to strangle her because of his blind jealousy and kill himself upon learning the truth.

Then she imagined the proud face of Faliero peering through the shutters of a low casement—Faliero, the doge who revenged a lady's honor and met a traitor's death. The memory of another Italian who paid a penalty for love assailed her. It was the sweet singer and composer Alessandro Stradella, who eloped with the fiancée of a Venetian senator only to die for his folly. At least eight nineteenth-century operas and one novel had canonized the legendary hero.

As the dark funereal boat glided underneath the Bridge of Sighs, connecting the Palace of the Doges with the prison, favorite lines from Byron's *Childe Harold's Pilgrimage* tumbled through Clara's mind:

> I stood in Venice on the Bridge of Sighs;
> A palace and a prison on each hand;
> I saw from out the wave her structures rise
> As from the stroke of the enchanter's wand
> A thousand years their cloudly wings expand
> Around me, and a dying Glory smiles
> O'er the far times, when many a subject land
> Looked to the winged Lion's marble piles
> Where Venice sate in state, throned on her hundred isles!

Clara attributed her rich power of recall to "the witching hour of night when the mind runs riot and intensifies . . . the thousand fanciful musings of the past."

On one side of the hotel was the Ducal Palace with its pillared arcades gleaming white in the moonlight, except for the red ones, from where in the days of the Republic death sentences were announced. Beyond was Saint Mark's Square with its pigeons, pedestaled lion, campanille tower, its shops, and cathedral.

Like all tourists, the girls spent much time in the square. They fed the pigeons, "so tame that they lighted on one's hand in friendly confidence." They wandered through the cool shadowy aisles of the cathedral, whose entrance of colorful mosaics was accentuated by the gilded horse monument. As always the foreign shops filled with exotic treasures lured the visitors. Venetian shops on the square offered a choice of old brocades, carved ivories from the East, delicate painted miniatures, the famous Venetian glass, rich mosaics, and pearls from the Orient. The ladies lunched at the little cafes overlooking the piazza. At times they strolled around the court enjoying the band music of Italy.

But mostly in the afternoons they repaired to the luxurious ease of their gondola letting the friendly gondolier follow his own inclination as a courier. They watched the action in the square from a distance, discovered the Lido (one of the four entrances to the open sea), and visited the lace factory and the glassworks. On the Grand Canal the boatman showed the girls the palaces of the ancient aristocracy of Venice, pointed out the abodes of the French writer Chateaubriand, the liberated English novelist George Eliot, and the German composer Richard Wagner. He showed them the Rezzonico, where Robert Browning died in 1899. He made certain that they noted the famous Rialto spanning the canal with its covered galleries of rounded arches which housed shops. Clara recalled that it was in the vicinity of the Rialto Bridge that the moneylender Shylock had bartered with Antonio in Shakespeare's *The Merchant of Venice* for the pound of flesh as a forfeit for his bond.

Again in the evening the ladies joined the flotilla of gondolas in order to enjoy the singers of the illuminated barges. It seemed to Clara that nowhere but in Italy could one hear such sweet, rich, full-throated tones. "And in Venice it is singing always. You are lulled to sleep by soft melodies, and snatches of song haunt your dreams."

The ladies had arrived in Venice when it was bathed by a midnight moon They left "the dream city" reluctantly when the rays of the sun had etched it with gold.

Of all the countries Clara visited, Greece interested her the most.

> We read the history of ancient Greece almost with the same feelings of admiration . . . that we have for a modern fictionist, so incredible . . . seem the facts . . . and so intermingled with realities are the stories of the gods and the mortals. We think of the classic land as peopled almost entirely with the beings of mythology and . . . we mix the fables of the inhabitants of Olympus with actual deeds of heroes. Of all the countries I visited . . . Greece held the most interest.

It was not because of the ruined splendors she viewed but "for the . . . profitable and enchanting thoughts" inspired by the crumbling temples and broken marbles. To her it did not require a long stretch of the imagination to people the land with the specters of those men who first gave the world inspiration in art, literature, and philosophy. "Here one can almost feel that Plato, Socrates, Phidias, and Aristotle were our warm friends. The objective point on a visit to Greece is Athens, 'City of the Violet Crown.'"

Thus as her ship that March afternoon plied its course through the multiplicity of islands in the Aegean Sea bound for the harbor of Piraeus, the ancient port of Athens, a flood of school day reminiscences consumed her. Once more the mighty Homer was regenerated in all of his glory and against the horizon of her imagination stretched the plains of Troy with its marching

legions and warriors clashing steel. Soon Odysseus, Menelaus, Achilles, Aga-
memnon, and a host of others returned in fantasy to play their parts, aided
and opposed by the gods of Mount Olympus.

As the vessel approached the entrance to the seaport, Clara was also reminded of historic heroes, who had contributed toward the long struggle for
Greek independence. To the left of the port was the bay and strait of Salamis,
where after Thermopylae, the Athenian naval commander, Themistocles de-
feated the great Persian fleet and put to rout an enemy far superior to the
Greek forces in numbers. Simultaneously Aristides had led the Athenian in-
fantry in the annihilation of the Persian forces on the island of Psyttaleis.
By the time the vessel had dropped anchor, Clara had already located the
Acropolis etched against the skyline, the mountain on whose summit sits the
Parthenon, the noted temple of Athena.

Arriving too late for sightseeing, Clara and her friend had to content themselves with checking in at their hotel situated at the Place de la Constitution
and dining on the diminutive balcony overlooking the piazza below. While
they sipped coffee and ate biscuits dipped in the famous honey of Hymettus,
they enjoyed the scene in the square. Mingling in the throng were Greeks of
all classes, from the highly sophisticated "Parisianized" to the ill-clothed peas-
ants late from the fields. Splashing the courtyard with color were the king's
soldiers in their handsome and well-tailored uniforms. Around small tables
in front of the cafes sat gentlemen drinking the wine of the country. A military band playing in the square added a touch of gaiety. The ladies watched
the drama below until the people dispersed and the lights came on in the shops
and cafes. With the square vacated, the girls sought again a glimpse of the
Acropolis, only six miles away. To their delight, "The white marble of the
ruined Parthenon took on the rose tints of the fading sun."

The visit to the Acropolis the next day was the highlight of the trip. To
reach the Parthenon, the ladies took a carriage and followed the road winding
up the western side of the incline. The limestone cliff rises nearly perpen-
dicular four hundred feet on all sides except the approach to the summit,
which is one thousand feet by five hundred. At the base of the citadel, on the
south slope, the ladies explored the theater of Dionysius, where Greek drama
had its inception and where Aeschylus, Sophocles, Euripides, and Aristophanes
had the distinction of giving it lifeblood. Clara noted that in the Greek theater, dating from the beginning of the fifth century B.C., with its circular orchestra, the marble seats in the front row around the stage were intact with
the titles of occupants carved on their fronts. These were the marble thrones
for the great while the ordinary limestone seats for spectators of less importance were behind.

At the entrance to the incline, and to the right, the ladies viewed the Propylaeum—a ruin of rocks—and the temple of Athena Nike. A little to the northwest they observed the bronze statue of Athena Promachos towering sixty-six feet in height and bearing a spear at rest. The point of the spear was said to have been a landmark by which early voyagers identified the coast of Greece.

The girls noted other ruins of the citadel but the main objective was the Parthenon at the top. Clara recounted in detail the chequered history of the Doric temple and its devastation through the centuries. She recalled that the Englishman, Lord Elgin, in more recent years appropriated the portable statuary and transported the treasures to London, where they are displayed in the British Museum under the caption of the "Elgin Marbles." Opposite the Parthenon, and only slightly less imposing, was the Erechtheum with its three types of Ionic columns and one of rare Caryatid figures—"Renowned in history as one of the most artistic creations of its kind."

Views from the summit of the Acropolis were superb. Visible, in addition to the layout of modern Athens designed in classic Greek style, were the site of Plato's garden where the philosopher and his disciples met; the spot where Aristotle kept school; the octagonal-shaped tower of Aeolus, the god of the winds; the prison on the hillside where Socrates was incarcerated and the Greeks administered to him the poison hemlock; and the Areopagus on Mars Hill, where Paul preached to the Athenians.

Upon departing, Clara was reminded once more of lines from Byron's *Childe Harold's Pilgrimage*:

> Come blue-eyed maid of heaven; but thou, alas!
> Didst never yet one mortal song inspire;
> Goddess of wisdom, here thy temple was.
> And is, despite of war and wasting fire,
> And years that bade thy worship to expire;
> But worse than steel, and flame, and ages slow,
> Is the dread sceptre and dominion dire
> Of men who never felt the sacred glow
> That thoughts of thee and thine on polished breasts bestow.

Clara Driscoll was more spiritually oriented than was generally known. This was due in part to the fact that she chose to live her religion rather than profess its tenets volubly. Mention has been made of her custom of collecting Bibles in the languages of the countries she visited. Wherever she traveled she also carried her own copy of the English version of the Bible. Because of her interest in religion as an adjunct of culture and her personal convictions, the visits to Jerusalem and Bethlehem, shortly after she concluded her European education, were memorable.

Her journey to Jerusalem, in particular, gave her the opportunity to observe the coexistence of the three religions of Judaism, Christianity, and Islam, together with their respective shrines all concentrated in a single location. It was of interest to her that the coexistence of the three forms of worship had not always been harmonious. The fact that the same holy places were revered by the adherents of more than one religion led to difficulties. For instance, the site of the ancient Jewish Temple, in the Haram ash-Sharif is regarded by Muslims as second in sanctity only to Mecca and Medina since they consider it the traditional scene of the ascension of Mohammed into heaven. The center of Haram, under the Dome of the Rock is sanctified by Muslims as the precise point from which the ascension was made.

Still Christian tradition accepts the site as the place on Mt. Moriah, where God commanded Abraham to sacrifice his son Isaac and where Solomon later erected the Temple. Built where the Jewish Temple of Solomon stood in previous centuries, the octagonal-shaped shrine encloses the sacred rock thought to be the center of the world. The shrine venerated by Christians, Muslims, and Jews alike, covers one-sixth of the Old Walled City of Jerusaleum in the southeastern angle.

The Wailing Wall in the southeast forms one side of an open enclosure outside the Haram. Considered the most sacred site in Judaism, it is the scene of constant Jewish worship, especially on the anniversary of the destruction of the Temple by the Romans in A.D. 70.

Another shrine that poses a major problem is the tomb of David on Mt. Zion, since it, too, is venerated by all three religions. The Christian belief is that it was the scene of the Last Supper and the descent of the Holy Spirit. However, David was a national figure whose line ruled Jerusalem for over four hundred years. He himself unified Israel, overcame the Philistines, and established a political and religious capital at Jerusalem—in short, created an empire. Under his leadership Israel had greater military and political achievement than in any subsequent era. As king, David also became the Messianic symbol through whom God mediated blessings to Israel. Hence Israelites, regardless of religious affiliation, claimed David as a national, as well as religious, hero. From the time of the crusades quarrels over David's tomb have been severe, especially between the Latins and the Orthodox.

Within the medieval walls of the Old Quarter, Clara probably found the Church of the Holy Sepulchre of equal interest to the Temple area and the Wailing Wall. Located in the northeast quarter of the walled city, the church had been destroyed and rebuilt many times. The present structure, dating from 1810, was ostensibly built on the site of Jesus' crucifixion and burial. Although the building is structurally weak and unimposing, the shrine is the center of Christian interest. Various Christian groups control parts of the building and hold services there regularly.

Special features of the shrine are the *Martyrion*, the presumed site of the Saviour's crucifixion, and the rotunda over the tomb of His burial and resurrection. Though recognized since the fourth century as the place where Jesus died, was buried, and rose from the dead, these claims have been contested. However, no rival site has been supported by any real evidence and, despite this uncertainty, many pilgrims pass through the shrine annually.

Sites of major interest outside the walls of Old Jerusalem included the tomb of the Virgin, the Garden of Gethsemane, and the mosque of the Ascension on the Mount of Olives. The view of the Holy City from the Mount of Olives was especially effective.

In addition to increasing Clara's respect for all religions, the visit to Jerusalem, where Jesus actually lived and taught, strengthened her own faith. Moreover, if the visit to Jerusalem was an excursion into Biblical history and an experience in religious research at first hand, the trek to Bethlehem was an intimate experience involving adoration.

As Clara vacated the old city with its shrines and its intricate maze of crowded houses, inner courtyards, narrow streets, and vaulted alleys, she had an even greater revelation in store in Bethlehem.

Leaving by the Jaffa Gate, she and her party covered the distance of five miles through the picturesque valleys of Gibeon and Hinnom. As usual, she traveled in an open, horse-drawn vehicle in order to enjoy the scenery en route. The first site of importance at the entrance to Bethlehem was the tomb of Rachael, another shrine held in equal reverence by Muslims, Jews, and Christians. The vehicle in which Clara was traveling passed the crop of stones. According to the legend, Jesus, seeing a man sowing seed, stopped and asked him what he was planting.

Sullenly the man replied, "Stones." From that time on, so the legend goes, stones have been the only crop.

Another stone by the roadside bearing an indentation was said to be the one on which Elijah slept one night when he was fleeing the wrath of Jezebel. Farther on, the travelers noticed the well of the Magi, at which the Wise Men from the East stopped to drink when the star appeared to them the second time.

In driving through Bethlehem's narrow streets, Clara was first impressed by the difference in the appearance of the inhabitants from other Orientals she had seen. Particularly was this true of the women. Bethlehem women were more attractive than others of Palestine. Fairer of skin, they were said to be descended from the Crusaders, "who for forty years had held a spot near Bethlehem while they were fighting to capture Jerusalem." The costume of the women appealed to Clara. The skirt, often of silk, was of a deep blue with a wide border of colorful embroidery around the hem. Worn with this was a rose-colored jacket likewise luxuriously embroidered. Completing the costume was a headdress of cream cloth with bright decoration around the edges. To distinguish themselves from their single sisters the married women wore tall, peaked headpieces covered with a white veil gathered together under their chins leaving their faces exposed.

When Clara Driscoll visited the Church of the Nativity in Bethlehem, it fronted on a cloistered forecourt. As she approached it, she was amazed at venders infesting the square and doing an enormous business in the sale of so-called sacred objects. The travelers were surprised at the severity and lack of architectural ornamentation of the complex of buildings comprising the area of the shrine. Excavations showed that the church was wholly rebuilt in the sixth century under Emperor Justinian I. It was of interest that Muslin conquerors had respected the church because of Mary's place in the Koran.

The interior of the Church of the Nativity was not so plain as the exterior. Decorations dating from the Crusades of the twelfth and thirteenth centuries had been preserved. Whereas the Greeks and the Armenians were said to own the Grotto of the Nativity, different Catholic nations shared in the ownership of the remainder of the building. Objects of particular attention were the caves known as the Chapel of St. Jerome, where the saint spent thirty years in translating the Bible into Latin as the Vulgate, and the Chapel of the Innocents, where the children hiding from Herod were slain.

But it was the Grotto of the Nativity itself that drew most of the visitors. Clara entered the crypt through a dark passageway and realized immediately that she had discovered the Grotto of the Nativity. As her mind tapped out the familiar words of Luke 2:7,

> And she brought forth her firstborn son, and wrapped him in swaddling clothes, and laid him in a manger; because there was no room for them in the inn,

the young girl from South Texas moved closer to the holy scene. In Jerusalem she had walked the same alleyways and streets the Saviour had trod, had meditated at Gethsemane, on the Mount of Olives, where He withdrew with His disciples on the eve of His crucifixion, had viewed the Holy Sepulchre. Now in Bethlehem she stood before Jesus' place of birth—*the most sacred spot in all Christendom!*

Two centers of interest mark the softly-lighted cave. They are the precise location where Jesus' birth occurred and the manger, opposite it in a recess, where the Christ Child was laid. The light emanates from suspended gold and silver lamps, upon one of which a silver star indicates the site of the Saviour's birthplace. A marble slab identifies the place of the manger. Walls of both the Grotto and the manger alcove are draped with rich tapestries and velvet hangings.

Clara observed other pilgrims in the performance of religious rites. Many knelt and touched their lips to the star and the marble slab over the manger. "In their eyes was a look of adoration bespeaking the feeling in their hearts." Clara Driscoll herself stood long in silence:

> One does not travel thousands of miles across foreign lands and strange seas to stand cool and emotionless beside the birthplace of the Saviour of mankind.

13

The Last Legacy

CLARA DRISCOLL HAD A QUESTING SPIRIT. All of her life she had been a seeker. She initiated her pilgrimage early to seek for her ultimate ideal. She sought it through a demonstration of patriotism, an appreciation of the arts, love of humanity, and through service to her fellowman. She sought it through romance, sought it through creativity. She sought it through travel, through religion. Courageously, endlessly, she pursued truth and her set goals. She searched throughout a life crowded with meaningful activity and crowned with signal success.

But the ideal for which Clara Driscoll searched was not only illusive, it was unattainable. The ideal escaped her for the reason that it, like the fabled Eldorado, was nonexistent in the temporal world. The ideal came to Clara Driscoll on July 17, 1945. Only death could bestow it: *Peace.*

Mrs. Driscoll died in her apartment on the twentieth floor of the Robert Driscoll Hotel a few minutes after nine o'clock on Tuesday evening, July 17, 1945. She was sixty-four. With her at the time were her physician, Dr. McIver Furman, and her nurse, Mrs. Thule Herbert. Death was attributed to a cerebral hemorrhage. Although Mrs. Driscoll had been in declining health for six months, she had been confined to bed for only three weeks and her death was unexpected.

The death of the most famous woman in the history of Corpus Christi and prominent national figure for seventeen years came as a shock to her legion of friends. Tributes and expressions of bereavement poured into Corpus Christi from over the nation and crossed political party lines.

On the evening of Mrs. Driscoll's decease a small group of close friends and business associates met at the apartment to arrange for the funeral. These included Dr. Furman and Mrs. Herbert, Philip Howerton (her agent and secretary), and Mrs. Howerton; Isaac W. Keys, W. Preston Pittman, and Shelton G. Hudson. The offer of a burial site in the State Cemetery in Austin, made

possible by the Daughters of the Republic of Texas, was declined by Philip
Howerton in deference to the deceased's previously expressed wishes to be interred in the family mausoleum in the Masonic Cemetery in San Antonio with
her father and brother. Prior to services to be held at Saint Mark's Episcopal
Church in San Antonio at two o'clock on Thursday afternoon, plans were to
have the body lie in state in the Alamo chapel from ten o'clock until one.

Again the story of how Clara Driscoll began her legendary career as "Saviour of the Alamo" was reviewed in the press.

> In fitting tribute to the woman, who single-handedly spared the shrine of Texas
> from demolition 40 years ago, Mrs. Driscoll's body will lie in state at the Alamo in
> San Antonio from 10 a.m. until 1 p.m. tomorrow.[1]

Once more eulogies praised Mrs. Driscoll's loyalty to the Democratic party
and to Franklin Delano Roosevelt:

> Always actively interested in politics and a lifelong Democrat, Mrs. Driscoll never
> sought nor accepted public office for herself. In 1928, however, she was elected
> Democratic National Committeewoman from Texas and from that date on she held
> the national spotlight as one of the most articulate women in the nation on the cause
> of democracy.
>
> An ardent champion of the late President Franklin D. Roosevelt, she made her
> last public appearance in Corpus Christi a year ago when she appeared before the
> Nueces County Democratic convention to fight against an uninstructed delegation.[2]

On the morning of July 20, as the remains of Clara Driscoll lay in state in
the Alamo chapel, honor guards from the San Antonio Police Department,
the Texas Federation of Women's Clubs, and the Daughters of the Republic
of Texas attended. For three hours thousands of admirers filed by the bronze
casket blanketed with pink daisies, carnations, and gladiolas—flowers of the
deceased's favorite color. Thus Texas's foremost patriot was reunited with
the shrine of the state's freedom that had exerted the greatest impact on her
life and career. Later she would join Travis and Bowie and Crockett in her
choice of San Antonio as her place of interment.

Many who filed by the bier in silence must have remembered Clara Dricsoll's
fervent phrases:

> Watch it . . . in the silence of eventide, when the glow of a departing day throws its
> radiant color like a brilliant crimson mantle about the old ruin. . . . Look at it in the
> busy hurry of everday life. . . . Then go and stand before it on a night when the
> moon throws a white halo over the plaza; when the lights of the city are darkened,
> the winds of heaven hushed. . . .

Simple funeral rites were conducted at two P. M., as planned, from Saint

Mark's Episcopal Church. Officiating were the Right Reverend Everett H. Jones, bishop of West Texas, and the Reverend Dr. Thomas H. Wright, rector of Saint Mark's. Burial followed in the family mausoleum in San Antonio's Masonic Cemetery.

Active pallbearers were Richard King, president of the Corpus Christi National Bank; Maston Nixon, vice-president of Southern Minerals; Roy Miller, acting president of the Intracoastal Canal Association; A. Eugene Dabney, Jr., vice-president of the Corpus Christi Bank and Trust Company—all of Corpus Christi; Jack Locke and Joe Frost of San Antonio; Mayor Tom Miller and Collector of Internal Revenue Frank Schofield—both of Austin.[3]

The list of honorary pallbearers, including both close personal friends and personages of national note read like a roster of the Democratic party's hall of fame and represented a cross section of the nation: Cordell Hull, architect of the United Nations and secretary of state; Speaker of the House Sam Rayburn; Postmaster General Robert A. Hannegan; Senator Tom Connally; Texas representatives Lyndon Johnson and John Lyle—all of Washington, D.C.; former postmaster general James A. Farley of New York; former vice-president John Nance Garner of Uvalde; Colonel Ernest O. Thompson, Beauford Jester, Dan Moody, and Colbert Green—all of Austin;

John T. O'Neil, A. J. McKenzie, Dr. Ferdinand P. Herff, and R. W. Morrison—all of San Antonio; Pat M. Neff of Waco; Richard J. Kleberg, Burton Dunn, Edwin Flato, Dr. McIver Furman, C. D. Johns, M. M. Gabriel, former mayor A. C. McCaughan, and Mayor Roy L. Self—all of Corpus Christi;

John Kenedy, Sarita; Doss Seago, San Diego; Claude E. Heard, Beeville; H. H. Bahn, Driscoll; Morris Gouger and W. S. Gandy, Robstown; Dudley Tarlton and Robert R. Hall, Corpus Christi; Dr. Conrado Sorolla, Santiago, Chile; Amon G. Carter of Fort Worth, James V. Allred and Dan Moran of Houston.[4]

Clara Driscoll's death marked the extinction of one of the finest families in the American Southwest. Not only that, the decease of the great lady signified the end of an era. It underscored the passing of an epoch that began roughly with the end of World War I, reached its peak under the leadership of Franklin Delano Roosevelt, and ended with World War II and its aftermath. Despite the two wars and a depression, the period typified one of the most phenomenal in American political as well as cultural history. It was an era in which new concepts in the fields of economics, sociology, and political theory were born. In addition there was a resurgence of appreciation for American art and culture. Not only did Clara Driscoll's death mark its close. Along with that of Franklin Roosevelt her life had made a major contribution to it.

In death, as in life, Clara Driscoll thought not of herself but of others. Deprived by nature of the privilege of bearing children, she, nevertheless, reserved a special place in her heart for them. In her will dated April 17, 1945, she left the bulk of a cattle, oil, and land fortune valued in excess of $7 million[5] to provide for the construction and maintenance of a free clinic and hospital for indigent children:

> I have recently become indebted to certain persons, firms, or corporations on large sums in the construction of . . . the Robert Driscoll Hotel and Office Building in Corpus Christi, Texas; nevertheless, it has always been my wish that the estate created by my father, Robert Driscoll, and my mother, Julia Driscoll, and preserved by my brother, Robert Driscoll, Jr., and me be used after my death for the amelioration of the condition of those Texans, and particularly those of Southwest Texas, who may need aid, and I have with much thought determined the use I shall make of this property with this aim in mind. It is my purpose, therefore . . . and my will and desire, and I so direct my Trustees, after the payment of my just debts, to create an endowment fund from the residue of my estate to be known as the 'Robert Driscoll and Julia Driscoll and Robert Driscoll, Jr. Foundation' . . . for the construction, equipment, and operation of a free clinic and hospital for crippled, maimed, or diseased children, with all necessary and desirable appurtenances, supplies, and professional medical attention as may be practicable under the circumstances. . . .[6]

To administer the estate and supervise the operation of the hopsital, Mrs. Driscoll named as trustees John T. O'Neil of Bexar County and Dr. McIver Furman and I. W. Keys of Corpus Christi.

In addition, she named employees and business associates as beneficiaries. To Luis Adrian she willed $50 per month so long as he was employed as foreman of Palo Alto Ranch and $425 per month thereafter for the remainder of his life; to N. Galvan, caretaker of Laguna Gloria, $10 per week for life; to W. Preston Pittman and A. E. Dabney, 133 shares each of Corpus Christi Bank and Trust Company stock valued at $26,000. (Estate tax was filed on the basis of $150 per share on the bank stock, but the Internal Revenue Service raised the value to $200 per share.)

Philip Howerton, Mrs. Driscoll's secretary, and Phil L. Highshew, her chauffeur, received bequests valued at $46,800 and $10,000, respectively. Howeton's inheritance also included the cancellation of a note for $1,050.

Cristobal Saenz, who was to have drawn an annuity after the termination of his services as a ranchhand, was automatically removed from the list of beneficiaries by his death on March 10, 1946.

By almost any standard Mrs. Driscoll's gifts were generous. Equally liberal were her instructions to her trustees in the administration of the foundation funds. The trustees were appointed to serve without bond and were responsible to no one in the discharge of their duties. In many instances they were empowered to act upon their own discretion and judgment and, in case of disagreement, were to abide by majority rule.[7]

The twelve-page document was a study in the humanities. *It was the last legacy* of the Driscoll line.

14

Driscoll Foundation Children's Hospital

THE DRISCOLL FOUNDATION CHILDREN'S Hospital in Corpus Christi, Texas, occupies a unique position in the history of such institutions. First, it was the reason for the creation of the Robert Driscoll and Julia Driscoll and Robert Driscoll, Jr. Foundation, which originally subsidized it on net income. Secondly, in providing free medical care to underpriviliged children of South Texas, it antedated present-day state and federal programs to administer similar services.

More significant, now in its twenty-fifth year of operation, the hospital has provided medical care for over forty thousand children admitted to the facility and more than one million in the outpatient department, at a cost of over $30 million; and it is beginning to serve a second generation of patients. Built at a modest cost of $4 million, the facility, after extensive modification and expansion, is valued at $8.5 million with a replacement value of from $12 to $15 million.[1]

The hospital was formally dedicated on February 22, 1953. It is to the credit of the prudent trustees—presently consisting of Dr. McIver Furman, W. Preston Pittman, and T. S. Scibienski[2]—that only after meticulous planning did they execute the directives of the Driscoll will. From 1945 to 1950 the trustees conducted a nationwide study of pediatric hospitals. In addition, they conducted surveys on the incidence of child mortality and the principal diseases affecting children in Nueces County, Texas.[3] Quite literally the Driscoll Foundation pioneered pediatric hospital services in Texas and the Southwest. Moreover, it is testimony to the trustees' wise judgment that they delayed the beginning of the project until they had the assurance that foundation funds could sustain it.

However, almost two decades of administering the hospital solely as a charity institution demonstrated the necessity for a change. Fortunately, in creating the foundation, Mrs. Driscoll foresaw the possible need for innovation to keep abreast of the evolution of health care for the children of Nueces County and provided for it in her will. Consequently, to extend its services to all children of South Texas, regardless of economic status, the trustees obtained legal authority in February, 1970 to operate the institution as a nonprofit facility. Since the transition, or for a period of eight years, the services of Driscoll Hospital have been available to all South Texas children. This extension of medical care to all children, regardless of economy, has not only contributed to the healthful climate of the community as a whole, it has made the public more health conscious in regard to children and more aware of the services available to them at Driscoll.

While the current annual budget is approximately $10 million, well over a million of that amount is provided by the foundation.[4] To meet the increased costs of medical care and to support the budget, the trustees, from time to time, have evaluated the capability of the foundation's assets to produce revenue. It was apparent that the Driscoll Hotel had begun to show a substantial loss in net income because of the competition of plush waterfront motels and hotels. After unsuccessful attempts to interest national hotel chains in the property in order to preserve its use for Corpus Christi, the foundation sold it to a group of local businessmen to be converted into an office building. Thus it was closed in 1970 and remodeled. In conformity with sound business practice, the trustees continue to adjust other assets of the foundation as the need arises.

Of the many excellent departments in the Driscoll Hospital, three merit special scrutiny. They are the Outpatient Department and facilities, the Department of Cardiac Care, and the Intensive Care Unit for Newborns. Outpatient facilities at the hospital have contributed to the success of the Preventive Medical Program. Total health care under the supervision of the patient's family doctor is provided in this department. The unit is equipped for eye, ear, nose, and throat treatment, along with audio testing and dentistry.

For over two decades the Driscoll Outpatient Division has provided medical services through more than one million visitations by South Texas children.[5] Even so, many young patients from outlying areas were unable to get to the Outpatient Department and frequently became acutely ill before receiving treatment. To offset this condition the trustees, recognizing the need for an off-campus clinic to reach these children, initiated plans to provide one.

With the aid of a grant awarded by the United States Department of Health, Education, and Welfare, the Children and Youth Project Clinic was established in Robstown, on January 11, 1970. A demonstration project designed to provide comprehensive health care to a specific target population of children and youth, the facility is strategically located. The geographic location encompasses the northwest quarter of Nueces County—an area of 200 square miles with a total population of 22,000. This includes approximately nine thousand children with an age range up to sixteen years.[6] The clinic extends medical, dental, and nursing care, together with the provision of nutrition, psychological aid, and social and physical therapy to those eligible.

In the first quarter of the clinic's operation—from January through March, 1971—394 hospital days of care per 1,000 patients were necessary. In scarcely more than two years—from April through June, 1973—hospital days per 1,000 patients were reduced by 37.4 percent.[7]

As a result of the clinic's extension of services to the child where he lives, emphasis from crisis-oriented care has been shifted to preventive care. In the first six months ending in 1973 the Robstown Clinic performed thirty thousand services for the children of the area. Even though emphasis is on preventive medicine, hospital care is available when necessary. Mobile vans are employed to transport acutely ill patients from the Robstown area to the Driscoll Hospital in Corpus Christi for this treatment. Approximately 25 percent of Driscoll's cases are surgical.

Driscoll's Pediatric Cardiology Department has achieved marked success in the treatment it provides. Since heart disease in South Texas affects from eight to ten infants out of every thousand born, it is recognized as a major problem. The initial attempt at a solution was the development of the Children's Heart Program of South Texas. Originally founded by a stipend from the Texas Regional Medical Program, the project is now subsidized by a grant from the federal government, the Driscoll Foundation, and other private sources. Dr. James Simpson, noted pediatric cardiologist, directs the program.

As an area-wide effort, the heart program brings together pediatricians, family physicians, cardiologists, heart surgeons, nurses and technicians from various hospitals, heart clinics, and health departments, all working together in close harmony with the staff of Driscoll. One aspect of the activity permits satellite clinics to be held regularly in various parts of South Texas bringing patient care closer to home communities. In studying the region's population and culture, the cardiac care team is enabled to work more effectively with heart patients and their families. These teams deal with the actual physical problems as well as related emotional difficulties and tensions. A medical team includes a physician, nurses, a cultural anthropologist, a psychiatric social worker, and cardiology technologists. The Children's Heart Program of South Texas provides training for pediatric cardiology associates who then dispense patient care to their own communities.

The hospital's Cardiac Diagnostic Clinic was begun in 1957 in conjunction with the Corpus Christi Heart Association. In 1956 funds from the Ford

Foundation Hospital Grants permitted the purchase of initial equipment. Since its opening the clinic has received donations from municipal and area organizations to purchase additional equipment. In 1960 the Corpus Christi Heart Association subsidized the gift of a Pemco Heart Pump. A later grant of $100,000 from the Moody Foundation in Galveston has insured further efficiency through the installation of additional highly sophisticated catheterization equipment in the hospital's Pediatric Cardiology Department. In April, 1967, a highlight in Driscoll's medical history was attained when the first open-heart surgery was performed.[8]

Installed in 1974 under the supervision of a neonatologist, the Intensive Care Unit for Newborns represents Driscoll's most recent area of child concern. Based upon neonatological science, to which recent space-age programs added dimension, the hospital's Neonate Nursery was the first in South Texas and remains the only complete service of this nature south of San Antonio and west of Houston.

In this department high risk newborns are treated until their conditions become stable, usually in from one to four weeks. Some of the infants requiring this treatment are premature from birth and weigh less than five pounds. Some have problems related to their mother's pregnancy, labor, or delivery. Others may have respiratory distress, irregular heartbeat, or birth defects of either mental or physical nature.

The treatment, which requires trained medical personnel and special equipment, with highly skilled technicians to operate it, embraces three areas: intensive care, intermediate care, and transitional care. Statistics confirm that 50 percent of high risk infants respond successfully to treatment and that it reduces infant mortality substantially.

Resident training for doctors, dentists, nurses, and various technicians is a vital aspect of Driscoll's Medical Education Program. The program was organized by Dr. Joseph McBride Sloan, who upon his retirement was succeeded by Dr. Meyer Kurzner, an enthusiastic supporter of the institution since its inception. Driscoll maintains active affiliation with medical and dental schools, other hospitals, and universities to insure quality care for its patients while simultaneously offering the best in training for medical professionals. The hospital maintains a tripartite relationship with the University of Texas Medical School at Galveston involving residents, students, and a special training program in the discipline of anesthesiology. It is affiliated with the Memorial Medical Center of Corpus Christi in intern and resident training, along with a family practice program, nurses training, and care of newborns. Driscoll is also affiliated with the Corpus Christi State University Nursing Program, and with Spohn Hospital.

The Pediatric Dental Department works with the Dental Branch of the University of Texas at Houston for the training of pedodontists. The two-year program embraces one year of study in Houston and a second with the children at Driscoll. Future registered nurses obtain clinic pediatric training through Driscoll's association with Corpus Christi's Del Mar College for Professional Nursing. For licensed vocational nurses (LVNs) Driscoll has developed its own postgraduate course in pediatric nursing. The twenty-six-week course provides the hospital with a continuing source of professionally trained personnel. Instruction in the course is given by local doctors, nurses, and technicians.

The training at Driscoll is comprehensive and is supported by a splendid medical library. Resident pediatricians spend twelve to thirty-six months in training at the hospital under the supervision of the staff and local specialists in cooperation with the Pediatric Department of the University of Texas Medical School under Dr. Charles W. Daeschner, Jr., chairman. As a part of the routine, these residents make supervised ward rounds and work daily with patients in the Driscoll Hospital and the clinic in Robstown. An important phase of the training is that of Pediatric Cardiology Associates as a part of the Children's Heart Program of South Texas. This intensive eight-month program of specialized training, under the direction of Dr. Simpson, equips nurses to assist doctors in obtaining heart-patient histories, in conducting preliminary examinations, and in preparing x-rays and electrocardiograms.

The wide representation of Driscoll graduates over the world is a barometer of the Medical Education Program's effectiveness and the institution's far-reaching contribution to medical service. Driscoll graduates have extended professional services to Mexico, Nigeria, Turkey, Thailand, Paraguay, Korea, Argentina, Denmark, Iran, the Philippines, in addition to states throughout America.[9]

According to Dr. Kurzner, the patient loads have increased and as the hospital is becoming increasingly a tertiary referral center for South Texas, more residents have become necessary so that in the 1978–79 fiscal year, eighteen pediatric residents and one pedodontic resident are funded.[10]

From the date of its opening in 1953, Driscoll Hospital has maintained a full-time staff of professionals outstanding in their fields. In addition to those mentioned, key personnel of the medical staff include Dr. Roberto Mejia, director of the Child and Youth Project and director of Outpatient Services; Dr. Alfonso Prado, neonatologist; Dr. Joseph Jackson, radiologist; Dr. Joseph Rupp, pathologist; Dr. Charles Daeschner, Jr., chairman of the Department of Pediatrics; and Dr. James F. Arens, chairman of the Department of Anaesthesiology, the University of Texas Medical School at Galveston.[11]

The hospital is under the direction of a board of directors approved by the Driscoll Foundation trustees. They include Colonel Floyd Buch, F. B. Cochran, Jr., Mark Hulings, Dr. Claude McLelland, Arturo Vasquez, Newton Warzecha, Mrs. Harvie Branscomb, Jr., and Joe Jessel.

The trustees of Driscoll Foundation have been assisted for twenty-seven years by Nettie Ruth Hoskins, executive secretary and accountant. There are three advisory trustees to the Driscoll Foundation who are appointed on a yearly basis and as of April 30, 1978, they include Dr. Lowell J. Kepp, E. A. Durham, II, and Fred W. Heldenfels, III.[12]

Mr. Gordon Epperson, F.A.C.H.A., former administrator from 1947 to 1967, rejoined the staff as president and chief executive officer of Driscoll Hospital in 1976. With the appointment of Mr. Epperson to head the overall operation the managerial structure has become streamlined. A clean-cut man of few words but one who translates words into action, President Epperson is optimistic about the future of Driscoll:[13]

> The technical system of delivering medical care in this hospital has changed drastically during this quarter of a century. *Technology will continue to advance.*
>
> With all these past changes and the trauma associated with change, the basic goal of the hospital has changed little, if any. That goal is to provide quality medical and patient care to each child brought to Driscoll for treatment. This goal is unlikely to change during the next twenty-five years. . . .[14]

For twenty-five years members of the Auxiliary to Driscoll Foundation Children's Hospital have given thousands of hours of service. These dedicated women assist with hospital and clinic patients, provide secretarial services, arrange for parties, toys, films, television and education materials for the children, and staff the snack bar and gift shop. In addition, they award scholarships for student nurses and donate equipment for the hospital.

Although the hospital is endowed by a foundation named for her parents and brother, the institution is a living memorial that testifies to the magnanimity of the childless woman who dreamed of its creation. In a rather real sense Driscoll Foundation Children's Hospital typifies not only the immortality of Clara Driscoll's dream, but the perpetuation of the American tradition she became.

Appendixes

APPEALS FOR THE ALAMO FUND

THE FIRST

A PLEA FOR THE ALAMO

The Daughters of the Republic of Texas have undertaken to raise a sum sufficient to purchase the property adjoining the Alamo in order to improve the surroundings, so that they may be in keeping with the dignity and glory of the old ruin.

It is their desire to make of this building, sacred to the hearts of all Americans, a worthy and artistic monument to the memory of those valiant martyrs who fell inside its walls.

The Daughters of the Republic of Texas is a chartered association for the following object:

1. To perpetuate the memory and spirit of the men and women who have achieved and maintained the Independence of Texas.

2. To encourage historical research into the earliest records of Texas, especially those relating to the Revolution of 1835, and the events which followed; to foster the preservation of documents and relics, and to encourage the publication of records of individual service of soldiers and patriots of the Republic.

3. To promote the celebration of March 2nd (Independence Day) and April 21st (San Jacinto Day); and to secure and hallow historic spots, by erecting monuments thereon, and to cherish and preserve the unity of Texas, as achieved and established by the fathers and mothers of the Texas Revolution.

They only ask you for the small sum of Fifty Cents to help accomplish the patriotic cause.

Please enclose the money and the names of three of your friends. If you should not feel inclined to aid in this movement, please return this to

[MISS] CLARA DRISCOLL
Chairman Alamo Mission Fund

P.O. Box 1021
San Antonio, Texas

THE SECOND

**TO THE SCHOOL BOARDS, SCHOOL TRUSTEES,
SUPERINTENDENTS AND TEACHERS:**

The Daughters of the Republic of Texas are, as you doubtless know, a society composed of the descendants of the early pioneers and heroes of the Republic of Texas. The society has among its objects the fostering of the study of Texas history, the erection of monuments to the memory of the early fathers and statesmen, and the preservation of relics and landmarks relating to the early days.

They wish to save the old Mission del Alamo. The State already owns a small part, but the value of what it owns will be impaired if the plan contemplated by Eastern capitalists be carried out—that of purchasing the remainder of the old Mission, buying the surrounding property and enclosing the Alamo, as it were, using the sacred spot where the blood of our Texas heroes was shed as an advertisement of the scheme. De Zavala Chapter, Daughters of the Republic of Texas, is trying to save it, and asks your cooperation. The children can help much. Let no name be refused, be the amount ever so small. To any child contributing or collecting one dollar we will send the story of "The Fall of the Alamo" and a photograph of the Mission.

Very truly,

[MISS] CLARA DRISCOLL
Chairman Alamo Mission Fund

Send donations to me and receipt for same will be forwarded immediately.

P.O. Box 1021, San Antonio, Texas.

LETTERS FROM RESPONDENTS

The following specimens of letters from Clara Driscoll's Alamo files selected at random reveal the type of people who responded to her appeals for aid and their individual reactions to the project. Furthermore, some of the names of donors and those recommended for solicitation have since become household words for their subsequent contributions to humanity on both national and local levels—Kleberg, Gould, Moody, Sealy, Groce, Gibbs. In some instances donors, including prominent businessmen, even bank presidents, took Clara Driscoll quite literally and sent only the fifty cents she requested. There were a few, however, who donated larger amounts.

The first letter written by Sarah Kleberg merits attention for the suggestions Robert J. Kleberg, her father, made for the success of the venture. As indicated elsewhere in the text, the two families of Driscolls and Klebergs owned adjoining ranches and were close friends. Undated, the letter might have preceded the second appeal as Clara's proposals to school children were similar to those proffered by Kleberg. Sarah's "Grandma" was Mrs. Henrietta King, who was listed on the letterhead stationery as proprietor of the King Ranche [*sic*], with Kleberg as manager. The unusual letterhead also carried a photo of Captain Richard King, who founded the ranch in 1854.

Dear Miss Clara

As you know, Papa is unusually busy at this time of year and so he has been unable to answer your letter in regard to the Alamo. He wrote a rough outline of a few suggestions, which he thought might help in the future to support the Alamo. I will quote his suggestions.

"I suggest this thought that the chief purpose in taking care of the Alamo should be to promote patriotism, as the greatness of any state or nation depends upon the patriotism of its citizens. I know of no more effective way of teaching and promoting patriotism than by encouraging the citizens to practice that virtue, by doing patriotic deeds.

"It occurs to me that it would present a great opportunity to the citizens of Texto call upon them to aid on the upkeep of the Alamo by each adult contributing $1.00 and each child attending the public schools, to contribute say 10 cents on March 2nd or on April 21st. One of our great poets has said, 'A land without memories is a land without Liberty.' Large contributions from a few would not cultivate or instill patriotism in the great mass of the people as would several contributions from the masses. As both of the days mentioned are public holidays, it might be well to ask for a legislative act calling on all children attending the Public Schools for a small contribution, thus memorializing the deeds of the heroes of the Alamo. Possibly a small button or pin and a picture of the Alamo could go with each contribution which is more than a dollar."

Papa and Grandma both asked me to say that they would be glad to contribute to the Alamo fund if you will tell them when you are ready for their contributions. Mama is well and sends her dearest love.

Sincerely

Sarah Kleberg

The next letter from Helen Miller Gould (1868–1938) of New York, daughter of the powerful railroad tycoon Jay Gould, was a notable exception to those who gave only the paltry amount requested. Miss Gould became widely known as a philanthropist for her gifts to the United States Army hospitals during the war with Spain in 1898.

579 Fifth Avenue
New York City

April 8th, 1903.

Miss Clara Driscoll,
Menger Hotel, San Antonio, Texas,

Dear Miss Driscoll:

Miss Gould asks me to acknowledge the receipt of your letter of March 16th, calling her attention to the fund which is being raised to buy some of the property adjoining the Alamo, and to assure you that she was interested in what you wrote.

She takes pleasure in sending the enclosed check, drawn to your order for Fifty Dollars, which she will be glad to add to the fund.

With her kind regards, believe me,

Very truly,

/s/ Elizabeth Altman
Secretary.

Dict. to L.A.H.

The following letter from attorney Charles Fowler of Galveston is important for its inclusion of the galaxy of persons who became famous for their own good deeds. For instance, W. L. Moody, the multi-millionaire founder of the American National Insurance empire, who later established a State School for Cerebral Palsied Children in Galveston, among other benefactions; John Sealy, the humanitarian, whose hospital erected by the Sealy Foundation in Galveston in 1887, with services available to everyone regardless of ability to pay, is today a part of the medical branch of the University of Texas system and one of the most noted in the Southwest; and the Texas pioneer and American patriot Leonard W. Groce, who provided funds, animals, and provisions to support the United States war with Mexico and later the Confederacy during the Civil War. During the war between the North and South Liendo Plantation in Waller County, Texas, was the site of a Confederate recruiting station and a prisoner-of-war camp. After the war it was occupied by 4,000 federal troops under the command of Brigadier General George A. Custer to enforce the Reconstruction measures.

Galveston, Texas
April 28, 1903

Miss Clara Driscoll, Chairman
San Antonio,

Dear Miss:

Replying to your esteemed communication relative to the restoration of the Alamo, I take pleasure in handing you herewith the contribution asked for by you and would suggest your addressing Messrs., R. Waverley Smith, John Sealy, I. H. Kempner, Judge M. E. Kleberg, Jas. A. Crocker, W. R. A. Rogers, Aaron Blum, Leon Blum, T. J. Groce, W. L. Moody, H. J. Runge and L. J. Polk, who I hope will respond to your eloquent plea in such a good cause.

Your respectfully,

/s/ Chas Fowler

Nor did Clara Driscoll overlook personnel of the institutions in submitting her pleas. This reply from A. (Alexander) Caswell Ellis, who was a distinguished University of Texas professor for thirty-seven years, is an example. From 1897 to 1926 Ellis was professor of philosophy and psychology of education. Like himself, the three professors he recommended were all members of the University of Texas faculty during its infancy and each made a notable contribution. Dr. W. J. Battle, a professor of Greek who also served as academic dean for a number of years was a baldheaded bachelor, whose shiny dome and horn-rimmed glasses were his trademark. Judge John C. Townes, a well-known Austin attorney, joined the university staff as professor of law in 1896 and was made dean of the school of law in 1902. Townes was the author of several books dealing with the legal profession, among which were *Studies of American Elementary Law* (1903 and 1911) and *Civil Government in the United States and in Texas* (1908). Dr. George P. Garrison joined the faculty in 1884 as instructor of English literature and history. When the two subjects were divided in 1888 he became head of the history department. Garrison, one of the most popular professors on the campus, established a graduate course in Texas history at the university in 1897 and wrote several books, including *Westward Extension* (1906).

The University of Texas
Austin

Office of
Committee on Affiliated Schools

Miss Clara Driscoll,
Chm. Alamo Mission Fund,
P.O. Box 1021.
San Antonio, Texas.

Dear Madam:

I thank you for giving me the privilege of contributing in this modest way towards your worthy enterprise.

You might write to Dr. W. J. Battle, Judge Jno. C. Townes, Dr. Geo. P. Garrison, and all the rest of the University faculty.

Wishing you success in your noble undertaking, I am,

Very truly yours,

/s/ A. Caswell Ellis

A similar specimen bears the letterhead of the Southwestern Insane Asylum of San Antonio:

June 4, 1903.

Miss Clara Driscoll,
Chairman, Alamo Mission Fund, Box 1021, San Antonio, Texas.

Dear Madam:

Replying to your favor I cheerfully enclose 50 cents and the names of three friends,—viz.—Dr. B. M. Worsham, Sup't. Austin, Texas; Dr. John S. Turner, Sup't. Terrell, Texas; Mr. John H. Chiles, Austin, Texas.

Trusting you may accomplish your object, I am,—

Very truly yours,
/s/ Marvin L. Graves
Superintendent

Another letter from an early Texas financier and civic-minded man was one signed by W. S. (Wilburn Sandford) Gibbs of Huntsville. Gibbs and his forebears, wealthy landowners and bankers, contributed substantially toward the economic development of Walker County and other areas of Texas. The two Huntsville men he mentioned were persons of stature. Robert Bonner Halley was a professor of physics at Sam Houston State Teachers College, as it was then known, and Charles G. Barrett was a businessman.

Dear Miss Driscoll:

I take pleasure in complying with your request, and wish you and your associates success in your undertaking.

I suggest the names and addresses below:

Prof. R. B. Halley, Huntsville, Texas.

Mr. C. G. Barrett,   ”   ”

” Callum H. Brown, c/o Menger Hotel, San Antonio, Texas.

> Very respectfully,
> /s/ W. S. Gibbs

Frederick Hadra responded to Clara Driscoll's appeal from Fort Saint Philip, Louisiana:

> Fort Saint Philip La.
> July 6 1903

Miss Clara Driscoll
Chairman Alamo Mission Fund
San Antonio, Texas

Dear Madame—

I have the honor to enclose a P.M.O. for One Dollar. I hope it will find sufficient company to enable you to accomplish your most laudable object.

> Very Respectfully,
> /s/ Frederick Hadra.

A. D. Evans of St. Louis, Missouri, invested a dollar in the project.

> St. Louis 7/4/03

Miss Driscoll:

With pleasure I enclose one dollar & hope you will receive enough more to save the Alamo.

Sincerely

/s/ A D Evans

Children of Morril Chapel School, San Antonio, pooled their small change to make up a pot of almost five dollars for the fund:

San Antonio, Texas
Feb. 2, 1904.

Miss C. Driscoll
Chairman Alamo Mission Fund,

Dear Miss Driscoll: Enclosed find ($4.67) Four Dollars and Sixty-seven cents, which I have collected from the pupils and patrons of my school, Morril Chapel.

I am sorry I could not send more to help in this great cause; wishing you success, I am,

Respectfully,

/s/ (Miss) Ernestine Edmunds

LAURELS

Although Clara Driscoll neither coveted nor competed for honors, she was a frequent recipient. Many of these have already been incorporated into the text. It seems appropriate to mention others.

When she was a young girl of fifteen or sixteen Clara Driscoll was chosen queen of the first San Antonio Fiesta. Introduced in 1896 to commemorate the victory at San Jacinto on April 21, 1836, the annual fiesta originally featured a mock battle in which occupants of decorated vehicles pelted each other with blossoms. The event was called the Battle of Flowers. Shortly before her marriage in 1906 Clara Driscoll also presided over the San Antonio festival as queen.

Attention has been given to the Clara Driscoll Day, October 4, 1939, proclaimed by Governor W. Lee O'Daniel, and the many tributes paid to the honoree, including one by the artist Clinton King, whose life-size portrait of her hangs in the state headquarters of the Texas Federation of Women's Clubs in Austin. A handwritten-and-delivered note from the artist to the honor guest is an interesting personal postscript to the event.

[Letterhead stationery]

Hotel Stephen F. Austin
Austin, Texas

Evening, Oct. 4th [1939]

Darling

I know you are so very tired after this day of Clara Driscoll Dedication. Not that it all wasn't beautiful & sincere. But no human being could go through it all without being slightly weary. I'm so sorry I didn't get to the dinner earlier. I did hear part of your talk & it was fine. I'm also sorry that you didn't get to the clubhouse earlier to have heard a few humble words directed toward a very great woman. I called you the Winged Victory of Samothrace & meant it *Straight* from my heart. Will call you around noon tomorrow.

Bless you, dear.

Clinton King

P.S. I was late to the dinner because they couldn't find my dinner jacket at the valet's.[1]

Recognition of Mrs. Driscoll in her native state of Texas is perhaps best attested to by another life-size portrait that was hung in the capitol in Austin in 1921. Painted by Wayman Adams of New York, the canvas was the second of a woman to adorn the Senate walls. The first was of Mrs. Rebecca Fisher of Austin, president of the Daughters of the Republic of Texas, who was present for the ceremony honoring Mrs. Driscoll.[2] Later two other portraits joined company with these. Both were likenesses of Miriam A. Ferguson, Texas's only woman governor.[3]

Reference has also been made to the awarding of the Distinguished Citizenship Medal of the Veterans of Foreign Wars to Mrs. Driscoll in impressive ceremonies on June 17, 1943. Other honors conferred upon the lady in that year included a Doctor of Laws degree from Baylor University; a seven-thousand-dollar Texas history scholarship named for her and established at the University of Texas at Austin by the Daughters of the Republic of Texas; and the choice of Mrs. Driscoll to sponsor the launching of the U.S.S. *Corpus Christi* at Wilmington, California, August 17, 1943.[4]

Historian Marquis James acclaimed Clara Driscoll in the *Saturday Evening*

Post as "The Bestloved Woman of Texas." Books have been dedicated to her. Brochures designed to acknowledge appreciation for her generosity and thoughtfulness have been issued by organizations. It was said that the song "Miss Clara," composed in her honor by the blind musician and World War I hero, was an especial favorite. Lexi Dean Robertson, Texas Poet Laureate in 1939, dedicated a sonnet to her.[5] One of the first books inscribed to Clara Driscoll was *Indianola And Other Poems* by Jeff McLemore in 1904:

Stanzas to Clara
(Composed while standing by the San Antonio River)

Here, by this clear and winding stream,
    Whose waters murmur to the sea;
Where languid nature seems to dream—
    My fancy wings its flight to thee.
The river slowly winds along,
    Its ripples laughing far and near;
The mockingbird sings his sweet song,
    And tells of one to me so dear.
Yet sweeter still his song would be
If *thou* could'st hear it sung with me.

And musing by this stream alone,
    And listening to this song-bird's lay,
My spirit could not help but own
    Its love for one so far away.
The night-winds round me softly sigh,
    And linger, that they might beguile;
The stars look sweetly from the sky,
    And Nature wears her softest smile.
All form a scene that were divine
If *thy* dear hand were clasped in mine.

May, 1903.[6]

Assuredly the young lover's dedication of his book and declaration of love must have been treasured by Clara Driscoll, who preserved a personal copy of the volume of verse throughout her life.

Another memorial, also relating to San Antonio and the shrine—one which surpassed all others as an incentive for personal gratification—was a bronze tablet placed on the walls of the Alamo chapel by the Daughters of the Republic of Texas and unveiled on March 2, Texas Independence Day, 1927:

Lest We Forget

Title to the Alamo Mission property

Acquired by her Efforts and her Personal Fortune

Was Conveyed by

Clara Driscoll

To the State of Texas

Sept. 5, 1905

That the Sacred Shrine be Saved

From the encroachments of Commercialism

And Stand through Eternity

A Monument Incomparable

To the Immortal Heroes

Who Died that Texas might not Perish

March 2, 1927[9]

Notes

CHAPTER ONE
ANTECEDENTS

1 Grants from Coahuila and Texas to Power and Hewetson, Archives General Land Office, Austin, Texas.

2 *Empresario Contract* between Coahuila and Texas and Power and Hewetson, dated June 11, 1826, and April 21, 1830, Archives of General Land Office, Austin, Texas. See also County Deed Records, Refugio County, Texas, vol. 45, p 637.

3 Walter Prescott Webb et al., eds., *The Handbook of Texas*, 2 vols. (Austin, 1952), 2:404.

4 Mary Virginia Henderson, "Minor Empresario Contracts for the Colonization of Texas, 1825–1834," *Southwestern Historical Quarterly* 32 (1928–29), pp. 10–13. See also William H. Oberste, *History of the Missions of Refugio*, Refugio *Timely Remarks*, Refugio, Texas, 1942, passim.

5 Camille Yeamans Neighbors, "The Old Town of Saint Mary's on Copano Bay And Some Interesting People Who Once Lived There" (M.A. thesis, Southwest Texas State Teachers College, San Marcos, Texas, August, 1942), p. 19.

6 James M. Day, comp., *The Texas Almanac 1857–1873* (Waco, 1967), p. 238. See also L. W. Kemp and Thomas L. Miller, comps., *The Honor Roll of The Battle of San Jacinto* (Houston, 1965), San Jacinto Museum of History Association.

7 Van Chandler, "Leaders During Lifetime, Driscolls Left Rich Legacy To Community," Corpus Christi *Caller*, January 18, 1959.

8 Webb and others, eds., *The Handbook of Texas*, 2:457

9 Ibid.

10 Journal of Constitutional Convention, 1869, H. P. S. Gammel, *Laws of*

Texas, 10 vols. (Austin, 1822–1897), 2 and 3, passim. See also Neighbors, *The Old Town of Saint Mary's* . . . , p. 78.

11 Refugio *Timely Remarks*, Centennial Edition, December 14, 1934.

12 Neighbors, "The Old Town of Saint Mary's . . . ," p. 23.

13 John J. Linn, *Reminiscences of Fifty Years in Texas* (New York, 1883), pp. 30–32. See also Robert Huson, *El Copano, Ancient Port of Bexar and La Bahia* (Refugio *Timely Remarks*, Refugio, 1936), pp. 6, 15, 30.

14 Neighbors, *The Old Town of Saint Mary's* . . . , p. 30.

15 Lyman Brightman Russell, *Grandad's Autobiography* (Comanche, Texas, 1930), pp. 17, 19. See also Neighbors *The Old Town of Saint Mary's* . . . , pp. 91–93.

16 Lyman Brightman Russell, "Recollections" manuscript. See also Neighbors as cited, p. 93.

17 Refugio *Timely Remarks*, Centennial Edition, December, 1934. For text of "A Night in Tilden" see the Refugio *Review*, March 17, 1911.

18 Andy Brightman, "Recollections" manuscript. See also Neighbors, as cited, p. 104.

19 Ibid. See also files of Refugio *Review* for years up to 1912.

20 Sallis J. Burmeister, "Reminiscences" manuscript. See also Neighbors, p. 106.

21 Neighbors as previously cited, p. 100. See also William Louis Rea, "Memoirs" manuscript.

22 *Indianola Scrap Book*, compiled and published by The Victoria *Advocate*, Victoria, Texas, 1936, pp. 70–84.

23 Neighbors, p. 120.

24 Webb and others, eds., *The Handbook of Texas*, 2:530.

25 Joe B. Frantz and Julian Choate, Jr., *The American Cowboy: The Myth & The Reality* (Norman, 1955), p. 17.

26 Ima King Curlott, "Foundations of a Family," Corpus Christi *Reporter*, December 10, 1950. See also Webb and others, eds., *The Handbook of Texas*, 1:341–342.

27 J. Frank Dobie, *A Vaquero of the Brush Country* (Dallas, 1929), p. 12. In the statement Dobie quotes John Young, who knew the Driscolls personally.

28 Ibid., p. 120.

29 Hobart Huson, "Rooke Family Always Faced Goodwill Projects of This Area," Woodsboro, *Refugio County*, August 9, 1957.

30 Bernard Brister, "The Story and Tradition of the Driscolls," The *Cattleman*, December, 1940, p. 85.

31 "Empress Clara," *Time*, July 30, 1945, p. 23.

32 "Driscoll Program Advances," The Corpus Christi *Caller–Times*, October 29, 1939, p. 5C.

33 Brister, "The Story and Tradition of the Driscolls," The *Cattleman*, December, 1940, pp. 85–87.

34 "Driscoll Program Advances," The Corpus Christi *Caller–Times*, October 29, 1939.

35 Jack C. Butterfield, *Clara Driscoll Rescued The Alamo—A Brief Biograpy* (San Antonio, 1961), pamphlet, np.

36 Paul Horgan, *Great River: The Rio Grande in North American History*, 2 vols. (New York, 1954), *The Indians & Spain*, 1:83–89.

37 Ibid., pp. 98–100.

38 Henry Reed Stiles, ed., *Joutel's Journal of La Salle's Last Voyage*, 1689–1693 (Albany, New York, 1906), passim. See also Francis Parkman, *La Salle and the Discovery of the Great West* (New York, 1963), pp. 308 ff.

39 Herbert Eugene Bolton, *Texas In The Middle Eighteenth Century* (Austin, 1970), pp. 57–63.

40 J. Frank Davis (State Supervisor Texas Writers' Project), *Corpus Christi: A History and Guide* (Corpus Christi, 1942), p. 52.

41 Ibid., p. 56.

42 Walter Prescott Webb, *The Texas Rangers* (Austin, 1935), p. 91.

43 Ibid., pp. 114–116. See also Richard N. Current, T. Hardy Williams, and Frank Freidel, *American History: A Survey* (New York, 1961), pp. 348–349.

44 Walter Prescott Webb, *The Great Plains* (Austin, 1931), p. 210. See also Frantz and Choate, *The American Cowboy*, p. 20.

45 E. P. Felger, "Texas in the War for Southern Independence" (Ph.D. diss., The University of Texas at Austin, 1935).

46 Mary A. Sutherland, *The Story of Corpus Christi* (Houston, 1916), pp. 19–31. See also J. Frank Davis, comp., *Corpus Christi, A History and Guide* (Corpus Christi, 1942), pp. 99–121.

47 Butterfield, *Clara Driscoll Rescued The Alamo*, np.

CHAPTER TWO
THE BIRTH OF A LEGEND

1 Travel file, the Driscoll Archives, Robert Driscoll And Julia Driscoll And Robert Driscoll, Jr. Foundation, Bank & Trust Bldg., Corpus Christi, Tex.

2 "The Alamo Is Run Down," The San Antonio *Express*, January 14, 1901. See also Mrs. Cora Carleton Glassford, ed., *Fifty Years of Achievement:*

History Of The Daughters Of The Republic Of Texas (Dallas, 1942), pp. 184–185.

3 Clara Driscoll, *In the Shadow of the Alamo* (New York, 1906), p. 26.

4 Deed Records Bexar County, Texas, Book 106, p. 162.

5 Deed Records Bexar County, Texas, Boox 223, p. 261. See also San Antonio *Express*, January 29, 1905, p. 4; Ibid., April 19, 1903, p. 16.

6 *Annual Report of the Daughters of the Republic of Texas*, April 20–21, 1894, p. 4. See also Mrs. A. B. Looscan, "Daughters of the Republic of Texas," *The Texas Magazine*, 4:112.

7 O. B. Colquitt, *Message to the Thirty-third Legislature concerning the Alamo* (Austin, 1913), pp. 1–2, 4.

8 Ibid., p. 10. See also Surveyors' Records of Bexar County, Book F-1, p. 28.

9 H. P. N. Gammel, *The Laws of Texas* (Austin, 1822–1897), 2:26.

10 *Reports of the Supreme Court of Texas*, 15:539–546; see also San Antonio *Light*, May 17, 1883, p. 1.

11 C. W. Barnes, *Combats and Conquests of Immortal Heroes* (San Antonio, 1910), p. 47. See also N. O. Winter, *Texas The Marvelous* (Boston, 1916), p. 108.

12 Barnes, *Combats and Conquests of Immortal Heroes*, p. 46.

13 Viktor Bracht, *Texas in 1848* (San Antonio, 1931), pp. 174, 177.

14 *Official Records*, Series 1, vol. 1, p. 517. See also San Antonio *Light*, September 16, 1904, p. 1.

15 Anna B. Story, "The Alamo From Its Founding To 1937" (M. A. thesis, The University of Texas at Austin, August, 1938), p. 45.

16 Deed Records Bexar County, Texas, Book 5, p. 538; Book A-2, p. 470.

17 Story, "The Alamo From Its Founding To 1937," p. 50.

18 William Corner, *San Antonio de Bexar* (San Antonio, 1890), p. 11. See also *House Journal Eighteenth Legislature*, p. 140.

19 Deed Records Bexar County, Texas, Book 48, p. 50.

20 San Antonio *Express*, July 28, 1907, p. 1.

21 *Texas Field and National Guardsman*, May 12, 1912, p. 347. See also Story, "The Alamo From Its Founding To 1937," p. 59.

22 Story, "The Alamo From Its Founding To 1937," pp. 63–64.

23 J. Frank Dobie, "The Line That Travis Drew," *In The Shadow of History* (Austin, 1939), pp. 13–16.

24 Martha Anne Turner, *William Barret Travis: His Sword And His Pen* (Waco, 1972), pp. 241–257. See also Walter Lord, *A Time To Stand* (New York, 1961) for authentic details of the Alamo siege.

25 Turner, *William Barret Travis . . .*, p. 214.

26 Clara Driscoll, *In the Shadow of the Alamo* (New York, 1906), p. 25.

27 Ibid., p. 27.

28 Ibid., pp. 28–29.

29 Clara Driscoll to Mr. Charles Hugo, February 5, 1903, Alamo correspondence file, Driscoll Archives, The Driscoll Foundation.

30 Story, *The Alamo From Its Founding To 1937*, pp. 65–66. See also the San Antonio *Light*, April 29, 1906; and *Fifty Years of Achievement* . . . , pp. 182–183.

31 *Fifteenth Annual Report of the Daughters of the Republic of Texas*, April 20–21, 1906, p. 20.

32 Molyneaux, "How The Alamo Was Saved," p. 425.

33 San Antonio *Express*, June 21, 1903.

34 *Fifteenth Annual Report of the Daughters of the Republic of Texas*, April 20–21, 1906, p. 29.

35 San Antonio *Express*, May 5, 1903. See also *House Journal Twenty-eighth Legislature*, 1903, pp. 296, 347.

36 San Antonio Express, April 16, 1903; October 18, 1904.

37 Lockhart *Post*, February 20, 1904, p. 1. See also San Antonio *Light*, February 27, 1904.

38 Butterfield, *Clara Driscoll Rescued the Alamo*, np.

39 *Fifteenth Annual Report of the Daughters of the Republic of Texas*, April 20–21, 1906, p. 18.

40 *Fifty Years Of Achievement* . . . , pp. 181–182. See also Molyneaux, "How The Alamo Was Saved," p. 429.

41 Deed Records Bexar County, Texas, Book 223, p. 261. See also Legal Papers File, Driscoll Archives, The Driscoll Foundation. Although paid on or before February 10, 1904, the document bears the date of April 15, 1904.

42 Molyneaux, "How The Alamo Was Saved," p. 420.

43. Ibid., p. 430. See also *Fifty Years Of Achievement* . . . , p. 189.

44 San Antonio *Express*, April 19, 1904, p. 20.

45 *Fourteenth Annual Report of the Daughters of the Republic of Texas*, April 18–19, 1905, p. 28.

46 Ibid., p. 36.

47 Story, *The Alamo From Its Founding To 1937*, p. 72.

48 San Antonio *Express*, February 5, 1905.

49 *General Laws of Texas, First Regular Session, Twenty-ninth Legislature*, 1905, pp. 7–8. See also San Antonio *Express*, January 25, 1905, p. 1.

50 *General Laws of Texas, Twenty-ninth Legislature*, 1905, p. 8.

51 San Antonio *Express*, August 31, 1905, p. 8.

52 Ibid., September 2, 1905, p. 6. See also O. B. Colquitt, *Message to the Thirty-third Legislature*, pp. 65–66.
53 Story, *The Alamo From Its Founding To 1937*, p. 77. See also *Fifty Years Of Achievement . . .* , p. 189.

CHAPTER THREE
AUTHOR AND PLAYWRIGHT

1 *Dramatic Compositions Copyrighted In The United States: 1870–1916* (Washington, D.C., 1918), vol 1 (A to N), First Reprint, 1968, 29351.
2 David Ewen, *The Complete Book Of The American Theater* (New York, 1958), p. 153.
3 Ibid. See also "Miss Clara Driscoll, A Bride," San Antonio *Semi-Weekly Express*, August 3, 1906.
4 *Mexicana* File, Driscoll Archives, The Driscoll Foundation.
5 Ibid.
6 Ibid.
7 Legal File, Driscoll Archives, The Driscoll Foundation.
8 Original program for *Mexicana*, *Mexicana* File, Driscoll Archives, The Driscoll Foundation.
9 Ibid.
10 Ibid.
11 Reviews and press notices, *Mexicana* File, Driscoll Archives, The Driscoll Foundation.

CHAPTER FOUR
ROMANCE OF THE ALAMO

1 Maurine Eastus, "Clara Driscoll's Personal Effects Reflect Vivid Life," Corpus Christi *Caller-Times*, October 4, 1953.
2 Fannie Ratchford, "About Your Ancestors: The Sevier Family," Dallas *News*, June 26, 1932.
3 Zella Armstrong, *Notable Southern Families*, 2 vols., (Chattanooga, Tennessee, 1918), 1:180–181.
4 Ibid.
5 Ratchford, "About Your Ancestors: The Sevier Family," Dallas *News*, June 26, 1932.
6 Armstrong, *Notable Southern Families*, 1:182.

7 Ibid., p. 189. See also Ratchford, "About Your Ancestors . . . ," Dallas *News*, June 26, 1932.

8 Richard N. Current and others, *American History: A Survey* (New York, 1961), pp. 116, 119.

9 Ratchford, "About Your Ancestors . . . ," Dallas *News*, June 26, 1932.

10 Will L. Smith, ed., *Members of the Texas Legislature 1846-1962* (Austin, 1962), pp. 200-209. See also Tommy Yett, ed., *Members of the Legislature of the State of Texas from 1846 to 1930* (Austin, 1939) pp. 200, 209.

11 Ibid. See also the San Antonio *Semi-Weekly Express*, August 3, 1906.

12 "Miss Clara Driscoll, A Bride," San Antonio *Semi-Weekly Express*, August 3, 1906.

13 Ibid.

14 Maurine Eastus, "Clara Driscoll's Personal Effects Reflect Vivid Life," Corpus Christi *Caller-Times*, October 4, 1952.

15 The San Antonio *Daily Express*, April 18, 1906.

16 "Miss Clara Driscoll, A Bride," San Antonio *Semi-Weekly Express*, August 3, 1906.

17 Ibid.

CHAPTER FIVE
THE NEW YORK YEARS

1 New York File, Driscoll Archives, The Driscoll Foundation.

2 "Artistic Effects In New Long Island," and other New York newspaper clippings in New York File, Driscoll Archives, The Driscoll Foundation.

3 Ibid.

4 Eastus, "Clara Driscoll's Personal Effects Reflect Vivid Life," Corpus Christi *Caller-Times*, October 4, 1953. See also Recipe Files, Driscoll Archives, The Driscoll Foundation.

5 Ibid.

6 Eastus, "Clara Driscoll's Personal Effects . . ."

7 Ibid. See also New York File, Driscoll Archives, The Driscoll Foundation.

8 Literary File, Driscoll Archives, The Driscoll Foundation.

9 Clara Driscoll, "The Angel of Banquete," Driscoll Archives, The Driscoll Foundation.

10 Sherwin R. Mills, "The Texas Club: A New York Organization of Which Mrs. Driscoll Servier is President," *Texas Magazine* 7 (February, 1913), p. 311.

11 Ibid., p. 312.

12 Ibid.

13 Programs, Carnival cotillion in celebration of the Battle of San Jacinto, given by the Texas Club of New York City, Friday, April 21, 1911, The Plaza Hotel, New York City. New York File, Driscoll Archives, The Driscoll Foundation.

14 Ibid.

15 Mills, "The Texas Club . . . ," p. 312.

16 The Dallas *Morning News*, March 11, 1940.

CHAPTER SIX
LAGUNA GLORIA

1 Butterfield, *Clara Driscoll Rescued The Alamo*, np.

2 Ruth Kluge, *Laguna Gloria, A Manuscript Pamphlet for Visitors at Laguna Gloria Art Gallery* (Austin, 1975), Item 7.

3 Ibid.

4 Alex W. Terrell, "The City of Austin from 1839 to 1865," *Quarterly of the Texas State Historical Association* 14 (October, 1910), p. 114. See also Martha Anne Turner, *The Life and Times Of Jane Long* (Waco, 1969), p. 143.

5 Kluge, *Laguna Gloria . . .* , as previously cited.

6 Ibid.

7 Kluge, *Laguna Gloria . . .* , as previously cited. See also Rudolph Bresie, "Laguna Gloria," unpublished term paper, 1968, Architecture Archives, The University of Texas at Austin, for pertinent detail.

8 Ibid.

9 Clara Driscoll, "The Red Rose of San José," *In The Shadow of The Alamo*, pp. 163–205.

10 Butterfield, *Clara Driscoll Rescued The Alamo*, np.

11 Mary Laswell, "Clara Driscoll Sevier As I Knew Her," Introduction to *Clara Driscoll Rescued The Alamo*, np.

12 Ibid.

13 Ibid.

14 Ibid.

15 Ibid.

16 "Hal Sevier, Former Chile Envoy Dies," Dallas *News*, March 11, 1940, p. 1. See also Webb, et al., eds., *The Handbook of Texas*, 2:594.

17 Fort Worth *Star Telegram*, July 31, 1934.

18 The Dallas *News*, March 11, 1940.

19 Current and others, *American History: A Survey* (New York, 1961), pp. 676–679.

20 Fort Worth *Star Telegram*, July 31, 1934.

21 *Who's Who In America* (Chicago, 1943), 2:163.

22 "Hal Sevier, Former Chile Envoy Dies," Dallas *News*, March 11, 1940.

23 Fort Worth *Star Telegram*, July 21, 1934.

CHAPTER SEVEN
MINDING THE STORE

1 The Corpus Christi *Caller–Times*, July 18, 1945.

2 "Robert Driscoll Was the Director of Famous Estate," Corpus Christi *Caller–Times*, October 1, 1940. See also J. Frank Davis, ed., *Corpus Christi, A History and Guide* (Corpus Christi, 1942), p. 178.

3 The Corpus Christi *Caller–Times*, July 19, 1945.

4 "Control of Vast Driscoll Domain Leaves Hands of Family First Time ...," Fort Worth *Star Telegram*, July 31, 1934.

5 "Taft Properties Sold," The *Cattleman*, September, 1928.

6 Ibid.

7 Butterfield, *Clara Driscoll Rescued The Alamo*, np.

8 Brister, "The Story and Tradition of the Driscolls," The *Cattleman*, December, 1940, pp. 85–86. See also the Corpus Christi *Caller–Times*, December 1, 1940.

9 "Control of Vast Driscoll Domain Leaves Hands . . . ," Fort Worth *Star Telegram*, July 31, 1934.

10 Ibid.

11 The Corpus Christi *Caller–Times*, July 18, 1945.

12 Brister, "The Story and Tradition of the Driscolls," The *Cattleman*, December, 1940, p. 86.

13 Butterfield, *Clara Driscoll Rescued The Alamo*, np.

14 Brister, "The Story and Tradition of the Driscolls," Corpus Christi *Caller–Times*, December 1, 1940.

15 Ibid.

16 Clara Driscoll, *The Girl of La Gloria* (New York, 1905), pp. 68–69.

17 Ibid., pp. 174–175.

18 Ibid.

CHAPTER EIGHT
THE CHILE AMBASSADORSHIP AND DIVORCE

1 The Chile Ambassador File, Driscoll Archives, The Driscoll Foundation.

2 "Seviers Honored at Tonight's Banquet," *Under Six Flags*, official publication of the Young Democratic Clubs of Texas, October 20, 1933.

3 "Control of Vast Domain Leaves Hands of Family First Time When Ambassadorship Takes Hal Sevier and Saviour of Alamo Out of United States," Fort Worth *Star Telegram*, July 31, 1934.

4 Ibid.

5 Ibid.

6 Ibid.

7 "Seviers Honored at Tonight's Banquet," *Under Six Flags*, October 20, 1933. See also program, "Farewell Banquet Honoring Ambassador and Mrs. Hal. H. Sevier, Given by Young Democratic Club, Nueces County, Friday, October 20, 1933," Driscoll Archives, The Driscoll Foundation.

8 Bascom N. Timmons, *Garner of Texas: A Personal History* (New York, 1948), pp. 167–168.

9 Program, "Farewell Banquet Honoring Ambassador and Mrs. Hal H. Sevier," Driscoll Archives, The Driscoll Foundation.

10 "Seviers Honored at Tonight's Banquet," *Under Six Flags*, October 20, 1933. See also additional newspaper files, Driscoll Archives, The Driscoll Foundation.

11 K. H. Silvert, *Chile Yesterday and Today* (New York, 1965), pp. 71–72.

12 *Encyclopaedia Britannica*, 5:554.

13 Silvert, *Chile Yesterday and Today*, pp. 141–146. See also Agustin Edwards, *My Native Land* (London, 1928), pp. 155–159.

14 Ibid., p. 124.

15 Silvert, *Chile Yesterday and Today*, pp. 73–79.

16 Ibid., pp. 74–77.

17 Eastus, "Clara Driscoll's Personal Effects Reflect Vivid Life," Corpus Christi *Caller-Times*, October 4, 1953.

18 "Their Excellencies, Our Ambassadors," *Fortune Magazine*, 9 (April, 1934), p. 120.

19 "Mrs. Clara Driscoll Sevier is Seeking Divorce," San Antonio *Evening Sun*, May 21, 1937.

20 Ibid.

21 "No! Mrs. Sevier Tells Husband," San Antonio *Express*, May 23, 1937. See also "Reconciliation Between Seviers Not Reached," San Antonio *Evening News*, May 23, 1937.

22 Legal Papers, Driscoll Archives, The Driscoll Foundation. See also "Divorce Granted Mrs. Sevier," Corpus Christi *Caller-Times*, July 9, 1937, and the Dallas *News*, May 21, 1937.
23 Clara Driscoll, "Sister Genevieve," *In the Shadow of the Alamo*, p. 71.
24 Ibid., p. 67.
25 "Hal Sevier: Gentleman," Austin *American*, August 1, 1937.
26 Legal Papers, Driscoll Archives, The Driscoll Foundation. See also Newspaper Clipping File, Driscoll Archives, The Driscoll Foundation.
27 "Sevier Divorce Case Is Settled," Corpus Christi *Caller-Times*, February 17, 1938. See also Legal Papers, Driscoll Archives, Driscoll Foundation.
28 "Sevier Divorce Case Is Settled," Corpus Christi *Caller-Times*, February 17, 1938.
29 Ibid.
30 Legal Papers, Driscoll Archives, The Driscoll Foundation.
31 "Hal Sevier, Former Chile Envoy, Dies," Dallas *News*, March 11, 1940.
32 Ibid.

CHAPTER NINE
CLARA DRISCOLL—PHILANTHROPIST

1 *Twenty-Third Annual Report of The Daughters of The Republic of Texas*, April 22, 1934, p. 51.
2 *General Laws of Texas Forty-first Legislature, Fifth Called Session*, p. 266.
3 Deed Records Bexar County, Texas, Book 1281, pp. 438–440; Book 101, p. 62. See also Story, *The Alamo From Its Founding To 1937*, p. 184.
4 Mrs. Glassford, ed., *Fifty Years of Achievement . . .* , xii.
5 "Clara Driscoll Saves Women's Clubhouse by Assuming Debts," Austin *American*, October 5, 1939.
6 "Texas Club Leaders Gather Here For Festivities Today Honoring Mrs. Clara Driscoll," Austin *American*, October 4, 1939.
7 "Clara Driscoll Saves Women's Clubhouse by Assuming Debts," Austin *American*, October 5, 1939.
8 "Texas Club Women to Observe Clara Driscoll Day Wednesday," Austin *American*, October 1, 1939.
9 "Governor's Proclamation Sets Aside October 4 As Clara Driscoll Day," Corpus Christi *Caller-Times*, September 26, 1939. See also W. Lee O'Daniel, "Proclamation by the Governor of the State of Texas," September 23, 1939, La Retama Library, Corpus Christi.
10 "Texas Club Leaders Gather Here for Festivities Today Honoring Mrs.

Clara Driscoll," Austin *American*, October 4, 1939. "Coffee Given at Austin Hotel for Mrs. Clara Driscoll," Corpus Christi *Caller–Times*, October 4, 1939.

11 "Texas Club Women To Observe Clara Driscoll Day Wednesday," Austin *American*, October 1, 1939.

12 "Coffee Given at Austin Hotel for Mrs. Clara Driscoll," Corpus Christi *Caller–Times*, October 4, 1939.

13 "Clara Driscoll—Patriot," original copy of address in the Driscoll Archives, The Driscoll Foundation.

14 Roy Miller to Clara Driscoll, October 16, 1939, Personal Letter File, Driscoll Archives, The Driscoll Foundation.

15 "Clubwomen Pay Tribute To Mrs. Driscoll At Ceremonies," Corpus Christi *Caller–Times*, October 5, 1939.

16 "Governor O'Daniel Speaks at Unveiling," Austin *American*, October 4, 1939. See also "Clara Driscoll Texas' Foremost Patriot, Roy Miller says as He Unveils Portrait of Her," Austin *American*, October 5, 1939.

17 "Clubwomen Pay Tribute To Mrs. Driscoll At Ceremonies," Corpus Christi *Caller–Times*, October 5, 1939.

18 Fannie C. Potter, ed. and comp., *History of The Texas Federation of Women's Clubs 1918–1939* (Denton, Texas, 1941), 2:387.

19 Ibid., Dedication. See also pp. 40, 297.

20 Kluge, "Laguna Gloria," p. 2.

21 "Clara Driscoll Formally Presents Laguna Gloria to Art Association to Use as Gallery," Austin *American*, December 5, 1943.

22 "Mrs. Driscoll Presents Home, Laguna Gloria, for Use as Texas State Art Gallery," Austin *American*, October 7, 1943, p. 1.

23 "Clara Driscoll Formally Presents Laguna Gloria to Art Association to Use as Gallery," Austin *American*, December 5, 1943.

24 Ibid.

CHAPTER TEN

NATIONAL DEMOCRATIC COMMITTEEWOMAN

1 "Mrs. Driscoll Active Politically," Corpus Christi *Caller–Times*, October 6, 1940.

2 "Political, Business and Social Career of Mrs. Clara Driscoll Proves That Texas Still Produces the Great Ones In Any Line," *Texas Press Messenger*, April, 1939, pp. 22–23.

3 Richard N. Current, T. Harry Williams, and Frank Freidel, *American History: A Survey* (New York, 1961), pp. 710–712.

4 John A. Garraty, *The American Nation: A History of the United States* (New York, 1966), p. 891.

5 "Political, Business and Social Career of Mrs. Clara Driscoll . . . ," *Texas Press Messenger*, April, 1939, p. 23. See also "Mrs. Clara Driscoll Will Match—Two for One—Any Donation for Plane Base," Corpus Christi *Caller-Times*, May 21, 1939.

6 Garraty, *The American Nation* . . . , pp. 741, 891.

7 Ibid, p. 739.

8 Current et al., *American History* . . . , p. 758.

9 Ibid.

10 Bascom N. Timmons, *Garner of Texas: A Personal History* (New York, 1948), pp. 214–216.

11 Garraty, *The American Nation* . . . , pp. 744–745.

12 Ibid., pp. 742–743.

13 Ibid., p. 743.

14 Ibid., p. 745.

15 Timmons, *Garner of Texas* . . . , p. 241.

16 "Garner for President, Result of Mrs. Driscoll's Nominating Action, Group Headed By Mrs. Driscoll Push Garner For Presidential Post," Corpus Christi *Caller-Times*, October 29, 1939.

17 Ibid. See also Timmons, *Garner of Texas* . . . , pp. 250–251.

18 Current et al., *American History* . . . , p. 749.

19 Timmons, *Garner of Texas* . . . , p. 242.

20 Ibid.

21 Ibid., p. 243.

22 Current et al., *American History* . . . , p. 748.

23 Timmons, *Garner of Texas* . . . , p. 254.

24 Ibid., p. 253.

25 Ibid., pp. 251–252.

26 Ibid., p. 253.

27 Timmons, *Garner of Texas* . . . , p. 260.

28 Ibid.

29 Ibid., p. 262.

30 Current et al., *American History* . . . , p. 764.

31 Political Files, Driscoll Archives, The Driscoll Foundation. See also Timmons, *Garner of Texas*, p. 267.

32 Ibid.

33 Political Files, Driscoll Archives, The Driscoll Foundation.

34 "Mrs. Driscoll Attends State Democratic Convention," Corpus Christi *Caller-Times*, May 28, 1940.

35 "Mrs. Driscoll Active Politically," Corpus Christi *Caller-Times*, October 6, 1940.

36 "Mrs. Driscoll Active in State and National Affairs," Corpus Christi *Caller-Times*, October 29, 1939.

37 "Political, Business and Social Career of Mrs. Clara Driscoll . . . ," *Texas Press Messenger*, April, 1939, p. 22.

38 Garraty, *The American Nation* . . . , p. 761. See also Current et al., *American History* . . . , pp. 766–787.

39 "Empress Clara," *Time* (July 30, 1945), p. 23.

40 Timmons, *Garner of Texas* . . . , p. 174.

41 Ibid., p. 275.

42 "Empress Clara," *Time* (July 30, 1945), p. 23.

43 "Political, Business and Social Career of Mrs. Clara Driscoll . . . ," *Texas Press Messenger*, April, 1939, p. 23.

44 Current et al., *American History* . . . , p. 767.

45 "Mrs. Driscoll Active Politically," Corpus Christi *Caller-Times*, October 6, 1940.

46 "Texans Attend Inaugural," Dallas *News*, January 22, 1941.

47 Current et al., *American History* . . . , p. 790.

48 Corpus Christi *Times*, July 18, 1945.

49 "Mrs. Driscoll Dies in Corpus," Austin *American*, July 17, 1945.

50 "Mrs. Driscoll Active in State Democratic Politics, Business, and Many Philanthropies," Corpus Christi *Caller-Times*, July 18, 1945.

51 Ibid.

52 Current et al., *American History* . . . , pp. 790–791. While Roosevelt allegedly tried to divert national attention to the war effort as a means of distracting critics of the Pearl Harbor debacle, his supporters employed the veil of national security as an effective cover-up of the attack to insure his election to a fourth term. This, coupled with the strain of conducting the war and battling unsympathetic Republicans in Congress, proved to be an insurmountable ordeal.

53 Current et al., *American History* . . . , p. 791.

54 President Roosevelt and Clara Driscoll died within a few months of each other. Roosevelt's death occurred at Warm Springs, Georgia, on April 12, 1945. Mrs. Driscoll died on July 17, 1945, at Corpus Christi, Texas.

55 Garraty, *The American Nation* . . . , p. 748.

CHAPTER ELEVEN
CORPUS CHRISTI ENTREPRENEUR

1 "Mrs. Driscoll Active Politically," Corpus Christi *Caller-Times*, October

6, 1940.

2 Ibid. See also "Clara Driscoll Honored With Active Year," Corpus Christi *Caller–Times*, October 13, 1940.

3 "Driscoll Program Advances . . . ," Corpus Christi *Caller–Times*, October 29, 1939. See also "Driscoll Name Synonymous With Texas History," Corpus Christi *Caller–Times*, October 13, 1940.

4 "Driscoll Program Advances . . . ," Corpus Christi *Caller–Times*, October 29, 1939.

5 "Mrs. Clara Driscoll Will Match—Two for One—Any Donation for Plane Base," Corpus Christi *Caller–Times*, March 21, 1940.

6 "Driscoll Name Identified With South Texas Progress Since Close of Civil War," Corpus Christi *Caller–Times*, October 6, 1940.

7 "Corpus Christi's New Hotel Named for Late Robert Driscoll," Corpus Christi *Caller–Times*, October 29, 1939.

8 "Construction Is To Start Immediately: McKenzie Construction Co. Will Build The Robert Driscoll," Austin *American*, May 1, 1939.

9 Green Peyton, *The Faces of Texas* (New York, 1961), p. 224.

10 "Driscoll Program Advances . . . ," Corpus Christi *Caller–Times*, October 29, 1939.

11 Ibid.

12 Peyton, *The Face of Texas*, p. 224.

13 Ibid.

14 Ibid., p. 223.

15 The source of this information was Dr. McIver Furman, who was both Mrs. Driscoll's physician and personal friend. Personal interview with Dr. Furman, August 20, 1977.

16 Ibid.

17 "Empress Clara," *Time* (July 30, 1945), p. 24.

18 The Corpus Christi *Caller–Times*, June 19, 1943.

19 Letter File, Driscoll Archives, The Driscoll Foundation.

CHAPTER TWELVE
WORLD TRAVELER

Unless otherwise identified, the source of all quotations in this chapter is the Travel File in the Driscoll Archives, The Driscoll Foundation, Corpus Christi, Texas. The file contains travel itineraries, personal handwritten notes, clipped copies of the "Texas Girl" travel sketches submitted to various Texas newspapers from around the world, some dated and some undated, post cards, souvenirs, and other ephemera.

1 Travel File, Driscoll Archives, The Driscoll Foundation.
2 Ibid.
3 Eastus, "Clara Driscoll's Personal Effects Reflect Vivid Life," Corpus Christi *Caller-Times*, October 4, 1953.
4 Ibid.

CHAPTER THIRTEEN
THE LAST LEGACY

1 "Mrs. Driscoll Will Be Buried in San Antonio," Corpus Christi *Caller-Times*, July 20, 1945.
2 Ibid. Mrs. Driscoll's loyalty to the Democratic party gave the impression that she was an ardent supporter of Roosevelt. While she liked him as a casual friend, his politics failed to measure up to her standards.
3 "Clara Driscoll's Body To Lie in State in Alamo," Austin *American*, July 18, 1945.
4 Ibid.
5 "Value of Driscoll Estate Placed at $7,022,706," Corpus Christi *Caller-Times*, April 7, 1946. This estimation was reached as the result of an appriasal with documents docketed in Nueces County court April 16, 1946.
6 Last Will and Testament of Clara Driscoll, Filed, July 26, 1945, Mrs. Henry E. Gouger, County Clerk, Nueces Couty, Texas, by Claudine Troupe, Deputy; Docketed, Keys, Holt, and Head, attorneys at Law, Corpus Christi, Texas, Vol. 29, pp. 121–126. See also Driscoll Archives, the Driscoll Foundation.
7 Ibid.

CHAPTER FOURTEEN
DRISCOLL FOUNDATION CHILDREN'S HOSPITAL

1 Official Records, Driscoll Foundation Children's Hospital, Corpus Christi, Texas.
2 Of the three original appointees to administer the Driscoll Foundation, only Dr. McIver Furman remains. W. Preston Pittman replaced John T. O'Neill (deceased, 1950) and T. S. Scibienski replaced I. W. Keys (deceased, 1955).
3 Driscoll Foundation Children's Hospital, Quinquennial Report, 1969-

1972, np. See also Official Records.

4 Statement of Dr. Furman and Mr. Pittman to author, April 17, 1978.

5 Interview with Dr. Furman, April 18, 1978. See also Official Records, Driscoll Archives, The Driscoll Foundation.

6 Ibid.

7 Driscoll Foundation Children's Hospital, Quinquennial Report, 1969–1972, np.

8 Official Records, Driscoll Foundation Children's Hospital.

9 Roster prepared by Dr. Joe Sloan, medical director of Driscoll (1952–1972). Original on file in Official Records.

10 Hospital Bulletin, *The Driscollite*, January–February, 1978, p. 5.

11 Statement released by Driscoll Foundation trustees. See also Official Records.

12 Statement released by President Epperson and confirmed by trustees.

13 Personal interview with Mr. Gordon Epperson, April 18, 1978.

14 Ibid. See also Hospital Bulletin, *The Driscollite*, January–February, 1978, p. 2.

APPENDIX
LAURELS

1 Clinton King to Clara Driscoll, Personal Letter File, Driscoll Archives, The Driscoll Foundation.

2 "Woman's Portrait Placed in Senate," Dallas *Morning News*, August 12, 1921.

3 Ibid.

4 *Who Was Who in America* 2 (1943), p. 163.

5 Program "Clara Driscoll Day," La Retama Library, Corpus Christi; Driscoll Archives, the Driscoll Foundation.

6 Jeff McLemore, *Indianola And Other Poems* (San Antonio, 1904), p. 104.

7 The inscription quoted here is in the same form as that of the tablet in the Alamo Chapel and as it is carried in *Fifty Years Of Achievement*, pp. 181–182.

Index

Driscoll, 82

O'Driscoll, Daniel: paternal grandfather of Clara Driscoll, 1–2; officer at the Battle of San Jacinto, 3

O'Neil, John T.: pallbearer at Driscoll funeral, 140

Palo Alto: base of Driscoll ranching operations, 9, 13, 14; removal of Seviers to, 66–68 passim

Paris: visited by Seviers on honeymoon, 45–47

Perkins, Mrs. Joseph M.: 84

Philwin, Harry, blind veteran of World War I: assists Mrs. Driscoll in bond rally, 112

Piñeda, Alonzo Alvarez: 10

Pittman, W. Preston: assists in making Driscoll funeral arrangements, 138; named heir in Driscoll will, 141; trustee of Driscoll Foundation, 143

Power, Colonel James: colonizer, 1–3

Prado, Dr. Alfonso: 147

Rayburn, Sam: Speaker of the House and good friend of Clara Driscoll, 104; honorary pallbearer at Driscoll funeral, 140

Refugio County: 1, 2, 3, 7

Republican Party: 2, 88

Robeadeau, Mrs. Roger: president of the Texas Fine Arts Association, accepts gift of Laguna Gloria, 85, 86

Robertson, Lexie Dean: dedicates sonnet to Clara Driscoll, 158

Robstown: named for Robert Driscoll, Jr., 9

Rockport: 3

Rooke, Frank B.: husband of Roberta Driscoll, 4

Roosevelt, Franklin Delano: names Hal Sevier ambassador to the Republic of Chile, 69–70; Preface, xi–xv passim; as candidate for office and as New Deal president, 87–106 passim; see also Garner, John Nance; Driscoll, Clara; and Sevier, Hal; Clara Driscoll's loyalty to, recalled, 139; mentioned, 140

Roosevelt, former president Theodore: neighbor to the Seviers on Oyster Bay, 50

Rose, Louis Moses: Alamo defector, 21

Rupp, Dr. Joseph: 147

Sabinal, Texas: home of Hal Sevier, 44

Sabinal *Sentinel*: newspaper established by Sevier, 44

San Antonio, Texas: birthplace of independence, 16; and the Alamo, 18–19, 20, 23, 46, 87

San Jacinto, Battle of: 2, 3

Santa Anna, Antonio Lopez de: mentioned, 21

Schofield, Collector of Internal Revenue Frank: pallbearer at Driscoll funeral, 140

Scibienski, T. S.: member of the trustees of the Driscoll Foundation, 143

Scott, General Winfield: victory celebrated in halls of Montezuma, 13

Seago, Doss: 140

Sealy, John: 152

Self, Mayor Roy L. of Corpus Christi: named honorary pallbearer for Driscoll funeral, 140

Sevier, Henry Hulme (Hal): introduces bill in Legislature to repay Clara Driscoll, 43; family background, 43; distinguished forebears, 43–44; education and early career as newspaperman, 44; member of the House of Representatives, 43, 45; marries Clara Driscoll, 45–46; on European honeymoon, 46–48 passim; editor of the New York *Sun*, 45, 46, 48; as cotton merchant in New York, 52; resignation from the *Sun*, 54; see also Chapter Five, The New York Years, and Driscoll, Clara; removal with wife to Austin, 55; founds the Austin *American*, 55; accepts diplomatic post in South America, 62; attends peace conference with E. M. House, 62; sells Austin *American*, 62; establishes Austin Public Library, 62

—Appointed ambassador to Chile, 1933, 69–71; observes changes since 1918, 73–74; loses interest and obtains release, 75; object of criticism in national press, 75; maintains business relations with estranged wife, 76; returns to Chattanooga after divorce, 77; eulogy to, in Austin *American*, 77; settlement out of court of suit against wife, 77; death, 78; see also Chapter Eight, The Chile Ambassadorship and Divorce, 69–78 passim; mentioned, 85

Sevier, Mrs. Henry Hulme (Hal): see Driscoll, Clara

Sevier, John: governor of Tennessee, 43; marriages and political career, 44

Sevier, Mary Benton (Douglas): mother of Hal Sevier, 43; born in Republic of Texas, 43; effect of place of birth on son, 44

Sevier, Colonel Theodore Francis; serves in Confederate Army, 43; marriages, 43; distinguished ancestry, 41–44

Sloan, Dr. Joseph McBride; 146

Smith, Alfred E.: candidate for the presidency of the United States , 87; quoted, 98

Sorolla, Dr. Conrado of Santiago, Chile; named pallbearer for Driscoll funeral rites, 140

S. S. *Amerika*: ship on which Seviers sailed for honeymoon in Europe, 46

"St. Mary's of Aransas": birthplace of Clara Driscoll, 1; see also Driscoll, Clara

Tarlton, Dudley: 140

Texas Club of New York: 52–54 passim; see also

MARTHA ANNE TURNER is a native Texan and unreconstructed South-
erner. For more than two decades she was a member of the faculty of
Sam Houston State University, where she pursued the profession of
writing along with her academic duties. At Sam Houston, Miss Turner
had the pleasure of using her own books in an advanced course she introduced to the campus—Life and Literature of the Southwest.

She now devotes full time to writing and averages two books a year.
In addition she contributes to magazines and journals. Her 6000-word
article on the celebrated author-artist-Marine, John W. Thomason, was
published in the historic 204th anniversary issue of the *Marine Corps
Gazette* in November 1979. The writer's other areas of interest than
American literature are history and folklore.

Hailed as a grassroots historian by C. L. Sonnichsen, Miss Turner likes
to investigate subjects overlooked by other writers or that have not been
exhaustively researched. Sam Houston, Santa Anna, and William Barret
Travis have come under the author's dissecting pen with the revelation
of fresh or relatively unplowed ground.

Clara Driscoll: An American Tradition is the first book-length treatment of the subject and contains material heretofore unpublished.

Miss Turner is listed in *Who's Who of American Women*, *Who's Who
in the United States*, and in the *Dictionary of International Biography*.

CLARA DRISCOLL

nineteenth book produced by Madrona Press
has been printed on Frostbrite Coated Matte paper.
Type used for text is twelve-point Aldine Roman,
two-point leaded, set on the IBM Electronic Selectric Composer.
Display type is Lydian Cursive and Korinna.
Printing: Capital Printing Company, Austin.
Binding: Custom Bookbinders, Austin.

MADRONA PRESS, INC.
Box 3750
Austin, Texas 78764